Blue River, Black Sea

Andrew Eames

BLACK SWAN

TRANSWORLD PUBLISHERS
61–63 Uxbridge Road, London W5 5SA
A Random House Group Company
www.rbooks.co.uk

BLUE RIVER, BLACK SEA
A BLACK SWAN BOOK: 9780552775076

First published in Great Britain
in 2009 by Bantam Press
an imprint of Transworld Publishers
Black Swan edition published 2010

Mixed Sources
Product group from well-managed
forests and other controlled sources
www.fsc.org Cert no. TT-COC-2139
© 1996 Forest Stewardship Council
FSC

Blue River, Black Sea

CONTENTS

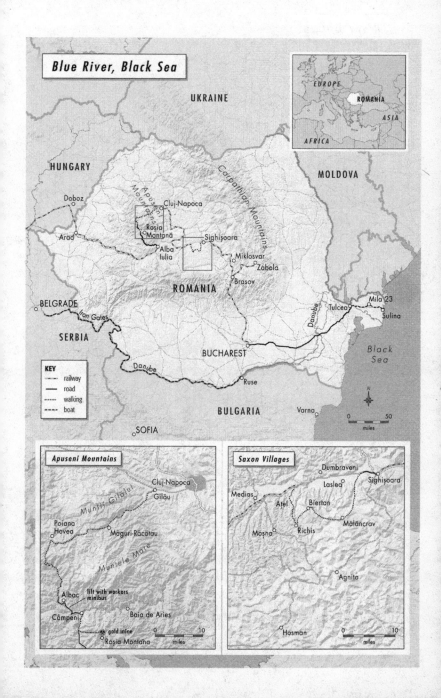

Blue River, Black Sea

UKRAINE

HUNGARY

Doboz

Arad

Apuseni Mountains

Cluj-Napoca

Roșia Montană

Alba Iulia

Sighișoara

Miklosvar

Zábola

Brasov

ROMANIA

Carpathian Mountains

MOLDOVA

BELGRADE

Iron Gates

SERBIA

Danube

Tulcea

Mila 23

Sulina

BUCHAREST

Danube

Ruse

Black Sea

BULGARIA

Varna

SOFIA

EUROPE

ROMANIA

ASIA

AFRICA

KEY
- - - railway
—— road
········· walking
– – – boat

N

0   50
miles

Apuseni Mountains

Muntii Gilăului

Cluj-Napoca

Gilău

Poiana Hovea

Măguri-Răcătau

Muntele Mare

Albac

lift with workers minibus

Câmpeni

Baia de Aries

gold mine

Roșia Montană

0   10
miles

Saxon Villages

Dumbraveni

Laslea

Medias

Atel

Biertan

Sighișoara

Moșna

Richis

Mălâncrav

Agnita

Hosman

0   10
miles

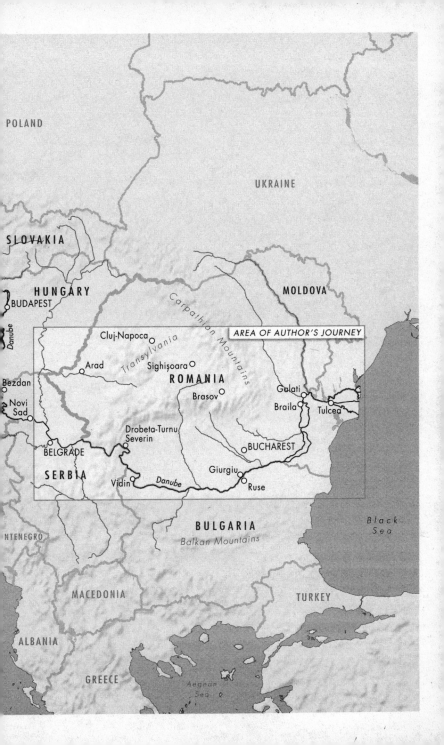

ACKNOWLEDGEMENTS

Although it was a true pleasure in the execution, this was a complex project in the planning, and many people deserve my heartfelt thanks for their suggestions and their hospitality. Pivotal in route-planning and contact-making were Count Tiber Kalnoky in Transylvania, Ursula Deutsch at the Danube Tourism Commission in Vienna, Barbara Geier at the German Tourist Office in London, Elizabeth Courage (formerly of the Hungarian tourist board) in London, Mark Andrews in Budapest, Count Jószef Hunyady in Hungary, Attila Munkas of the Argo and Branko Saviæ at YugoAgent in Serbia. Mike Morton of Beyond the Forest in the UK provided essential assistance with getting there and back. Big thanks to all of them, and particularly those among them who also put a roof over my head en route.

Various people opened their doors to me when they didn't need to. In particular I'd like to thank Prince Karl-Friedrich Hohenzollern, Archduke Alexander Habsburg-Lothringen, Princess Anita von Hohenburg, Abbot Gregor von Henckel Donnersmarck, Count László Karolyi, Countess Jean-Marie Wenckheim-Teleki, Julia Nótáros,

Carmen and Adi Costina, Gregor Roy Chowdury and Prince Paul-Phillippe Hohenzollern.

First mate Vlado on the Argo turned out to be an invaluable companion, and Barbaneagra Neculai in the Delta was (unknowingly) instrumental in my final chapters. For advice on walking through Transylvania I'm grateful to Nat Page of Fundatia Adept, to the Mihai Eminescu Trust, and Johan of Green Mountain holidays in Romania.

And finally this list would not be complete without a fulsome acknowledgement to those who stayed behind, particularly, Susanne, for essential cultural, emotional and topographical orientation. We call it home.

'Nothing great was ever achieved without a bit of enthusiasm.'

Rev. Lloyd Murdock, Presbyterian
church of St Mark, Cape Breton

Donaueschingen: the Danube Begins

I was deposited in Donaueschingen by a dibbly-dobbly railway which had trundled over the Black Forest from Freiburg, stopping at every cow-pat. The last of the winter snows had only been a month gone, but already the rolling hills of the Baar looked bleatingly fresh and glossy in the spring.

'Snow!' exclaimed a child a couple of seats behind me in the train, but it was only an echo of a season, a cloud of featherlike seeds slaloming through the trees, searching for new life, riding the breeze and catching the sun like soft, airborne skiers looking to go off-piste.

Donaueschingen itself turned out to be a pleasant, if unexceptional, pint-sized place with a Fürstenberg Prince's Palace in the style of a French chateau, an onion-domed church and an imposing selection of houses, some frescoed, some half-timbered, and many in pastel pinks and blues, like crayons in a tin or ballerinas waiting for the ball. Any pop-up book would have been pleased to have had it.

At the town's core was not the palace of the Fürstenbergs, but the home of something far closer to the hearts of modern Germans than the aristocracy: the giant Fürstenberg brewery, a rambling beer palace on a traffic island that puffed steam and smothered surrounding houses with its wet-wool smell. Unlike tobacco, bread or coffee, where the aroma is better than the product, beer is one of those commodities that delivers better than it promises. But the claggy smell didn't inhibit a selection of vigorous-looking pensioners, either with knapsacks or on bicycles or both, who circled the town's streets and greeted each other with the fellowship of the like-minded. They had the air of people who knew exactly what they were about to do, how they were going to do it, and the number of vitamin pills that would be required. Despite the earliness of the year they were already improbably tanned.

I had a plan, too. I was in town for two extremely important reasons: first to pay homage to the official source of the Danube, which rises in Donaueschingen; and second to buy a bicycle that would be capable of taking me all the way down the riverbank to Budapest.

As plans go, it was a fairly simple one, and one where you'd think that little could go wrong. Unfortunately, however, I'd arrived at lunchtime and all the shops were shut, so the pensioners and I were all revved up with no-where to go, circling the beer palace of a traffic island.

It happened to be market day in Donaueschingen, and stalls in a narrow clutch of streets had a selection of those gadgets used for cutting vegetables that somehow never ever make it into mainstream retailing, gadgets that are always demonstrated by men with toupees who once had careers as DJs until hair loss kicked in. Them aside, the remaining stallholders were Turks with worry beads and Sikhs in shades, and they were all talking amongst themselves in the lunchtime lull, knowing full well that pensioners fuelled by multivitamins were not going to be interested in denim fashion accessories fresh out of a crate from China. For this new arrival from London, that clutch of streets felt comfortably multicultural, and not claustrophobically small-town Baden-Württemberg at all.

It was on the other side of the market that I first came across the river, a slender and handsome chalk stream, beribboned with Ophelia tresses of weed which sheltered tail-flickering trout. But it wasn't the river I'd come for. A sign on the bridge indicated this was the Brigach, and I had known it and its colleague the Breg existed. Officially, these two 'send the Danube on its way', which makes them sound like a pair of proud parents waving from the bridge. Unofficially, the two B rivers merge, and are then joined by the baby Danube, which completely usurps their riverbed, chucking them out of the pram. A European cuckoo.

In the back of my mind I'd envisioned the Breg and Brigach as being tucked away out of sight and somehow sadly lacking in the river department, which would explain why no one mourned their passing. I hadn't expected either of them to be so handsome or so central to the town. Poor innocent Brigach, it didn't deserve to be treated with such contempt. And if the Brigach didn't deserve it, then probably neither did the Breg.

However, any concern over B-river discrimination was soon overtaken by a more pressing and selfish consideration, because Donaueschingen's bicycle shop had remained firmly closed well after the designated lunch break, despite the opening hours posted on the door. Departing from the norm is a rare state of events in

Germany, and I was worried. I knew the shop had a range of second-hand machines – I'd telephoned beforehand and I could see them through the window – so its continued closure was a setback, to say the least. Without a bicycle, the struggle for supremacy between B and D rivers didn't matter a bean; my journey was dead in the water before it had even begun.

At this point I had one of those strange moments of good fortune that have occasionally illuminated my life, for which I should be more than truly grateful, and for which I promise to be when I am old. The most recent was on the Spanish island of Fuerteventura, where I'd had my briefcase containing flight tickets and passport stolen from a hire car. I'd disconsolately set out to drive the 3 miles to report the loss at the nearest police station, met the eye of a smiley old man by the roadside, and just beyond him spotted the briefcase, inexplicably completely intact, sitting beside a bush by the road. As the tears of relief rolled down my cheeks, I felt as if I'd just taken part in some parable which I didn't have the wisdom, or the faith, to comprehend fully.

This time it was a bicycle journey, not a flight, that was at issue. So I wandered up the hill through the centre of Donaueschingen in the vain hope of giving the bike shop's long-lunchers more time to return to their posts. I didn't have a plan B.

Fortunately I didn't need one. Towards the top of the hill I passed a cluster of some twenty-five people gathered on the steps of the *Rathaus*, and twenty-five people, in a clump, in early spring, constitutes quite a crowd in Donaueschingen. My first thought was that it was a fire drill, but these were individuals, quietly waiting, not groups of work colleagues murmuring and giggling. My second thought was that it must be some sort of political demonstration, but there were no posters, nor any strutting rabble-rousers preparing to make their views heard. Apart from the two clerks sitting behind a desk, the only people who evidently knew each other were three council workers in bright orange dungarees who looked distinctly amused at the whole operation. They were smirking in particular at the behaviour of a small man who was doing his best to look important in the no-man's-land in front of the desk, but with no natural charisma, no podium, no microphone or other badge of authority, he didn't quite know how to start, where to stand or in which direction to face. This was their boss, the man who ruled their lives, and in the unforgiving light of the public gaze he was floundering. The council workers were plainly enjoying his discomfort.

As I came abreast of the crowd, this man just about managed to assemble everyone's attention by raising his voice until it squeaked, like a musical instrument which was being abused in the hands of a beginner. He nodded to one of the men in dungarees, who reached for a bicycle from the bicycle rank. But instead of swinging his leg across the saddle and heading off on some pre-arranged errand, he wheeled the bicycle forward and the burgermeister, or whoever he was, announced:

'So this one – how about ten?'

The crowd shuffled. No one volunteered.

'Five?'

'OK, I'll take it for five,' piped up a voice from behind the burgermeister's right shoulder, in a tone that suggested he was only doing it out of compassion for the homeless. A man who'd been lounging against the *Rathaus* wall produced a banknote, handed it to the girl behind the desk, and the bicycle was his.

Suddenly I was hyper-alert. Clearly I was witnessing

5

some kind of auction, of direct relevance to my immediate future: the bicycles drawn up outside the *Rathaus* didn't belong to council workers or shoppers at all, as I'd previously assumed. Plainly, fate intended me to take part.

'Can anyone . . . ?' I asked the man next to me.

'Sure, but you need to be quick.'

A couple of other bikes had already gone, both of them for laughably small sums, and judging by the way he was distributing them at the earliest possible bid, the burgermeister was clearly keen to get it all over and done with as quickly as he could, hankering for the security of his scrupulously tidy desk, his protective ring of staff and the reassuring familiarity of the daily routine.

The bike that had caught my eye was a Kettler, a well-known German make and practically new, so when its turn came to be wheeled forward I waved in the burgermeister's direction.

'Ten.'

It was a ridiculously small amount for a bike that probably cost 500 euros, but I wasn't the only one interested: a smart-looking mother had been waiting for this moment with her teenage son at the edge of the group, and she immediately jumped in.

'Twenty.'

This was a whole new dynamic on the steps of the *Rathaus*. The mother and I exchanged steely glares and traded bids steadily, while the burgermeister looked more and more embarrassed, as if he'd stepped inadvertently into the middle of a family dispute. The two of us became the focus of all attention: the yummy mummy versus the un-yummy bummy with the rucksack. This was real-life drama in Donaueschingen. We were clearly not stooges planted in the crowd by the *Rathaus* to drive the prices up. So who had the deeper pockets, the greater desire? As the temperature rose I could sense we were heading for the front page of the *Donaueschingen Gazette*.

Eventually the bidding neared 100 euros and I began to falter; and at this stage I made the fatal error of upping my offer in a two rather than a five. Sensing my weakness, the mother closed in for the kill.

'One hundred and five!' she said with great finality, trumping my puny two-step by a whole 8 euros.

I shook my head. She didn't look as if she was going to give up, and besides, I was saying to myself, I'd only be tempting fate with a bike so new and so appealing; it was such an evident thief magnet that I'd be constantly worrying about the responsibility of looking after it. So I let it slide, defeated, and my well-dressed enemy wheeled away her new acquisition, hostilities over, without favouring me with another look.

The only other bike I was interested in was a brown thing that looked OK, model unknown, relatively new. I got it for 20 euros, emphatically and viciously outbidding an elderly gentleman who quite thought he'd got it for half that price and was taken aback at being so savagely gazumped. I handed over the cash, signed a chit to prove that I hadn't stolen it, and wheeled it away down the hill. And although it was momentarily unridable because of flat tyres, I could tell that this brown thing was one of the best investments I'd ever made. It would only let me down once in the next 1,400 kilometres, and even that was to be my own stupid fault.

With the first reason for coming to Donaueschingen resolved, it was time to get on with the second: the Danube spring.

It would be disingenuous of me to pretend that I'd

arrived in the town completely ignorant of the source of the Danube debate. The official line is that the Danube starts at a spring in the town because the Romans said so, but Italian scholar Claudio Magris, in his book on the river, turns the whole issue into a preamble of *Tristram Shandy*-like proportions on the exact definition of source, possible whereabouts of said source, or even the need to find a source, which takes him forty-odd pages. I'd had Magris' book recommended to me again and again before I set out on this journey – it is the only relatively contemporary socio-historical account of the Danube – but found it almost impenetrably scholarly. The great man exercised his synapses through four hundred pages, displaying immense erudition, leaping between intellectual rooftops and poking his nose down the chimney stacks of downriver nations like a PhD chimney sweep from Mary Poppins. For my part, my synapses jumped through a few hoops and did a couple of short sprints to try to keep up, but after a while they were all tuckered out so they lay down and looked at the sky, and short of poking them with a sharp stick there was nothing much I could do about it.

Magris spends his first chapter striding (mainly metaphorically, I assume, because he didn't strike me as a strider) around the Black Forest hills from possible source to possible source, and I can imagine him with some of Donaueschingen's vitamin-filled pensioners in tow, seemingly attentive and impressed by the great man's digressions, but with their synapses even more tuckered out than mine.

He was by no means the first to have furrowed his brow over the Danube's origins. The German poet Heinrich Heine wandered over the source territory in the 1880s, and although he came to no definitive conclusion he clearly felt sympathy for the victimized B rivers. As he wrote in a letter to Karl Marx, 'clearly it would be easy to adhere to the thesis that there is no Danube at all, only Breg and Brigach. Thus the Danube becomes a fiction.' A fiction? It'd be a bugger for me and my book if it did.

Fortunately, local lore has a glib solution for us non-scholars: to find the source of the Danube, so they say, all you have to do is to find a river that could reasonably *be* the Danube and stroll up and down its banks mumbling continually, 'This is the Danube, this is the Danube,' and hey presto, the river exists.

In Donaueschingen itself, whose very name depends on the Danube, there was no room for debate. '*Hier entspringt die Donau*' (literally, 'Here springs the Danube') declared a categorical noticeboard between the Fürstenberg Palace and the Bohemian baroque St John's Church. 'And the Romans counted it a very important site.' I detected the hand of the burgermeister at work in invoking the Romans, because, being the architects of modern civilization, they would have known what they were talking about. So there.

Alongside the sign, a circle of balustrades opened to permit the visitor down to a wrought-iron fence. The fence surrounded a basin of clear water disturbed only by jelly-jewel bubbles of air rising to the surface, and the occasional plop of a coin going in the other direction as another visitor's wish sank into the depths. This was the Donauquelle, or the Danube Spring, and looming over it was the allegorical figure of Mother Baar pointing towards the Black Sea, telling the infant river where to go. From the air, what with the iron fence and the encircling stone balustrade, the translucence of the water and the glimmering of coins on the spring bed, it must have looked like an ornamental brooch pinned to the side of the palace's park. Or a turquoise rivet, if you were up at 35,000 feet.

On an adjacent wall, Donaueschingen's '*Hier entspringt die Donau*' proclamation was corroborated by a show of solidarity from all the countries that lie along the river's length. They demonstrated that solidarity through plaques which acted as multi-governmental witness statements to banish all doubts from the spectator's mind, because the Danube must start here if both the Romans *and* all these governments say so. Forget the Breg and Brigach, was the subtext to all these messages: they're history. In the making of a great river, somebody had to get hurt.

As for the wording on the plaques, it was pompous, sententious and bland. The Danube 'connects us with the great family of European nations' declared the Croats. Bulgaria soliloquized about being linked to the heart of Europe (i.e. please let us be one of the gang). Hungary quoted its suicidal tragi-poet József Attila about the Danube being a wonder of nature (so let's all jump in and drown), the Romanians declared that they were watching over the Delta on behalf of everyone (it's ours, don't even think about interfering), while the Ukrainians burbled on about how the Danube's water carries the hopes and prayers of millions of Europeans (the Russians told us to write that) and the Serbs declared that the great river brought 'something that man is lacking' (has anyone got a packet of fags?).

For a while I sat by the source in the sun, waiting to see if any Magris-like profundity would descend on my shoulders, too, but all I could think of was the fate of the poor B rivers. Then I began to be concerned about the possible impact of the slow rain of wish-impregnated coins down into the bed of the Donauquelle, blocking the flow. Presumably those same dungaree-clad council workers had the honour of stepping over the ironwork at regular intervals, to plunge into the hallowed water to remove the silver, or else the Danube would be in danger of becoming gummed up with loose change before it even started. That in itself was a novel idea. Could the B rivers suddenly be gifted a second chance? And what then if the council workers were summoned, with their plungers? Would the unblocking, the sudden shifting of silverware, have any consequences downriver? Surely if the butterfly-flapping-its-wings theory of climate was correct, then the removal of a single one-euro coin in Donaueschingen had the potential to produce a tidal wave in Novi Sad?

Anyway, as this was the official starting point of my journey, I felt the need to mark my departure with some kind of ceremony, and just flipping another coin into the water wasn't going to be enough. So when a desultory pair of tourists had drifted away, leaving me there on my own, I circled the spring, pumping my new bicycle pump, and muttering '*Drum bun, drum bun, drum bun,*' which is actually Romanian for 'good journey'. Warming to my task, I improvised a halting dance, like a Red Indian preparing for war. '*Drum bun, drum bun, Ma Baar.*' And then, with a last look at the plaque indicating that there were 2,840 kilometres to go, and at the allegorical figure of Mother Baar pointing me on my way, I mounted my 20-euro set of wheels and headed for Budapest.

The idea of a journey down the Danube was more of an accumulation than an inspiration. It all started a long, long time ago when, as a recent graduate, flying out to Asia, I remember looking down out of the aircraft window at a land that was russet-brown, wrinkled, veined and as bristly as the hide of a camel – Romania, according to the flight plan – and wondering what on earth it could be like down there, behind the Iron Curtain. It might have been a different planet. Then I promptly forgot all about it, because south-east Asia became all the rage. For many years Thailand was far more interesting than Transylvania, and destinations right under our noses, part of our own continent, remained far more foreign to us than many places halfway round the globe.

Then the Wall came down, and the West started to wrap its warm hands around the chilly East, and new airline routes started to stir the pot. Over succeeding years I dipped my toe into this new territory with journeys to Poland, to Bulgaria, to Romania, to Czechoslovakia and to the former Yugoslavia. But a lot of it made little lasting impression; the landscape was often neglected, the cities devastated by war and then badly mauled by peace. The architecture was unrewarding, the food forgettable, the history unknown and the languages unrelated to anything I had learned at school. The British press had lost interest in the region once the communist-overthrow stories were done, apart from a flurry of excitement over Romanian orphanages. It was hard to get a handle on the place.

But then it started to force itself on our attention. Eastern Europeans started arriving in the West, particularly once their home countries joined the EU, to do our plumbing and our loft conversions. Early in the new millennium I recall having a conversation with a typical British builder who complained that he didn't have any problem with the blacks and the Asians; he knew a bit about the British Empire and slavery, and he could see where these different ethnicities had come from and why they were in Britain. They were easy to pick out in a crowd and he knew what they were like and how to handle them.

Eastern Europeans, however, were a different matter, he said. Confusingly, they looked just like us, but he had no idea who they were or where they had come from. Nobody had taught him anything about them at school, there was never anything about their countries in the newspapers, there had never been anything about them on the TV, and now here they were, blending in and walking around as if they belonged. Some of them were even Muslim, whilst looking just like West Ham supporters. It was as if they were impostors who'd slipped in from Europe's backyard. 'Like having someone turn up on your doorstep claiming to be a brother, when you never knew you even had one,' the builder said. He was quite incensed.

The final catalyst for the book was a trip I made to Transylvania, where I stumbled into an almost medieval landscape that I never dreamed still existed in Europe, of scything farmers and their fruit-collecting children, of horses and carts, of wells in the villages, wolves in the woods and bears in the hills. The storybook detail was captivating. The storks on chimney stacks, clapping their beaks when their youngsters stood up. The chicks in home-made chicken runs on the roadside verges. The little smoking huts in every yard, breadmaking ovens for summer use. And the daily cow parade, when all the villagers' cattle brought themselves back from the fields punctually at milking time and wandered down the main street until they reached their owners' houses, where the gates would be standing open to welcome them home. Transylvania seemed a mythical place, one where you literally didn't count your chickens until they hatched, and one where you made sure you made hay while the sun shone.

The resident humanity was no less captivating. My host in this fairytale land turned out to be a Transylvanian count whose great-uncle had been the foreign minister of the Austro-Hungarian Empire, who had Habsburg

13

cousins, who knew the Prince of Wales, who was a Knight of Malta, who spoke many languages fluently, and who told me that most aristocrats of the region had once sent their children to British public schools. I thought such people only existed in stories.

On that Transylvanian trip, standing in a clocktower looking down over an ornate, belfried hilltop town that confusingly had three names – Sighişoara to the Romanians, Schässburg to the Germans and Segesvár to the Hungarians – I fell into conversation with a German tourist.

'Look at it,' he said, with a sweep of his hands over the red-tiled rooftops. 'Don't you recognize it?'

I shrugged. 'I've never been here before.'

'It's Germany, don't you see? It was built by Germans, lived in by Germans for hundreds of years, until they were all forced to leave. This should all be Germany. And Budapest – did you know about Budapest?' I shrugged again. A jingoistic, imperialistic German is not a common experience in the modern world, and it wasn't one I was enjoying.

'It was all German-speaking, Budapest. In the 1820s there were two daily newspapers in German, none at all in Hungarian, and Hungarians were only a third of the population. Same in Prague, it was all Germans, hardly any Czechs there at all. You never heard of the Banat? The Danube Swabians? Empress Maria Theresa?'

I had to shake my head again and again, and eventually the German despaired of teaching me any more.

'Then you don't know anything about European history,' he said, with great finality.

He was right, I didn't. Despite an expensive education my knowledge of the geo-politically enlarging and reuniting European continent in which I lived was sketchy at best, and it barely lapped up against the former Iron Curtain, let alone spilled over to the other side. I was one of those who knew far more about Thailand than I did about Transylvania.

The extent of that ignorance was driven home to me on the flight home, while running my eye over the map of Europe in the back of the inflight magazine. I found my eye following the route of the Danube. I knew approximately where it started, in southern Germany, and that it flowed through Austria and then through Hungary to Budapest, just like in the Strauss waltz:

> Danube so blue
> You flow straight through
> The meadows and dales . . .

but after that it simply vanished off the edge of my mental map. So to see it running onwards, through Slovakia, Serbia, Croatia, Bulgaria, Romania, and with sideways nods to Moldova and the Ukraine before making its exit into the Black Sea, came as a surprise. This was a European equator I hadn't realized existed, a European Amazon, far larger and longer than any other river in the region. It was a mighty liquid belt that held Europe's trousers up, and yet all I knew about it was that it was supposed to be blue, which turned out to be complete tosh. How come we didn't pay more attention to it at school?

So when I got back I looked it up. It was the European Union's longest river, said my encyclopaedia, at 2,840 kilometres, and the ten Danube countries it ran through had a combined population of a hundred million, about whom we knew practically nothing. As well as being the longest river in continental Europe, it was the only one that flowed west to east, a crucial fact that had saved Europe's bacon over the centuries. Had it flowed the other way, then the likes of Genghis Khan, the Almoravids and the Ottomans could have taken a watery conveyor belt right into the heart of the West, and the Western world would have ended up a very different place.

But the Danube was more than that. Rivers have their own narratives, with a beginning, middle and end; they are not just water that moves. They rise and fall, tumble and stall, breed life and generate their own personality, accelerating and slowing, chattering and slumbering at will. They are more than just a physical presence, more than just wet stuff in queues. Animal life, and human life, gather around them, and always have done. In his unusually titled book, *The Glance of Countess Hahn-Hahn (down the Danube)*, Hungarian author Peter Esterhazy writes that 'The difference between water and a river is that the latter has a memory, a past, a history.' And a river like the Danube has a lot more memory, past and history than most.

Its potential as a storyteller intrigued me greatly. I found myself believing that a river that had its head in old Europe and its tail in new would inevitably share some of its experiences with me. It had flowed, mutely and immutably, through centuries of tremendous change, carrying messengers, fugitives, emigrants and evacuees as well as tourists. It had soaked away any blood that had been shed, helped in the building of nations on its shores, and absorbed all the effluent of supposed progress, without passing judgement. Now, surely, it could be coaxed to reveal all to someone journeying along its length. I could just see the headlines in *Hello!* magazine: 'At home with the Danube; 50 years of war and peace and still smiling on.'

More than that, I envisaged the river as a reassuring presence that could accompany me through the ups and downs of a long, ambitious journey along Europe's watermark, the mark that authenticated Europe as truly European. It would always be there, an uncomplaining travel companion carrying me along in its slipstream right down to Europe's back door. A companion, a mentor, a guide, an interpreter, ever reliable and ever present. A touch inscrutable, maybe, but incapable of guile.

Logistically, too, it could help greatly with the process of the journey. The very concept of travelling along a river's route had a pleasing inevitability to it, making the journey instantly and easily defined. By plonking myself down in Donaueschingen I was connecting myself in one metaphorical stroke both with the guts of my journey and with my final destination, and although it wasn't quite like peering down a rifle barrel at the Black Sea, it did help remove the vagaries of a traveller's itinerary. I was plopping myself into Europe's open mouth, submitting myself to the whims of its interior plumbing, and hoping to emerge unscathed from its rear end. I was at the start of a 2,840-kilometre voyage, and the countdown started right here. I would know exactly when I was halfway, and equally exactly when I had just 20 kilometres to go. If ever I left the river for a detour, then the Danube would always be there waiting on my return to tell me in which direction I should turn and to tell me a few stories on the way. If ever I ran out of inspiration or energy, then I could always just throw myself in and float. And, of course, if the journey turned out to be dull, I'd always have something to blame.

Not that there'd be much danger of that, I hoped. The further it progressed in an easterly direction, the more there'd be to learn, because the more unknown, and undeveloped, would be the lands it passed through. The Donau became the Dunaj, the Duna, the Dunav, the Dunarea, and the Dunay, until finally it arrived at the Danube Delta, a wetland wilderness the size of Dorset, where Russian-speaking tribal fishermen lived in houses thatched with reeds and where colonies of Dalmatian pelicans gorged themselves on a hundred different species of fish. What could be better?

It all sounded incredibly exotic for somewhere just a low-cost flight away. The more I learned, the more I became convinced that the river, like Theseus's piece of string in his fight against the Minotaur, was a perfect vehicle for a journey into the labyrinth of the new Europe. An excuse for taking a literary swab of a newly united continent and colliding with the debris of the last seventy-five years of European history en route. A way of stumbling on broken dynasties and on people and places with gripping recent narratives of how their lives, and homelands, had changed.

I could see it becoming a metaphor in itself, in true Conradian tradition, having its starting point in Western civilization, in the world of broadband and plasma screens, and its destination in a social and political semi-wilderness where wolves still roam. As in Conrad's African or South American rivers, a journey along its length would be a journey back to the basics of existence, a journey back in time.

With all this in mind, I was contemplating a matey conversation when the Danube and I first met in Donaueschingen. I saw myself drawing up a chair to the river's edge and throwing a friendly arm around its shoulders, like two cowboys getting together in the saloon before their adventure begins. 'I hear you're heading for the Delta? Yup. Well, as it happens, me too.'

And off we'd go, sunset or no.

But you can't have a matey conversation with a mis-behaving toddler, especially if you suspect it of having just nicked someone else's pram. After my pre-lunch encounter with the poor innocent Brigach, I was beginning to have my doubts whether the Danube should have been allowed to exist at all.

However, the Danube is not blue, and the Black Sea is not black, and nothing en route is quite what it says on the tin. So I shouldn't have been surprised when, 22 kilometres after my optimistic departure from Donaueschingen on my 20-euro set of wheels, the river, on whose very existence my journey depended, suddenly disappeared.

2

Immendingen: the Danube Disappears

Logically, a journey down a river should be done by boat. Given that I would be travelling with the Danube's very considerable current in my favour, my first thought was of a rowing boat, and calling the resulting book 'Backwards to the Black Sea'. But on probing a little deeper the boat plan didn't seem such a good idea. For while the Upper Danube was widely celebrated in books and brochures, the Lower Danube was rarely mentioned in any traveller's accounts, and my 1994 edition of *Exploring Europe by Boat* went only as far as Budapest; beyond that, the river went off the edge of the boatie world.

I found a couple of diaries on the Internet about travelling beyond Budapest on a cruise boat, which weren't very encouraging: evidently the passengers had whiled away the time with napkin-folding demonstrations, strudel-making competitions and taking photographs of lock installations. Reading between the lines, I gathered that beyond Budapest the river became scenically dull, traversing great plains and incarcerated between high embankments to restrain it from invading people's homes. Huge stretches of riverbank had no real cultural or scenic interest at all, and humanity kept well away unless there was high ground to hand.

The alternatives to cruise boats didn't sound much better. Those books I did find that narrated small-boat journeys suggested that their authors were forever in awe of the river's power. They were so anxious about finding moorings and about their own security that they barely left the water or their precious craft, and consequently saw very little of anything on dry land, which wasn't what I wanted at all. An Italian yacht skipper who posted his log on the Internet went into detail about excessive mooring charges, difficult customs officers, industrial landscapes and debris in the water. It sounded as if he'd had a thoroughly bad time.

So then I did the journey digitally, with the help of Google Earth. Without budging from my front room I swooped down on Donaueschingen, where the palace and its parkland had obviously been captured in the early morning, even before the vitamin-powered pensioners were up, when the railed-in button of the Donauquelle was all but invisible and the embryonic river was still hidden by a curtain of heavy shadow created by the trees. When it finally emerged, the Danube was a thin, weedy thread snared in a bushy beard and where it became more substantial it was regularly blocked by barriers which I later discovered were hydroelectric dams. Plainly they wouldn't have been circumventable in anything bigger than a canoe.

The first rivercraft I spotted were two speedboats looking like a pair of feather-tailed swifts below Kelheim, where the Main-Donau Canal joined from the north. And here was my very first barge, followed by several more down below Regensburg, where there was big drama on the river. A barge had got stuck, and there were others skewed around it like woodlice chewing on bark, surrounded by a giant stain of mud as their propellers churned at the riverbed. Several skippers were evidently working their engines hard, unaware that their efforts were being captured by a passing satellite.

Then came Passau, whose most noticeable feature was a big railway yard and the luminous green river Inn, filled with meltwater from the Alps, which joined the jade-green Danube. And despite the Inn being the dominant partner and completely recolouring the combined waterway, it suffered from the same unwise marriage as the Breg and Brigach had done, because it too was forced to surrender its name and its bed.

Google Earth's detail continued as far as Vienna and then, where the river changed from Upper Danube to Lower, it went impressionistic, turning to Van Goghian swirls and Klee-like spangles of colour. Instead of mucky green it became a deep, idealized blue, as if someone in Google's Politburo had given the command that, in the absence of other info, it should be coloured to match the waltz. Occasionally details would resolve themselves out of the mist, such as the barge clusters below Belgrade, and it looked as if only one of Novi Sad's three bridges – all destroyed by NATO warplanes in the strikes against Serbia – was functioning normally when the Google camera had been overhead. Below Moldova Veche the banks were plainly steep and inaccessible, and then it all flattened out again and the Romanian side was covered in tiny strips, a carpet of rectangles in leftover colours of heather, russet and rust, offcuts from a lino factory. For hundreds of kilometres there was very little sign of substantial settlement anywhere near the river.

Eventually my mouse passed the point where the Black Sea Canal struck off out to Constanta, on the sea coast, but the river itself turned north, started to lose its composure and to fray distractedly into subsidiary channels. Finally it sprawled, exhausted and disintegrating, into the Delta, which looked like one of those school science projects where you take an unknown liquid and drop it on to blotting paper to see it separate into bands of constituent colours. My mouse could go no further.

So what sort of boat could cope with all these differing river states? A boat that was portable enough to get round the dams of the upper reaches; a boat that was powerful enough to cope with what was sometimes a 10 m.p.h. stream and which was fast enough to speed me through the sluggish, boring bits. It would have to be a boat big enough to sleep in, substantial enough to be spotted on a barge's radar after dark and secure enough for me to feel comfortable about locking it up and leaving it occasionally. This wonder-boat would be waiting for me at the top of the river, primed and ready to go; it wouldn't cost me much money, and it would be something I could easily sell to the fishermen of the Delta when my journey was done, despite the fact that they lived in what was essentially a barter economy and had no money. In short, it was a boat that didn't exist.

It was pretty much at this point that I started to re-read Patrick Leigh Fermor, the British travel writer who'd set out in 1933, aged eighteen, to walk from the Hook of Holland to Istanbul. The resulting books – *A Time of Gifts* and *Between the Woods and the Water* – are travel classics, and much of the route they describe lies along the Danube. A third volume (to describe the cross-country journey through Bulgaria and into Turkey) has not yet appeared, and Leigh Fermor, in his nineties at the time of writing, is cagey about whether it ever will.

The author was someone I had admired from afar, but until that point I wouldn't have called myself a fan. For him, the world is a great university, full of arts, literature, languages, history, biology, zoology, all of which enrich his work. Returning to his books with almost forensic interest, my admiration of his writing intensified and my resolution to do this journey weakened. How could his account ever be bettered, or even matched? Not by me, for sure, and I wasn't keen to invite the comparison.

But there was something else in Leigh Fermor's books, something which spurred me on. The author picks his way across the cultural tapestry of Europe, teasing away at selected threads until they unravel in his hands, revealing how they work and what binds them together. His account is very much a portrait of an era, of a Europe between the wars, a bucolic place whose old institutions and families were hanging on by their fingernails, about to be hit by a tidal wave of change. A handful of years after his passsing, half of the landscapes he described were smashed under the heel of fascism and vanished behind the expressionless mask of communism.

Today, seventy-five years on, the mask has slipped, the tidal wave has receded, the last lingering puddles have all but evaporated and much of the superficial damage has been repaired, so surely there was a value in retracing his steps, to see whether any of his old, romantic Europe had survived the three-quarter century of brutalization?

Crucially, as far as my logistics were concerned, Patrick Leigh Fermor hadn't stuck slavishly to the river, and that gave me a wonderful excuse not to do so either. Although his broad intention had been to walk, he'd also travelled by horse, boat and even car, wherever his story led him. I decided to do the same, to use whatever form of transport seemed most appropriate at the time. As it turned out, that would mean bicycle, boat, train, horse, barge, foot and rowing boat. And each stage would become a bigger adventure than the last.

Setting out from Donaueschingen that afternoon via the Fürstenberg Palace park, pursued by the sound of peacocks, it was impossible not to be optimistic. From beneath me came the reassuring susurration of bicycle tyres eating up a dedicated cycle track, and around me stretched carpets of dandelions *in excelsis*. Nature was in full riot mode, the bushes sizzling with birds and the ground creaking as it was forced asunder by spring's green shoots hungry for sun. Germany was looking good in a way I'd never really appreciated it could, with embankments of wild flowers, fields of rape, hedgerows of butterflies and distant church spires, shimmering like something new-baked. I had bread, cheese and a bottle of wine in my saddlebag, wind in my hair and a smear of suncream on my nose. The trees genuflected gently at my passing, congratulating me on my freedom and my weeks and months of unadulterated and unpredictable travel that lay ahead.

The Danube, however, was in playful mood, and showed little inclination to get on with the task we were both engaged on. Once it pulled clear of the park's regimental straitjacket of symmetrical tree lines, it started to roll around the flat valley like a ball-bearing on a plate. Still a toddler in riverine terms, it had already bullied the Breg and Brigach into submission, and now it was plainly enjoying the first chance to stretch its legs, get fat, knock into things and disobey Mother Baar's 'Get Thee to the Black Sea' instruction, as toddlers are wont to do.

That prim, railed-in button of water by the schloss, with its jelly-bubbles and pompous plaques, was already a distant memory, and the burgeoning river had already become a far less predictable thing. Given the right set of circumstances it could transform itself, rise up out of its bed and drown people, no matter how well prepared they thought they were for its bad behaviour. But right now it was unthreatening, unaware of its power, gathering strength by hungrily swallowing tributaries as it moved through an essentially flat land. There was no clear indication why or in which direction it should flow, but move it did, tickled onwards by an average drop of 0.00047 per cent over its 2,840 kilometres – barely worth leaving its bed for – and the rumour that somewhere to the east there was a whole sea waiting for its grand entrance. There was no suggestion that it was about to disappear.

After about a dozen kilometres the land rose up discreetly, disguised in woodland, as instructed by Mother Baar, to prevent the headstrong river making a run for the North Sea or the Mediterranean as all its fellow waterways did. The river, the cycle way, a road and a railway were all funnelled together into a tree-lined throat, four confederates each of whom had a different agenda: the railway was too lazy for corners, the road preferred to avoid trees, the river liked volleying off the valley walls and the cycle way didn't want any hills, so all four crossed and criss-crossed each other, as if knitting a giant patchwork pullover – a pullover that would eventually turn a lovely mellow red and yellow in autumn, but at this stage of the year was almost fluorescent with new spring.

In the midst of all this were farmers with tankers of diluted winter slurry, spraying it over their fields and thickening the air with the smell of rancid cheese. Cows, recently evicted from winter barns, were browsing between the river's bends and bellowing happily – or perhaps unhappily, I don't know, I don't speak cow. The riverside *Hintertupfingens** were quiet, staked out with a crucifix at either end, with a *Rathaus* in the middle and a couple of men in boilersuits fixing things in front yards, as men in boilersuits tend to do. I noticed that a couple of farms had proper little baroque-style multifloored schlosses for pigeons and doves mounted on staves in their courtyards, for even pigeons live in castles on the Danube. Most also had stacks of firewood piled up against the walls, a sign of good housekeeping. It reminded me of that much-loved German euphemism, '*Viel Holz vor der Hütte*' ('Lots of wood in front of the hut'), aka a well-stacked figure of a woman. *Hintertupfingens* are full of them.

Approaching Immendingen I crossed the river courtesy of what looked like an old disused barn, which had been knocked out at both ends and swung across the river so cattle could amble through. Just beyond it I was brought up short by a signboard which made a neat pair with Donaueschingen's '*Hier entspringt die Donau*'.

'*Hier versinkt die Donau*' it declared, with no attempt at an apology. One moment the Danube *entspringt*, and the next it *versinkt* again, as if it was a perfectly natural thing to do. Ashes to ashes, dust to dust, *springt* to *sinkt*. Now you see it, now you don't. Tempting though it could have been to interpret this as an act of God, demonstrating the transience of earthly matters and thereby the supremacy of the life eternal, there was a perfectly logical explanation. It was all to do with the

Hintertupfingen is a German byword for rural backwater. It refers to any mythical rural village 'behind Tupfingen', which itself is already the back end of beyond.

geology of the Swabian Alps, an area of limestone hills particularly rich in cave systems, as limestone does tend to be, and it was into one of these that the river had disappeared.

I read on, anxiously, because my journey needed – nay, required – a river, this river particularly. The notice said that the Danube vanished completely for 155 days in the year, but the rest of the time there was sufficient water to maintain a surface presence, and as far as I could see this was one of those rest-of-the-year moments. There was still plenty of water. I left the bicycle and walked along the bank to make sure it was going to stick with me through thick and thin, and although I could detect a certain thinning out, it continued merrily enough, at a good healthy size. Certainly the ducks and herons appeared completely unconcerned.

So I returned to my bicycle full of hope, but the next time the path and the river coincided, a couple of miles further on, the Danube had gone. Dematerialized while I wasn't looking, with no trap-doors left ajar. All that remained were a couple of putrid puddles in the riverbed, which was otherwise largely occupied by smug bushes, rushes and reeds, luxuriating in the unaccustomed space, pretending they belonged. It didn't look as if a serious amount of water had travelled this way for years.

Barely believing my eyes, I bumped my bicycle across the empty riverbed and deposited it under a bush, treading carefully lest I stood on one of the cracks and ended up being dematerialized too. All that water, gone. Fish and all.

My first thought was that the Breg and the Brigach had finally worked out a way to exact their revenge, and had somehow pulled the plug. In fact, the underground geology of the area is so arranged that most of the water masquerading as the Danube over that first 22 kilometres (which is heavily Breg- and Brigach-impregnated anyway) disappears underground and never reappears in the Danube riverbed at all, which makes the whole source-of-the-Danube debate pretty pointless. Seditious underground river-courses subvert it southwards to release it into Lake Constance, which forms the headwaters of the Rhine. So only when it rains hard does the source of the Danube actually keep its head above ground sufficiently to feed the Danube proper and end up heading east to the Black Sea; the rest of the time it evades Mother Baar's carefully arranged attempts to direct it, ducks out of sight *sans* ducks, and ultimately ends up going due north instead. How badly behaved is that!

An empty riverbed is a depressing sight, whichever way it is headed, and wherever it is in the world. It carries a more disturbing absence than a disused railway line or even a row of empty houses, because rivers represent the essence of life. For many kilometres after Immendingen I pedalled alongside a pathetic string of puddles, barely daring to look at them, lest they too shrank away into the earth with shame under my stare. The bed refilled only gradually, a poor sickly dribble contributed by tributaries, and it wasn't until the town of Tuttlingen that it could really be counted as a proper river again with anything approaching a decent cleavage. Even then it was shored up by a weir at the end of town, working like a padded bra to produce a fuller cup for the benefit of Tuttlingen's strollers. The Danube was back, but it was no longer the vigorous, impetuous toddler that had departed Donaueschingen, full of spirit. This was its anorexic, indecisive distant relative, and henceforth it would be regularly bullied to keep it on track on its route to the east.

*   *   *

On the outskirts of Tuttlingen the cyclepath ran alongside a small industrial estate. This was my first real taste of manufacturing along the river, with a collection of small companies producing the likes of dental instruments, computer accessories and egg noodles. Germany is full of small-scale manufacturing units like these, enterprises that had their origin in the economic miracle, the *Wirtschaftswunder*, of the post-war years. These enterprises have chosen to remain family-owned and specialist for the last five decades, only changing what they do to make the business better, not necessarily bigger.

On the whole, Germans have an inclination towards, and a propensity for, this sort of small-to-medium specialist enterprise. They have an ability to plough the same furrow, again and again, until they can do it to perfection – or ad nauseam, as the rest of Europe might say. They know what they can do, they do it well, and they go on doing it, on and on, comfortable within their own realm, largely without feeling a pressing need to get richer, or to swallow up other companies. The rest of us benefit from their mental rigour, because no one can match them when it comes to perfecting dental instruments and egg noodles, and ultimately their factory owners become wealthy because we appreciate the quality of what they've made.

This mentality has its beginning in an educational system that is more focused than ours, and is followed by apprenticeships, vocational qualifications and probationary periods. Combine this with a national characteristic of treating the wish of higher authority as law, and you have a formidable workforce, both obedient and productive. Thus the person behind the ticket window in the railway station will have spent a probationary period in all aspects of ticketing, including postings to other ticket windows in the region. He's done the training, so now he does the time, waiting for more senior management to retire or die before moving up the ticketing tree. By early middle age he knows absolutely everything there is to know about his station, the people in it, and the wider railway industry. In return, he has a job for life.

The downside of this predilection to be organized is that there's a good chance that the thoroughly informed ticket clerk is also thoroughly bored. There's nothing he hasn't seen, heard or said before, so he's not interested in his work any more. He has no inclination to do anything above and beyond what the job description requires of him, and must always go home at 5 p.m. (half day on Fridays). So while you'll certainly get the information and the ticket you want from him, a smile is not in the contract.

Such creeping dissatisfaction is made bearable by holidays, leisure activities, cable television and beer, plus the sense that everyone else is in pretty much the same boat. The harder task is for those unfortunates who suddenly realize they're in completely the wrong job, and who'd actually far prefer to be doing something else. In other cultures such career volte-faces are relatively easy: you can buy an answering machine, print yourself a business card and call yourself a plumber or a translator, and if someone actually pays you good money to do what you say you can do, then you can truly claim to be whatever it says on the card. But not in Germany; if you want to strike out as an individual, away from your chosen path, you must go back to the beginning to collect all the right certifications and apprenticeships again, and you don't pass Go or collect £200 until you've done so. Consequently not many people do.

This structured channelling of society produces people in boxes, and social stereotypes which we all recognize. These include the inflexible German who finds it hard to adapt when something in his or her environment doesn't turn out as it says in the brochure; the forward-planning German who gets up early to put his towel on the sun-lounger and can't understand why others don't do the same; the thorough German who is so emphatically confident about his area of knowledge that he is quite prepared to tell others when they've got something wrong.

In Germany these stereotypes operate within their own comfort zones, where the unexpected rarely happens and where their views and their expertise are repeatedly endorsed. The disinclination to disturb the status quo is a legacy of the post-war years, when everyone had something they'd rather not talk about, so they closed ranks and stuck to their own environment. It wasn't until the last decade or so, for example, that schoolteachers actually started to dwell at any length on the Nazi years. Before then, nobody dared mention the war at home or in the media, and it was not something that children studied, even though it was the invisible hand on everyone's shoulder.

For the older generations, those comfort zones helped to exclude all the awfulness of the twentieth century; they kept their heads down, worked hard and for God's sake didn't complain, because they'd lost the right to do that when they lost the war. All was fine as long as they remained behind their ticketing windows; stepping outside their comfort zones could be a real shock to the system, so on the whole they preferred not to.

Just occasionally you can come across a German in this advanced insular state, at large in the wider world. Some years ago I bumped into one in a hotel kiosk in

Tunisia, where he was in a state of outrage at being asked to pay three times the normal cover price for a copy of *Bild*, the most popular German newspaper. He simply couldn't understand the take-it-or-leave-it attitude of the shop's proprietor, who was charging on the basis of what holidaymakers were prepared to pay. As far as the tourist was concerned this was blatant profiteering at the expense of the unwary, and furthermore when he realized, having bought it, that it wasn't even that day's edition, he condemned Tunisia and all who lived in it with some fairly choice language. Plainly he hadn't left his home town for a while.

Back in Germany there are many major advantages to such an organized, channelled society, and the best amongst them is quality and reliability in workmanship, which are both still highly prized. When you call out a plumber or visit an optician you know your job will be done properly, within the time stipulated and for a justifiable price. The plumber or optician has a tradition and a reputation to maintain if he wants to stay in business, so he takes care. Even retailers take pride, refusing to obsess over increasing this month's turnover compared to last month's, because they're in business for the long term in high streets whose shops don't change from one year to the next.

Go to a German optician, for example, for an eye test and new glasses, and the latter will be produced as prescribed for a price that amounts to only a third of what you'd have been quoted in the UK. Tell the German sales assistant what you would have paid at home, and he'll be horrified. He'll sit down and work out the approximate cost of materials, the cost of labour and the rental cost of the shop, add his profit on top and demonstrate how the final price is a combination of all those elements.

'That may be how your retailing works,' you'll be forced to admit. 'But it is not ours.' Ours is increasingly based not on what things cost, but on what people are prepared to pay. Just as the right price for a house is not based on the number of bricks in its walls, but on perceived demand. Just as the right price for a German newspaper in Tunisia is not based on its cover price plus freight cost, but on how badly a holidaymaker wants to read it. It's a market-based approach that many Germans have yet to accept.

But that's where, sadly, German industry is beginning to go. Hundreds of small family-owned manufacturing operations like the dental equipment and egg noodle factories on the outskirts of Tuttlingen haven't been able to persuade the next generation to take over when dad, or grandad, retires. With nowhere to go, the latter are being hoovered up by American-style mergers and acquisitions specialists who are dressing them up and selling them on, pushing them into much larger conglomerations and corporations where the concern is shareholder value first, quality of product second, needs of workforce third. The emphasis of this new-look manufacturing is on increasing revenue, reducing costs and making more money. And the message to the ageing benevolent owners is that they'd better look lively or else they'll simply get edged out of their market by these hungrier, acquisitive animals who are crowding their space.

Meanwhile, aware that there are other, possibly easier and certainly more glamorous ways of making money, the younger generation, no longer restrained by the heavy hand of history, are reluctant to follow their parents into the family firms. These young Germans are emerging from the post-war tunnel, beginning to adjust to a bigger marketplace and a life of more change. They don't see the need to hide any more, because it wasn't their generation that caused the problem. They've travelled widely and they can see that there is a bigger stage waiting for them than their uncle's small manufacturing company in the neighbouring valley. They don't want to be tied to a niche enterprise that does its job well but isn't going anywhere in particular. They're resisting the rigour and insularity of their parents, and many will describe themselves as Europeans first, Germans second. In this, European marriage statistics bear them out, because in terms of mixed-nation relationships Germany tops the league: a German is more likely than any other European to marry someone from another country.

I have direct experience of this phenomenon, having married one myself, and I have to say it doesn't feel like a cross-cultural relationship at all. Like it or not, out of the whole range of Europeans we are closest in character to the Germans, and they closest to us. We are, after all, fundamentally Saxons at heart. And our Queen is a German too.

3

Sigmaringen: Encounter with a Prince

When Patrick Leigh Fermor set out for his long walk back in 1933 he made a point of staying with as many aristocrats as possible. He had the right social contacts before he left home and he made even better connections as he went along, so in the event he was virtually passed like a sociable parcel from schloss to schloss, from one four-poster to the next. Along the Upper Danube in particular he wrote that castles were seldom out of sight, and many of his days ended with the spying of a 'small and nearly amphibian schloss mouldering in the failing light', which would turn out to be lived in by the 'widowed descendant of the lady-in-waiting of Charlemagne', who would be pleased to see him.

In those days the life of an archduke, a baron or a count was essentially leisurely, the various households busy with guests as they all visited each other and made sure their children married within the right social milieu. In such gently paced existences Leigh Fermor must have been an exotic and engaging house guest, with plenty of anecdotes to tell of his unusual voyage thus far. The likes of Baron Rheinhard von Liphart-Ratshoff were happy to receive him in their studies, where they'd be wearing slippers and reading Proust, or at least that was the position they'd adopted to receive their English visitor. And for a day or two at each place – sometimes even several days when he felt particularly welcome – he'd enter a world of riding, shooting, dinners and servants, accompanying families on excursions in charabancs to riverside picnics and playing polo on bicycles around their ornamental gardens. Some of these families spoke French at home, had English nannies and international family networks, and they all knew everyone else along the river, irrespective of national borders. So when he announced it was time he was moving on they'd write a note to their noble cousins further east to arrange his next accommodation.

In an ideal world I would have loved to have done the same, but many of the aristocratic families of the 1930s were no longer in residence, particularly in former communist countries. Many of them had been 'all handle and no jug' – i.e. titled, but with no cash – and once the war and its aftermath had taken away their land and their privileges, they'd chosen to flee and to start again overseas. Those who were brave or foolish enough to stay were reclassified as political dissidents and incarcerated in labour camps, 100,000 of them from Hungary alone, where every fifth person had aristocratic blood. There they were literally worked to death, particularly the tens of thousands of dissidents who died while digging the Black Sea Canal in Romania, a project to join the Danube to the Black Sea avoiding the meandering Delta, which was still ongoing as recently as the 1970s. Of course the death toll of European aristocracy is dwarfed by the numbers of Jews who died in the Holocaust, but the cull of the gentry remains one of the untold stories of the aftermath of the Second World War.

With Leigh Fermor's experience in mind, I was keen to meet aristocrats on my journey too, but it didn't prove easy to arrange. I don't move in the right kind of social circles and so (with one or two exceptions) bumping into the blue bloods of the Danube was going to be a matter of banging on doors and begging an audience. Those exceptions were down to the Transylvanian count I mentioned earlier, Count Tibor Kalnoky, who gave me the benefit of his knowledge, his wisdom and the email addresses of his lordly cousins on the riverbank.

Back in 1933, Leigh Fermor had moved eastwards at a steady walking pace and yet he occasionally arrived at the next schloss ahead of the relevant letter of introduction. Despite this, his hosts would still admit him, and entertain him, without really having any idea who he was or why he'd pitched up on their doorstep. These days, sadly, people are more private, less trusting and less flexible. In theory, in an era of instant communication, it should be even more possible to make arrangements at the last minute, but in practice people now require exact timings, plus heaps of advance notice. At least they did with me.

It was thus, for example, with the Saxe-Coburg-Gothas of Grein, a dynasty whose UK arm is more familiar to us under its adoptive name the House of Windsor (changed in 1917 to avoid anti-German sentiment), and who are also the rootstock for the Bulgarian and Portuguese royal households. For them, I was told that unless I could give a time and date a month in advance there was no chance of an appointment. I responded with regret that I could not be so specific: the vagaries of the weather, of bicycle travel in general, of my stamina in particular, of the quality of the route over the 800 kilometres between Donaueschingen and Grein, and of all the other appointments I was making along the way meant that it was impossible to say, before I set out, when exactly I'd get there, but I would be only too happy to provide more accurate updates from the saddle as I got closer. But the Saxe-Coburg-Gotha answer was uncompromising: without a month's notice it would not be possible to meet any member of the family. It was a response that made me grind my teeth and envy Leigh Fermor his email- and mobile-free existence.

I had more luck with the Hohenzollerns, however, another name with plenty of history attached and one with more relevant connections on the Danube. As their castle was at Sigmaringen, only around 90 kilometres downriver from Donaueschingen, providing an ETA at the portcullis wasn't so difficult. I was particularly keen to make a date because the Hohenzollerns represented my first nobility along the river. There was a good chance they'd be my last, too, at the other end, because they'd also been the royal family of Romania who had been deposed by the communists. I'd been in touch with a Hohenzollern pretender to the throne in Bucharest, and he'd agreed in principle to meet when I got there, even though it was some months down the line. So with the promise of Hohenzollerns topping and tailing my journey, I pedalled hard towards Sigmaringen, while trying not to get too sweaty, for my appointment with Prince Karl-Friedrich Emich Meinrad Benedikt Fidelis Maria Michael Gerold von Hohenzollern. Or Charly to his mates.

The route to Sigmaringen lay through an extremely pretty riverscape where an increasingly self-assured Danube burrowed its way through the southern end of the Swabian Alps, a grand name for a range of limestone hills that struggled to reach 1,000 metres. For a while the river valley turned into a pint-sized gorge, punctuated by thumbs of limestone sticking out of the woods of beech and juniper like broken piano keys, some of them topped with castle ruins. The cyclepath started to wrestle with the scenery and my lungs had to wrestle too to keep up. All around me were explosions of blossom, stationary puffs of smoke that represented spring's heavy artillery, as fruit trees announced that they were back in business again and this year they were determined to do well.

I stopped briefly for refreshment at a pathside farm where a youngish and enterprising farmer's wife had installed a coffee machine and an ice-cream freezer. She'd put tables and chairs out in the sun to detain passersby, and a sign that read '*Fahrradeis*' (ice-cream for cyclists) with a strong hint at paradise. However, her husband seemed to be doing his best to ruin her little Eden. He shouted as he stomped from the barn to the toolshed. He shouted as he stomped from the toolshed to the tractor, and he shouted again as he stomped from the tractor to the byre. His accent made what he was saying fairly impenetrable to my ear, but I could tell that he was using a vocabulary that wasn't impressing his wife.

A few kilometres further on and the atmosphere was much more refined. The monastery town of Beuron turned out to be practically all monastery and practically no town. Although it had been founded back in the eleventh century, most of the buildings dated from the nineteenth century and their big roofs loomed over the river valley, in a setting that was immaculately groomed. It all looked very prosperous, and walkers who circled the monastery could buy Kloster *Wurst*, Kloster chocolates and even tins of Kloster spaghetti bolognaise in Kloster shops. Most of the surrounding houses were part of the Kloster estate, with saints' names on their gateposts.

Some were gaunt and rather grotesque guesthouses, the eaves covered in frescos and the entranceways choked with weeds, suggesting that, while prosperity wasn't a problem, numbers of visitors had been much reduced in recent decades. Money flowed, but people stayed away.

The whole place marched to a beat that I couldn't hear. Seeking enlightenment, I ordered a Kloster beer in the local café and fell into conversation with the only other drinker, a lively Swiss man in his thirties. His brother was one of the monks, and he was waiting to take him out for the day.

'Where are you going to go?'

'We usually have a round of mini golf just down the hill here. It's just one of our little routines. He's always been competitive – he gets quite cross when he misses his putts and accuses me of trying to get him to take the Lord's name in vain. Which of course I am.'

'Is that what he wants to do – mini golf?' It was hard to visualize: a monk desperate to get his hands on a putter.

'Usually we end up in the nearest McDonald's, too.'

I couldn't hide a look of surprise. 'You're joking?'

'No, we really do. McDonald's represents a moment of freedom. Something a little bit naughty. And we loved McDonald's when we were kids, it's what we have in common. God knows, there's not a lot else.'

I took my time over my drink, and then sauntered downhill to the monastery church. Dressed as I was in lycra cycling shorts, I didn't feel entirely comfortable going inside, but there was no congregation amongst the high baroque, with its fulsome confection of pink-and-white marble pillars, frescoed ceilings, robed saints, flamboyant stucco ogees and pediments and cherubs. If it wasn't painted, then it'd be gilded, and even the organ pipes were topped and tailed with gold. It wasn't the sort

41

of place to find peace of mind with all that ornamentation screaming at you. I found it an indecent display of wealth, but in case there is a God, I knelt in a pew and thanked Him for my Donaueschingen bicycle experience, and I asked for the Fuerteventura one to be taken into consideration too, just in case; I wouldn't want to be thought of as ungrateful. After all, even the Muslims have a saying: 'Trust in Allah, *and* tie your camel to the tree.'

Sigmaringen turned out to be a jovial, intimate town, with lots of pavement cafés clustered round a jagged knuckle of rock towering above the river. Its streets were busy with students and soldiers on leave from the Tenth Panzer Division, whose barracks were sufficiently nearby to keep Gaby's Exotic Cabaret in business. The Danube did a tight right turn around the town, and the jumble of streets at all angles and gradients would have been confusing were it not for the Hohenzollern castle rising above everything, the cock of the rock, a helpful way of getting one's bearings. In fact this was just one of several Hohenzollern properties, with another even bigger castle not far to the north at Hechingen, but this one at least had a Hohenzollern in residence, while the Hechingen castle was the official, unlived in, family seat.

There's Hohenzollern memorabilia all over town, recording the passing of each noble benefactor. An equestrian statue of Leopold von Hohenzollern in the main square, and a fountain presented by the Hohenzollerns in the pedestrianized centre, with copper figures holding flowers, shielding fires, cutting corn and presenting grapes. The schloss itself towered over a big, still pool in the river, something of a fearsome engineering achievement in the way it sprouted out of the rock. In terms of location, it looked as if it was designed for hot-oil-pouring on enemy heads, but its architecture was more ornamental than defensive, sending out a mixed message of intimidation and exhilaration. There was an odd mix of styles: a Dutch gable-end, some peaked towers that looked like they belonged to Tuscany, giant red roofs studded with tiers of dormer windows and spiked with chimneys, and painted red shutters on the main windows that could have been a job lot from Ikea. No surprise, then, to learn that when the original fortress-like building was damaged by fire in the 1870s, it was largely rebuilt in the eclectic style that was fashionable at the time. The net result reminded me of Mervyn Peake's Gormenghast, and I could imagine a pale, lonely prince peering down from behind those shuttered windows, wondering what it would have been like to have friends and mix with ordinary people.

Anxious about my first meeting with German aristocracy, I'd been careful to do a bit of research about their role in the territory and quickly realized that virtually the sum total of my knowledge of German history revolved around two key twentieth-century events. Those two world wars represent all we learn about Germany at school and completely mask how young a nation it actually is. We tend to bracket it with Britain and France as one of the long-standing powers of Europe, but actually Germany only formally became a single entity in 1871, when Bismarck's victories over France and Austria led to the proclamation of the German Empire. Up until then it had been a patchwork of 350-odd principalities, run by electors, margraves, counts and dukes, amongst whom were the Hohenzollerns. Today's Germany is an awkward but powerful young adult on the world stage, just emerging from a troubled adolescence during which it had put on muscle faster than brain.

A thousand years ago the land populated by Franks,

Alemanii, Saxons and Swabians extended eastwards into what is now Poland, the Czech Republic and Austria. All were loosely federated into something called the Holy Roman Empire, which saw itself as the successor to the Roman Empire, but historians usually point out that it was neither holy, nor Roman, nor an empire. The emperor (invariably also the German king) was based in Bavaria but he had little real authority beyond his own region.

The principalities in this empire of wishful thinking eventually sorted themselves out into two main camps, particularly after Martin Luther nailed his ninety-five theses on a church door in 1517, kick-starting the Reformation and demonstrating the potency of the printed word. Prussia, in the north, went largely under the thumb of the Brandenburgs, the Protestant arm of the Hohenzollern dynasty, which had split into two in the fifteenth century. And what was called Austria, to the south (including the whole of today's southern Germany), was run by the Habsburgs. Here the Catholic arm of the Hohenzollern dynasty had its territories, one of which was Sigmaringen.

Despite the 'empire' label, there had been little organization to any Holy Roman lands over and above a basic feudal system accorded to the local lord. Crucially there was no central taxation and no German army, so when Napoleon arrived in 1806 he skittled the electors one by one, as easily as knocking a row of bottles off a wall, and dissolved the Holy Roman Empire altogether. It was he who then amalgamated lots of the principalities, consigning hundreds of local ruling dynasties to the scrap heap and ending up with a list of thirty-five monarchies of various kinds, plus four free-standing cities: Hamburg, Bremen, Frankfurt and Lübeck.

In the southern region of Germany he rationalized

121 principalities down into three regions. While doing so he allowed the southern Hohenzollerns to keep (and even expand) their authority, principally because Princess Amalie Hohenzollern had been brought up in France and was a friend of Josephine Bonaparte. They'd gone shopping in Paris together.

Napoleon then moved on eastwards to make the mistake of taking on the Russians, a famous error that others have made since. Encouraged by his defeat, the Prussians, the Austrians and the British took him on at Leipzig in 1813 and spanked him too. The Congress of Vienna in 1815 sorted out the aftermath of conflict and set Germany's national borders close to where they are today, but it didn't go so far as to create a unified German state. Instead a loose German Customs Union, incorporating eighteen states and twenty-three million inhabitants, was formed in 1834, but the whole federalization process stalled until the arrival of beefy Bismarck, who rose through the ranks of the Prussian army in the north. It was he who took on the Habsburgs, controllers of southern Germany, and forced them off German soil. He then used his political and military power to coerce the remaining local aristocracy to accept the authority of one unified German state, with Prussia the dominant partner. And Germany was born.

The Hohenzollerns cleverly rode out all these changes. The schism between the northern Protestant and southern Catholic branches of the dynasty had been patched up in the mid-nineteenth century, and they agreed to share the family castle at Hechingen as the official family seat. Thanks to Bismarck's efforts, the Protestant branch was by far the stronger of the two, and both of the kaisers of the newly formed German Empire were northern Hohenzollerns, including the much-derided Kaiser

Wilhelm II, who made the unfortunate decision to go to war in 1914. And this is the moment when most school history books turn their searchlights on Germany for the first time.

Frankly, I was a bit relieved to learn that the Sigmaringen end was the less powerful of the two dynasties, less instrumental in world history, because meeting Kaiser Wilhelm's son or grandson could have been uncomfortable given what had transpired: 'So it was your grandpa who started fifty years of war?' Happily, the Sigmaringen family's dabbling with kingship was restricted to a brief flirtation with the Spanish throne in 1869 and to the invitation extended to a spare son to become prince of Romania in 1866, thus starting a Hohenzollern-Sigmaringen Romanian royal family. At the time of that invitation from Romania the intervening Habsburg-ruled lands had been hostile to the Hohenzollerns, so twenty-seven-year-old Karl (the future King Carol I of Romania) had had to board a Danube steamer disguised as a travelling salesman in order to collect his throne. To us it seems odd to hear how an obscure land on the eastern side of Europe could invite a relatively minor nobleman from the western side to cross the continent to take their crown, but that's how it happened in those days, even in the UK, which at the time was being ruled by a family from a northern German town called Hanover. And as a king, Karl/Carol turned out to be a jolly good thing.

These incidents apart, the Hohenzollern-Sigmaringen dynasty had bumped along neither prospering unduly nor threatening to fade away until it arrived at the gateway to the twenty-first century with handy assets of a steel factory, extensive forestry, a Bavarian ski resort and half of Vancouver Island, not to mention a few other small castles and manor houses in the neighbourhood. All of

46

which was controlled by the prince I was about to see.

I pitched up outside the castle at the appointed time, and *seine Durchlaucht* – His Serene Highness – sent one of his staff to escort me through to his offices. The castle's interiors looked relatively unchanged since the fire that prompted the remodelling of the 1870s. That fire had been caused by great-great-grandfather Prince Leopold's interest in technology: he'd installed a hydropower unit down on the river below in order to supply one of the first electric lighting systems in Germany, and a fault on the circuit had started the conflagration.

Apart from this early venture into son et lumière, Leopold had also installed the first flushing toilets in Germany, still in place in the castle, but elsewhere the interiors were pretty timeless: the usual grandeur of velvets, tapestries, portraits and hand-carved Louis XV furniture. There were ladies' quarters, a long chandeliered ballroom and a dark-walled gentlemen's smoking room with slate-topped tables for the menfolk to play cards and chalk up the scores. The walls of the Hubertus Hall were covered in hunting trophies, usually one representative beast from each of the Hohenzollern's extensive domains, including a moose from Sweden and a stuffed Romanian bear snarling from the top of a rock. The accumulated testosterone from all these shot animals added to the perceived potency of the Hohenzollerns themselves. A goodly horn collection signified a spunky duke.

There was, however, no visible souvenir of Sigmaringen's most celebrated temporary residents, the less-spunky pro-Nazi Vichy government. This French government-by-proxy had been moved here in the latter stages of the Second World War. The Hohenzollerns had had to pack their bags and move out in order to make way for Marshal Pétain and his staff of eighty, in order that the Vichy administration could churn out the necessary paperwork under the ceiling frescos and the close supervision of their German 'allies'. By this stage Hitler didn't trust them an inch so they were effectively under house arrest atop the rock in Sigmaringen, and the view of the Danube stretching away unimpeded from virtually every window must have been difficult to bear. Fortunately the French treated the schloss with the greatest respect and their temporary residence did it no harm, but the emotional impact on the Hohenzollerns was significant.

Following their eviction, the family was temporarily rehoused in the von Stauffenberg castle near Ulm, which had not surprisingly fallen empty after Claus von Stauffenberg's bomb-in-the-bunker plot to kill Hitler had missed its target. Von Stauffenberg had been summarily executed and his family dispersed to concentration camps, so the family home was unexpectedly vacant. Handy for the Hohenzollerns, but these were not comfortable circumstances in which to lose your main residence, or to go housesitting for old friends, especially when fanatical Nazis wanted to burn the von Stauffenberg castle down, no matter who might be inside.

'The family never really returned to live in Schloss Sigmaringen after that,' explained Prince Karl-Friedrich, when we finally met in his smart suite of offices somewhere up on the fifth floor. 'I have an apartment here, but our main house is a few kilometres away. It is rather smaller.' I tried to visualize what 'rather smaller' meant – presumably not a 'small' that I would recognize.

Various of his female staff fluttered around, producing coffee and waving diaries, treating him with a reverence and formality that made me feel nervous, acutely aware of the wear and tear of travelling by bicycle: 'This man's feet smell. Chop off his head!' And I'd end up on the wall of the Hubertus Hall, between the Swedish moose and the Romanian bear, my dark glasses still hanging around my neck.

Contrary to my expectation of a sort of leisurely bicycling aristocracy, Scandinavian style, Karl-Friedrich was a steely, formal character in his mid-fifties, dressed in the sort of Savile Row suit you see in the smarter gentlemen's clubs of St James's, with yellow tie and a silk handkerchief in his top pocket. A captain of industry, British style, with very little of the idle rich about him. The message I got was that he was a very busy man, and he seemed impatient with my vicarious interest in Hohenzollern life and times.

To my opening questions about the family's resources he suggested, almost with a touch of severity, that I should have consulted the Hohenzollern website, which had all necessary details. He wasn't much more expansive on the subject of his wider relatives, either, barely acknowledging the greetings I brought from his cousin in Romania, the (self-proclaimed) heir to the yet-to-be-reinstated Romanian throne. In fact, although he mentioned nothing of it then, I later discovered that he was in far closer contact with Romania than I could have guessed, being touted in some circles as a possible future king.

'It's hard to keep up with the whole family,' he said, passing his hand repeatedly over his brow in a gesture I wasn't sure was habitual or just the stress of dealing with me. 'There are so many cousins, so many of them, and there are invitations every month. In the old days there were lots of visits, but these days when communication is so easy, paradoxically we don't meet nearly so much, and then it's usually brief. Sometimes there are family shooting parties and traditional events like weddings, but mostly I travel for business.'

I asked what sort of business, and again he referred me to a website for the details of the steel factory, the forestry and the ski resort. 'And I have an investment company for business start-ups.'

I had the distinct feeling that he would be happier discussing the state of the Dow Jones index than the life and times of the German aristocracy.

'So do you get involved in town life?' I persisted, thinking of the various statues in the streets below.

'Obviously the castle is a big attraction for tourists, so inevitably I am involved.'

I tried a different tack, thinking of the Leigh Fermor era. 'Would family life have been much different in the 1930s?'

'Of course. In those days the land was enough to support the castle, there was no need for all the other businesses and there was a lot more leisure time. Now we have a hard time keeping up. We've sold seven castles in the last twenty years, just to keep costs down. Initially we tried to find tenants, but these are big properties. One of them was formerly a monastery. It is not easy to find buyers for places that size in the middle of the countryside.'

He seemed to lose a little stature as he talked about the necessary disposal of family property. Plainly it was a matter of huge personal pride whether or not the dynasty prospered under his control.

'I guess it must seem a big responsibility, keeping the whole show on the road. Did it ever occur to you to do something else?'

'My father left the choice to me. I wasn't forced into it.'

'Did you at least do other things for a while?'

'I had to decide before university.'

That seemed tough, and I said so. 'So what about the next generation?'

'I'm guiding my son. I've said he can have a gap year, but he's got to make his mind up. He's beginning to show the right aptitude.'

Poor kid, was my first thought, swiftly followed by a second thought that the word 'poor' didn't really apply. 'And if he doesn't want to?'

'Then I have to make preparations for the future. Possibly a nephew.'

It turned out that his son had just finished at an upmarket English boarding school, which Karl-Friedrich had presumably considered to be a better education for a German prince than his own experience in a Swiss international school. I wondered whether the future prince had made any unsuitable liaisons with young assistant matrons away from the watchful eye of his parents.

'And what about future marriage partners? Do your children have to marry into the nobility?' I knew that he himself had, to a von Stauffenberg countess, which must have seemed absolutely the right thing to do given that uncomfortable housesitting during the war.

'I wouldn't disapprove if they didn't,' he said, somewhat unconvincingly. And then, perhaps aware that he hadn't been definitive, he added, 'The point is that they've got to have the same ideas as each other to make the relationship work, ideas about responsibility towards society, etc., about having to give as well as take. Inevitably that means a similar social background. You have to accept that as an aristocrat you are a person of public interest, like it or not. It is not as if we have to arrange meetings for the children as they did in the old days, when sometimes marriages would take place without both partners even being present. My children are finding family connections via the Internet and arranging to meet up anyway.'

They were, however, getting a helping hand in real time, too, because the prince and his wife were hosting a party in the castle's ballroom later in the year, with a guest list of 250–300. Like as not most of the A-list of suitable marriage partners would be assembled, because a Hohenzollern was quite a catch.

'Will there be some families you don't invite? Old enmities?' I was thinking in particular of the Habsburgs, and it must have been written on my forehead.

'The Hohenzollerns weren't friends with the Habsburgs in the past,' he said, 'but there's no particular frostiness when we meet these days.'

No, his main concerns were plainly the status quo of his business, and building up sufficient momentum to be able to pass on the estate in a healthier state than when he found it. 'Besides, I couldn't live a life without work, it would be too boring.'

'You could say the same of all work and no play.'

'Well of course I like to ski,' he said impatiently. 'And to sail. When I can. And I play in a band, a jazz band.' He rootled around in a drawer and pulled out a CD for a band called Charly and the Jivemates, which he gave me as a parting gift as he showed me to the door.

'Which is you?' I asked, looking down at the smouldering, slightly sleazy, figures in shades on the cover.

'That's me, the other me,' said Prince Karl-Friedrich von Hohenzollern, pointing to the one in the middle wearing the snakeskin shoes and the leopardskin jacket. 'Charly.'

I should have known.

I left Sigmaringen thinking that my first contact with Danube aristocracy had gone reasonably well, but it hadn't produced a string of downriver addresses as it had for Leigh Fermor. The prince had seemed defensive and rather private, but it had seemed unrealistic to expect anything else. Why should he invite an unknown, slightly smelly writer any further into his life than necessary? What benefit could it be to him? If he had, I might have found out more than he was prepared for me to know, and put it in a book like this. They may not be in each others' houses any more, these Danube aristocrats, but there's plenty of gossip along the riverbank, most of which I'd forgotten by the time I got back to London and listened to Prince Charly's Jivemates CD. Listening to it, all those weeks later, I realized that somewhere underneath that frosty exterior there'd lurked a whole personality I'd barely noticed, that of a serious musician shackled by his position in life, trying to get out. The recording was remarkably good.

On my way out of Sigmaringen I had one final storyline to pursue. I was keeping a weather eye open for anything called the Fishermen's Rendezvous, aka the Treffpunkt der Fischer. An inn of this name in Sigmaringen hosts the opening scene of Jules Verne's little-known book *Le pilote du Danube*, where members of the Danube League, a fishermen's society, met in 1876 for their annual boozy lunch.

At the meeting, a Hungarian called Ilia Brusch, whom no one in the society had heard of before, bragged that he was going to descend the Danube from source to mouth, surviving solely on the fish he would catch all the way down and making a large profit by selling what he didn't need. He was prepared to take on any bets that it could be done.

The League was intrigued, particularly because in those

days the Danube had a big problem with piracy and theft affecting noble properties along the banks, and members were of the opinion that the enterprise was very risky. But then, once Brusch had left the meeting, another previously unknown new member suggested they send someone (i.e. himself) with the Hungarian, to verify whether or not he did as he promised. The League's membership agreed.

Unaware that he was to have a companion, Brusch started from the Breg and Brigach intersection on what he estimated to be a two-month journey, and caught his first fish within sight of his sending-off party. In Ulm, a couple of days downriver, he was joined by the mysterious new member of the League, who persuaded his way on to the boat as a passenger. The reader knew by now that the latter was no fisherman but the Danube's chief of police, and of course that Brusch was no fisherman either, but a prince amongst thieves looking for a good cover story to travel the river. The rest of the book is an account of how the two men try to find out more about each other as the journey becomes more dangerous, and how they finally become firm friends, bonded by common enemies – pirates, and the Danube itself.

Whether or not Jules Verne ever travelled the river I don't know. His account is very imprecise, and even in the days before hydroelectric dams it would still have been practically impossible for a fisherman to descend by boat from the Breg and Brigach intersection, bearing in mind the sunken section by Immendingen. So I wasn't surprised when I didn't find any evidence of a Fishermen's Rendez-vous on the outskirts of Sigmaringen.

But I did discover one at the end of that day's pedalling, by a village called Rottenackers. With Jules Verne in mind, I stopped off for a shandy at the Rottenackers Fischhütte, which turned out to be a glorified garden shed with a terrace and bar overlooking three artificial fishing ponds fed by the Danube. I was hoping to meet wise old Danubian fishermen who might be able to tell me a thing or two about the lifecycle of the sturgeon, but the only drinker was a young man too pale for anyone who spent any time out of doors, with the sort of face that had been rendered immobile by too much beer. Like the fish in the ponds, his expressions struggled to reach the surface through an opaque soup. They were too sluggish to respond to any emotions that he might have been feeling underneath. Talking to him was a matter of throwing bait on to the water to see if there was anything that caught his interest, and I didn't have much luck with traditional openers. But when I mentioned my bicycle, his lips puckered up into a question. Where was I headed?

'Budapest.'

'Ah, Poland,' he slurred.

'No, no, not Poland,' I corrected, and I filled him in on the list of countries that the Danube flowed through, most of which I don't think he even heard. But the talk of destinations unlocked another pattern of sentences in his brain, and he started to give me directions on how to get to the autobahn that headed east.

'I'm on a bicycle,' I reminded him. 'And I'm following the river.'

'Which river?'

I was already beginning to tire of his company. When I'd finally managed to get him to understand where I was going, and where I was coming from, he asked the only logical question.

'Why?'

I explained about being a writer, in my experience usually a mistake. His eyes grew wide.

'So when you get back to London, big big city, you're

going to be writing about how you stopped in a fisher-men's hut by Rottenackers, small small place?'

I nodded. I was thinking I probably would, now that I'd met him.

This thought seemed to worry my companion.

'I don't know how many people in London know about Rottenackers,' he said, dubiously.

I agreed that not many would have had the Rottenackers experience. But added that, after a few days on a bicycle, I was beginning to get some inkling of it myself.

4

Ulm and the Danube Swabians

German schoolchildren invariably learn two things about the Danube. The first is the mnemonic that helps them remember its tributaries, which runs thus: '*Iller, Lech, Isar, Inn fliessen rechts der Donau hin/Altmühl, Naab und Regen sind dagegen links gelegen*' ('The Iller, Lech, Isar and Inn join from the right, and the Altmühl, Naab and Regen come from the left').

The second is the tongue-twister about the river's first substantial city, '*In Ulm und um Ulm und um Ulm herum*', which means 'In Ulm, in the vicinity of Ulm and around Ulm', and when muttered repeatedly from the handlebars of a 20-euro bicycle fits neatly with Rossini's gallop from the *William Tell Overture*: Diddle-er diddle-er diddle-rum-tum-tum. *In Ulm und um Ulm und um Ulm herum*. Diddle-er diddle-er diddle-rum-tum-tum. *In Ulm und um Ulm . . .*

I was diddle-ering towards Ulm, giving thanks for the consistently good weather, when it occurred to me that an *Ulm herum* – a slight detour – might be a good wheeze, to take in a couple of the tributaries that weren't large enough to make it into the river mnemonic despite pretty mnemonical names. The Ach and the Blau.

So I had a salami sandwich in Riedlingen's market square, near a fountain of tumbling storks, and got out the map to think it over. Around me a clutch of market stalls were selling fruit, cheese, meat and vegetables, and a roaming dachshund was doing a circuit of us bench-lunchers with an intense, quizzical expression that said 'I'm not actually begging, I'm just doing a survey of what people are putting in their sandwiches this year. For which I require samples, please.'

Riedlingen's centre was a cobbled *Altstadt* full of gabled and shuttered houses in a tight fist of alleys on the flank of a riverside hill. At cobble level around the main square were two bakeries, an optician, a pharmacy, a *Gasthof*, a bookshop and a Greek restaurant, most of them with the owner's name and trade painted in Gothic script on the plasterwork above the awning, indicating that they'd been there for years and had no intention of moving on for years to come. It is hard to imagine such a state of perseverance on the British high street, where most retailers expect to move, be it up or down the retailing ladder, in the not-too-distant future. British retailing, with hungry franchising and prowling bully brands, is subject to true capitalist ethics: grow or die. Staying still is tantamount to an admission of defeat.

Meanwhile in Riedlingen, above and around the long-staying shops, the truly elderly properties bent a bit at the knee in tacit acknowledgement of each other's longevity, a nod here, a curtsey there, frozen in the act of shivering, huddling together for protection against the traffic. Some of them were so ancient that their half-timbering looked positively skeletal, but they still managed to puff out their chests in their upper storeys and look down their noses at neighbours who'd been done up by banks to become unfeasibly smooth-walled and straight in the limb, like film stars whose skin had become surprisingly wrinkle-free and who no longer sagged at their gable-ends.

From my map I gathered that my choice of route ahead lay between sticking to the modern river-course east of Riedlingen and heading straight for Ulm, or following the Danube's original glacial route *herum*, through prehistory around the edges of the Swabian hills. And heruming through prehistory sounded the more interesting of the two.

The asparagus season was in full swing as I turned my handlebars north in search of the Ach, mumbling, 'So, the Ach. Ach so.' This was prime *Spargel* territory, and it had been on menus all the way from Donaueschingen; I'd even seen mention of an asparagus museum in one of the local towns, and found it hard to imagine how you'd derive a whole cultural experience out of a single vegetable (unless of course it was the potato, upon which complete nations have depended). I didn't need a museum to tell me that this *Spargel* thingy was not the green spear that we think of at home. Germans like their asparagus to be pale and anaemic, or at best straw-coloured thanks to lashings of butter. To keep it pale and soft necessitates making sure it never breaks through the topsoil into daylight, and therefore as it grows, by the force of nature, so does the pile of earth above it, by the hand of man. The Ach valley north of Ehingen was one of those places where this tussle between man and nature was being acted out on a daily basis. Below ground, millions of tumescent spears were straining every sinew for a glimpse of the sun, while above ground a farmer had time to berate his teenage daughter, leaning out of an upper window in a dressing gown on a long phone call about last night, before climbing on his tractor and entombing his rows of straining *Spargel* into even deeper piles of earth. Sooner or later the *Spargel* race would end in *Spargel* tears, when groups of Hungarian or Romanian labourers would arrive by the vanload, plunge their hands into the moist earth and cut the poor buggers out of their darkness. They would finally have their wish for their moment in the sun granted, but too late to go stiff and green with pleasure, because they would be viewing it through a film of butter. So, the Ach. Ach so.

For a river with a highly noticeable name, the Ach made a comparatively low-key entry into the Danube's former valley, threading between the fields trailing a thin and sickly streamer of bushes, a kite's tail looking for a kite. On my bicycle I found myself weaving from one valley flank to the other, trying to avoid the main road. Around me the season was moving fast and my exuberant dandelions *in excelsis* of the first few days of the journey were now being overtaken by highly regimented fields of wheat, marching in fascist phalanxes along the valley floor and rudely thrusting the wild flowers to the sides. The untidiness of spring, which had threatened momentarily to get out of hand, had been quickly brought to heel.

Eventually the Ach and I arrived simultaneously in Blaubeuren, a handsome resort town with yet more fifteenth-century half-timbered houses, here with windows inturned and latticed wood in *mashrabia* style, like something you might see in Cairo. The Ach changed nationalities too, becoming bridged, canalized and neat, and threading between and under the houses, as if auditioning for a walk-on part in Amsterdam.

At the far end of Blaubeuren, where the town rammed its head against wooded hills, I came across its main attraction – a jewel of a spring called the Blautopf (the

Blue Pot) that would have done a far better job of being the designated starting point of the Danube than the spring at Donaueschingen, particularly now that I knew that most of the water emerging at Donaueschingen ended up in the Rhine.

Actually 'spring' was a misnomer for what I found at Blaubeuren. A spring is something that slakes your thirst by burbling out from under a tussock, but this Blautopf was a vertical cave filled with water, the big front door for a whole underground river system. Its throat descended deep into the ground and its mouth opened wide to gargle out a glassy lagoon, whose superficial stillness belied the massive movement of H_2O taking place below. That throat fed the mouth incessantly, at up to 32,000 litres per second, but only the lip of the lagoon quivered where it became an instant river, the Blau. I knew it eventually joined the Danube in Ulm, having snaffled up the Ach like a truffling pig just outside town. If only the Romans had designated this as the source of the longest river in continental Europe, then my journey would have been following the blue Blau, and not the blue Danube, which of course is decidedly not *blau*. And there was no denying the blueness of the shimmering Blautopf. Apparently, after rain, the blue turned lighter and cloudier, and after a lot of rain it could even turn green or yellow as the power of the extra rushing water released yellow particles of lime from the rock in underground chasms, but that day it was practically forget-me-not hue. The hole it emerged from was so deep – over 60 feet – that you couldn't see the bottom, and the lagoon so calm and flat that it was hard to believe that the whole thing was on the move, and at a riverine rate which was more than enough to turn the wheel in an old smithy on the lagoon's southern side.

Below ground, the river flowed through caverns which

were only starting to be explored. Sadly, I could find no mention of any direct connection with the Danube-sinking system, which was a shame; it would have made a dazzling, glamorous resurrection for the lost waters of Immendingen if some of it could have emerged here.

That day a group of divers was going through slow predive checks by the smithy, surrounded by a small crowd of admirers. I could see a couple of air tanks anchored to the bed of the lagoon, presumably for emergencies, for there had been accidents here, including deaths, in recent years, but there had also been major finds. A German archaeologist had recently discovered Europe's oldest art, 30,000–33,000-year-old ivory carvings of a duck, a horse's head and a mammoth, in a cave system connected to the Blau. These finds confirmed the theory that Europe's first human beings had been adventurous ancestors of the Assyrians and the Chaldeans of Mesopotamia and Ur, who moved west from what is now Syria and Iraq. When they reached Europe they followed the only obvious route, the original course of the Danube, making their homes in riverside caves as they went. If this theory is correct, then the Danube valley becomes Europe's equivalent of East Africa's Rift Valley, the cradle of European civilization, and so by heading downriver I could feasibly claim (cue portentous music) to be heading back to the dawn of time. Until someone finds something older somewhere else, that is.

Certainly there was something primeval, compelling and unsettling about the presence of that giant hole in the ground and its silent, smooth delivery of so much pure water. Miraculous, even, and the presence of a Benedictine monastery next to the Blautopf, next to such a wonder of nature, came as no surprise. But it was the Blautopf that visitors walked around, talking in subdued voices, not the monastery church, and the spirituality they demonstrated was based more upon superstition than religious belief.

'Can I throw money in?' asked a little girl of her parents.

'Better not.'

'But I want to make a wish!'

From the corner of my eye I watched how her parents would respond, and they in turn looked at each other, uncertain. The spring at Donaueschingen had been full of coins, but this fathomless hole into prehistory was a different matter.

'You might hit one of the divers coming up,' said her father, eventually. It was a convincing enough argument, but there was more to it than that. To toss a coin into the Blautopf would be a bit like lobbing bits of metal into the works of the world. And nobody would want to be the one who choked the blue Blau.

A couple of hours later I was in Ulm, cycling past furniture warehouses and table-dancing clubs in the suburbs, not enjoying my first big city on the river. Meanwhile the Blau was still doing its tumbling watercourse act somewhere over to my right, gushing through the Fishermen's Quarter (now reinvigorated with art galleries and designer B&Bs) where visitors sat out on terraces and little bridges and ate grilled trout. Eventually it would slide anticlimactically into the dung-coloured Danube below the city's long medieval ramparts, and nothing *blau* would remain.

Ulm had been one of the Holy Roman Empire's first free towns, and one of the richest towns in Europe in the fifteenth century, which was why its cathedral had been endowed with the highest church spire (161 metres) in the world. Much of the town centre was pedestrianized, and although it looked old, it had actually been largely rebuilt after a severe pummelling during the Second World War. Allied bombers had theoretically been targeting Ulm's giant fortress and barracks – one of five Federal Fortresses in Germany, with a resident fighting force of 10,000 men – but the bombing ended up being pretty indiscriminate and most parts of the old city were destroyed.

The intriguingly translated city brochure I picked up in the tourist office was determined to look on the bright side. The net result of the bombing, it said, was that the city had become 'an Eldorado of modern architecture', which made it sound far worse than it was. The same translator described Ulm's most famous son, Albert Einstein, as being 'at the very top of the list of go-getting Ulmites' – ah yes, that list of go-getting Ulmites; I wonder who filled positions two and three? And he (or she) went on to characterize the city's various cultural offerings as 'extremely pleasant alternatives to twiddling one's thumbs'. Wrong choice of language, or taking the piss?

The translator's post-modernist take softened the sense of alienation I was feeling on my arrival in Ulm, which was essentially the result of the stark contrast between my rural ride through pastoral Baden-Württemberg, where I was a monarch of the path, and the altogether faster, dirtier, noisier city streets, where I was cannon fodder for cars. I'd felt like a figure in an artist's landscape in Baden-Württemberg, a figure that belonged, but in Ulm I was an anachronism, completely out of step with the urban pace. Cities diminish their visitors, and foreign visitors are the easiest targets. Only once you are sure of where you are going to sleep, earning you a little bit of belonging, can you start to feel braver again. Confidence begins with a bedroom of one's own.

In Ulm, the place I found to stay was rather different to the quiet guesthouses I'd frequented upriver. Mind you, I had had a couple of unlikely overnights even in the countryside, and on my very first night on the road out of Donaueschingen I'd ended up in a *Gasthof* frequented by lorrydrivers, a twenty-four-hour place with a giant car park attached in which the 40-tonners were lined up in rows. The drivers assembled here in the evenings like sparrows on a wire, seeking community amongst other habitual migrants, even though they spoke little of each others' languages.

'You don't need to worry about your bicycle,' the proprietress had said to me as I parked it amongst the behemoths, hoping they'd notice it in their rearview mirrors when they reversed out in the morning. 'We don't need to have guard dogs – our drivers all sleep in their cabs.'

Inside, the *Gasthof* smelled of deep-fat frying, 'Rhinestone Cowboy' played endlessly on the sound system, and the drivers had beer and cigarettes with dinner, beer and cigarettes with breakfast, and beer and cigarettes with midnight snacks. I'm not sure how alert they'd be to anything by the time they'd staggered back out into the lorry park, unless perhaps you tried to steal their cigarettes.

I had woken to a dawn chorus of Volvos clearing their throats of diesel phlegm, to realize that nicotine had prematurely aged everything around me: tablecloths, curtains, wall colour, skin. The woman who served breakfast looked like a cross between a bullfrog and a dragon, and the breakfast coffee tasted like it had been made by adding boiling water to last night's ashtrays.

The place I found in Ulm was not dissimilar. It was called the Schwarzer Adler, which coincidentally happened to be the name of Leigh Fermor's first hotel in Germany, and it too was a largely male doss-house that stank of old cigarettes, with a shared bathroom at the end of each corridor. The manager was a Brazilian called Mrs Herring, and she ran the place single-handed while Mr Herring (not Brazilian, but not German either) sat out on a small first-floor terrace with his ghetto-blaster and worked his way steadily through a crate of beer. In the evenings he would be joined in this activity by other long-term residents, presumably after they'd finished work, and they'd light candles and get maudlin together, singing along to Mr Herring's CDs. How long you'd have to be resident in the Schwarzer Adler to qualify for this elite karaoke club I don't know, but you couldn't come or go from the hotel without passing the Herring *Stammtisch*, exchanging greetings as you went.

Besides me, there were a couple of genuine tourists who flitted like ghosts along the Schwarzer Adler's corridors, bemused by where they'd ended up, but the rest of the clientele were plainly regulars, mostly from Eastern Europe, and by the look of their footwear mostly here to work on construction sites. At the weekend they all disappeared over the side, including the Herrings, and the Schwarzer Adler became like a ghost ship.

Early that Sunday morning, to celebrate my first actual path-crossing with Leigh Fermor, who'd walked over the Danube at Ulm en route for Munich, I climbed the *Münster* (minster) spire as he had done, all 768 steps of it, the only time I could be sure of putting my feet exactly where he'd put his. From the outside, the spire was not particularly beautiful to look at, knobbled as it was with decorative excrescences and patched with repairs from different eras, which all contrived to make it look rather gaunt and threadbare. Inside, there was no warning about quite how narrow, winding and claustrophobic the stair would become. It was something of a human experiment in a medieval capillary – an experiment where you'd embark a normal cross-section of people at the base, people who obviously thought they were up to climbing a tall, tapering cathedral tower, and then watch to see how far they percolated upwards and what kind of excuses were deployed as they realized they couldn't go any further. The interest in the experiment would lie in which nationalities would push on, doggedly, and which individuals would turn back, and how the increasing physical demands would affect the dynamics of a family or a group of friends.

If I hadn't already spent many days on a bicycle, I would have struggled to reach the top myself. At around step number four hundred I was grateful to feel a breeze begin, and a little beyond was a scrawled message suggesting I had 'just passed the best bit', but I wasn't going back to look. Not far short of the top the *Münster*'s bells started to toll, thankfully not from anywhere in the immediate vicinity, but the sound swam around the spire obliterating all other noise, coming from all angles at once as it reflected upwards off the Eldorado of modern architecture spread out below. I regretted not bringing the city brochure up with me; the author would no doubt have had some encouraging bon mots about the health benefits of twiddling one's legs up the spire. When I finally reached the ledge below the peak I felt nothing but admiration for the people who'd actually built this Gothic rocket back in 1377. Many of them must have died so that future generations could twiddle to their hearts' content.

The *Münster* has an organ concert every Sunday, which was a good opportunity to get my breath back, swallowed up once again by the womb of the building. Inside, the nave was too tall to be beautiful, but it made a great echo chamber for the organ. This was not twiddling; the sound was mighty enough to make the flagstones rumble and vibrate my bones inside my flesh.

Afterwards I was reunited with the Danube over a pike and chips on the city's riverside ramparts, in a part of town that Leigh Fermor described as 'containing nothing later than the Middle Ages', but which now boasted a heavy concentration of very un-medieval Internet cafés. Just along the wall was the Eagles' Bastion where the Tailor of Ulm, another go-getting Ulmite called Albrecht Berblinger, had attempted to fly the first ever hang-glider, back in 1811. 'The Ulm tailor attempted to fly on a whim/But the devil led him into the Danube to swim' runs the local rhyme, making fun of the poor chap quite unnecessarily. Berblinger's plan had been to cross the width of the river, but the reality was that he'd barely managed halfway, and compounded his failure by doing so in the presence of the king. There was nothing wrong with his design, which was well ahead of its time, but what he hadn't allowed for was the descending column of cold air above the river, which is particularly chilly in Ulm thanks to its union with the Iller (as in *Iller, Lech, Isar, Inn fliessen rechts der Donau hin*), which brings meltwater from the Alps. Afterwards, the discouraged inventor moved on to make artificial limbs for the war-wounded, which counted as a more productive use of his time.

A hazard for low-flying hang-gliders it may be, but the Danube's union with the swollen Iller at Ulm is enough to render the river officially navigable for the first time, and over my pike and chips I watched a smattering of leisure and pleasure boats struggling to hold their own against the stream. For the first time on my journey I felt that I was sitting alongside a mighty, trans-European waterway, a transport artery which the EU has prosaically designated as 'Corridor VII', and as such I felt connected to the cities and nations that lay ahead of me. But reading *The Glance of Countess Hahn-Hahn (down the Danube)*, I found that Peter Esterhazy felt no such connection in Ulm. On the contrary, it was his belief that the German Danubians didn't look any further east than the ends of their noses. 'An Ulmer can only see as far as Regensburg, a Regensburger only as far as Passau, and as for the good people of Passau: they're blind.'

Certainly over the centuries various points of the river have viewed themselves as the last bastion of Western civilization, believing that barbarism began at their eastern gate. As recently as 1815, at the Congress of Vienna which was to set the template for modern Europe, Austro-Hungarian Chancellor Metternich declared, 'East of Vienna the Orient begins.' At the time, the concept 'Europe' referred to everything west of Vienna, while countries to the east were for guest appearances by semi-mythical entities like Attila the Hun, Mongols, and empires called Byzantine and Ottoman, whose cities had exotic names like Constantinople. To most minds these names could as easily belong to Greek legend as to relatively recent European history. These days, however, Western civilization goes all the way to the Black Sea, or so the EU concept suggests. But many cities on the upper reaches of the river nevertheless stick to the Esterhazy line, and show little interest in what happens on their downriver side.

Ulm, however, is an exception, and that week the city was hosting a festival of modern music from eastern Danubian countries, with a particular emphasis on love songs from Bulgaria and the Balkans. Not that I needed to attend any official concerts, given what was taking place on the Schwarzer Adler's terrace every night.

Mr Herring's soirées aside, the Ulmite institution that peered downriver with the most intensity was the new Danube Swabian Museum, close to the Fishermen's Quarter in one of the giant barrack buildings that hadn't been destroyed by Allied bombs. The story of the there-and-back migration of Danube Swabians, as narrated within its walls, is one of the lesser-known dramas of Central Europe, and one which doesn't yet have a proper happy ending.

From the mid-eighteenth century onwards, 200,000 economic migrants set off from Ulm to float down the Danube to new lives in a promised land in Central Europe, just as in later centuries the Irish would head off across the Atlantic or the Greeks would set off for Australia. Except that, unlike the Irish or the Greeks, huge numbers of their descendants reversed the process two hundred years later and came back again in a hurry, with nothing but the shirts on their backs. The net result for the likes of Baden-Württemberg is that a quarter of the state's population today comes from behind the Iron Curtain. It's a back-and-forth migration that Germans have been reluctant to talk about.

The story starts at the end of the seventeenth century, when the Austro-Hungarians had finally driven the Ottoman Empire out of Central Europe. Although their passing was a huge relief for the oppressed locals, it created something of a vacuum in whole swathes of what is now Hungary, northern Serbia and eastern Romania (then just Greater Hungary). Management and manpower in these areas had been swept away when the Turks were evicted, so at the instigation of Austro-Hungarian Empress Maria Theresa, administrators set about refilling the vacated spaces so that good arable land could be put to work.

Much of this land had been given to Austro-Hungarian

aristocrats as a reward for contributing their soldiers to the imperial army, and it was those aristocrats who sent their beadles to Germany's market squares to recruit the craftsmen, labourers and farmers for this supposed new Eden in the East. Their efforts were particularly successful in southern Germany because people were ready to listen. Crop failures, combined with the effects of the Thirty Years War, and an inheritance system that subdivided property into ever-smaller plots, meant that many families were very interested in the talk of free and fruitful land that lay downriver, and the Danube was there on their doorsteps to deliver them.

The empire designated the upriver port of Ulm as the embarkation point and commissioned the building of *Ulmer Schachteln* (literally Ulm Crates), ponderous and heavy wooden rafts with a cabin and four steering oars, whose only motive power was the river current. In those days climbing aboard was a bit like setting off for the moon knowing that your spacecraft didn't have enough fuel to come back again. Whole families embarked on these craft on the promise of houses and land in villages and towns which were mostly drawn up on paper but had not yet been built (as happened a century later in North America). The land, however, was good, and although they had a hard time initially, the communities prospered as one generation succeeded the other, as the saying goes:

> *Dem Ersten der Tod*
> *Dem Zweiten die Not*
> *Dem Dritten das Brot*

which roughly translates as 'First death, then hard living, then prosperity.'

The original 200,000 migrants multiplied rapidly, and by the turn of the nineteenth century there were some two million ethnic Germans living in pockets of Central and Eastern Europe, in chessboard urbanizations which had been planned in Vienna. Their children were educated in schools founded by the empire, and although they were bilingual, these communities rarely intermarried with the Hungarians, the Serbs or the Romanians they lived amongst. They maintained their own language and folk traditions, but they didn't see themselves necessarily as Germans, because Germany per se hadn't yet come into existence; their main identity came from the village to which they belonged, as it did for a lot of other ethnic groups around them.

But a hundred years later they were being forced by pan-European change to think again. In the late nineteenth century most of these ethnic Germans found themselves in a land now called Greater Hungary, where the Hungarians were going through a strongly nationalistic phase as part of a power struggle with the Austrian half of the Austro-Hungarian Empire. The nationalists were putting pressure on all ethnic groups to think of themselves as Magyar, forcing them to speak Hungarian, and eradicating German-medium schools. If you accepted this Magyarization, you could have a good career, but if not, your community was effectively ignored. Of course this attempt to eradicate ethnic minorities had the opposite effect, as it regularly has done throughout history all across the globe. Forced to choose between host country and origin, the two million Danube Swabians suddenly found themselves looking back to the distant fatherland for cultural input and support. They realized they were not just villagers with different traditions: they were German.

Not long afterwards the ugly face of nationalism began to show itself in Germany, too, in the shape of national socialism, aka Nazism, and the Nazi message to those German communities out there in Central Europe was simple: 'You are our bridgehead.' The implication was that allegiance and loyalty to the fatherland would be rewarded, never mind that they had left that fatherland 150 years earlier. Hitler made no secret of the fact that he saw the East as Germany's *Lebensraum*, as his chance to create an empire through what he called his *Drang nach Osten*, desire for the East. All the other major powers had overseas dominions in the form of colonies, but his would be right under his nose. He saw countries like Poland, Czechoslovakia and Hungary as easy meat, already pre-tenderized with their strong Germanic content, and he was surprised that anyone in the West actually cared about them. Especially when they cared enough to fight.

When war came, Hitler made an agreement with his ally, Hungary, that the Danube Swabians would not be conscripted into the Hungarian army but into the German army instead. Moreover, they were expected to join the SS, the supposed protective force originally created as a personal guard for Hitler, but which became the most aggressive element of the whole army. So when the war ended badly for Germans everywhere, these satellite Swabian communities found themselves branded as the breeding grounds of extremism. Many of those whose homes had been on Romanian soil, and were therefore now Soviet-controlled, were taken to labour camps in Russia and never seen again. Those in what became Yugoslavia had their citizenship removed and were gathered together into designated villages which were surrounded by fencing to become concentration camps. The best treated were the 550,000 in Hungary, of whom 240,000 fled, mostly back to Germany, before the Iron Curtain closed the door.

Communism was tough on ethnic minorities, so for the next fifty years the remaining isolated Danube Swabians (an estimated 500,000) kept their heads down, and many of them eventually gave up on the idea of German identity altogether to be absorbed into mainstream life. Tens of thousands didn't, however, and longed to go 'home', spurred on by Germany's gradual post-war economic revival and by the German government's eventual declaration that anyone who could prove German parentage, no matter how long ago, had a right to German citizenship. When the Wall collapsed in 1989, many thousands of these *Aussiedler* (settlers outside) flocked back to 'their' country, and had full claim to pensions and benefits. Meanwhile the seven million *Ausländer* (foreigners) living in Germany, including two million Turks, were denied the privilege.

In the years since the war, plenty of Danube Swabians had returned to Ulm, the river port where the original migration had started, and I'd arranged to meet one of them in the museum.

Franz Flock turned out to be a rumpled, tufty-haired, whiskery and twinkly seventy-year-old, so keen to tell his story to an interested party that he greeted me like a long-lost friend. I wouldn't have picked him out from the crowd as being any less German than anyone else in Ulm, but one of the first things he did was to declare that he was not German at all, but *Donau-Schwabe*, Danube Swabian. It was, he said, something very different.

Herr Flock's ancestors had left the Rhineland back in the 1780s, originally emigrating as farmers, although his grandfather had been a dyer of cloth, specializing in indigo. The family had completed the water-whipped journey, bumping downriver on the *Ulmer Schachteln* and eventually settling in a region he called the Batschka, now the north-eastern region of Serbia. (This area is better known today as Vojvodina, a region riven with ethnic difficulties following the recent disintegration of Yugoslavia. I was to find myself stumbling through it later in my own journey.)

As a boy Franz had grown up on the Danube riverbank in Palanka, between Vukovar and Novi Sad, both familiar names from world news in the late 1990s, when they were hard hit by NATO bombers. During the difficult years of the Second World War his parents had moved across to what they hoped might be the relative safety of the Sudetenland, now in the Czech Republic but at that time another region of Europe that had been settled extensively by three million Germans. But when the war ended with no obvious sanctuary for Danube Swabians – the Sudetenland was reclaimed by Czechoslovakia and Germany itself didn't look like a good prospect – the ten-year-old Franz and his family set off by train to travel back home across Czechoslovakia and Hungary to Yugoslavia.

It had suddenly become a very dangerous thing to be a German-speaker in Central Europe. 'In Hungary we had to pretend to be Yugoslavs returning home from forced labour camps,' Franz recalls. 'I could only speak German then, but my mother spoke good Croatian and my father could manage Hungarian.'

They got as far as the Yugoslav border (at the same location where I was to find myself making an on-foot crossing in the weeks ahead), but the border guards were not so easily fooled by their stumbling second languages and the labour-camp cover story, and refused to let them across to go home.

They had no plan B. Like many millions of ethnic Germans living outside the borders of Germany, they found themselves homeless, stateless and distrusted, thanks to the outcome of a war started by a nation with which they'd only had long-distance cultural ties. In another time and another set of circumstances, their plight might have been labelled 'ethnic cleansing', and a United Nations might have come to their rescue.

'We didn't have anywhere else to go, so we had to camp out under open skies, waiting until the border guards changed their minds,' said Franz. In the event it was lucky they didn't. Partisans turned up on the southern side of the border, partisans who'd fought against the SS troops, and they weren't going to treat them well. The families fled back north into the relative safety of Hungary, where Hungarian Swabians took them in. The mayor of the village where they ended up told every household to help, and the eight-member Flock family were given two rooms in another family's house. But Franz was clearly not inclined to dwell on difficult times.

'My parents were teachers and they got work, doing private lessons. Then my mother founded a school for Croatian minorities who were also isolated in Hungary.' The language spoken at home swiftly became Hungarian, and German was relegated to the language of his grand-parents.

'Those ten years in Hungary were very happy ones, probably the happiest of my life,' continued Franz. Hungarian communism was a liberal strain that per-secuted intellectuals, not minorities, and although the Swabians were regarded as strict, precise and mean, always with money squirreled away, they weren't persecuted. So he was able to complete his education in Budapest without difficulty.

The mid-1950s was a good time to be a Hungarian. The nation had moved steadily away from Stalinism. Writers were becoming increasingly bold, and anything and everything was being discussed in the press. László Rajk, a leader who'd been hung years earlier as an arch-criminal, had been reburied as a hero, and there was a call for more democracy, more independence. As for Franz, he'd qualified as an electronics engineer and in 1956 he'd just got a good job with the Hungarian postal service when the nation's slow waltz towards democratization came to a sudden crunching halt.

That October some 300,000 people had set out on a great march, arm in arm, through Budapest. Initially it had all been good humoured, and how the fighting started is still not universally agreed. It is thought that the AVO, the Hungarian secret police, had machine guns posted on the tops of buildings and started to fire over the marchers' heads to disperse them. The marchers, however, were incensed; they seized weapons from friendly troops on the ground and fired back, and for a while they were successful. The AVO melted away and the Soviets withdrew their troops, allowing the brief establishment of a new, liberal government. A real mood of exhilaration swept through the city. People power had been honoured, the Soviet juggernaut had been faced down, and freedom was in their grasp. But future Soviet leader Yuri Andropov, on a state visit at the time, had been caught up in the demonstration's traffic and he was determined not to let a satellite state like Hungary slip the Soviet leash, lest others might want to do the same.

That November the city exploded under an onslaught from heavy artillery, bombers and tanks as the Soviets returned. They reduced to rubble every building from which a shot was fired, killing up to 50,000 Hungarians, while a further 20,000 fled abroad. After eight days of fighting there was no more resistance, and the inquisitions began, neighbour against neighbour. Budapest felt violated, its people in despair. There was no food, no money, no hope, and living conditions were appalling.

The brutal way in which Hungary's 1956 Revolution was suppressed shocked Soviet-dominated Eastern Europe into another three decades of submission, and without it the communist experiment might have ended far earlier. But it also destroyed communism's image in the rest of Europe, where the ideology had had plenty of supporters until then. In Britain, the Communist Party lost one third of its membership almost overnight.

As for Franz and his friends, they could see there was no future in staying where they were.

'Hungary was full of Russians. The towns, the villages. Full of Russians. Everything stopped, the trains, everything. We could see no hope.' So along with eight others, he crossed the border back into Yugoslavia, where he was picked up by the Red Cross and transferred to a camp in Italy. From there the other escapees went on to settle in Canada, but Franz's eventual destination was Germany, a village where his uncle lived, and it wasn't what he'd expected.

'In my youth Germany had been glorified – just to set foot in it was regarded as a privilege. But since then it had become the starter of disastrous wars, and suddenly nobody wanted to go there at all. The place my uncle lived was a real *Kuhdorf* – cow village. Food was basically just potatoes and more potatoes. It was such a disappointment.'

Still, he'd knuckled down, relearned his German and got a job with Siemens before eventually changing careers to become a teacher, just like his parents. For their part, his parents had stayed behind in Hungary, and for decades Franz had returned twice a year, crossing difficult borders as regularly as clockwork in order to visit them. It was enough to bring him to the attention of the CIA, then still a force in reconstructing Germany, who'd sent an agent to recruit him.

Herr Flock had had no desire to get involved, and told them so. 'I was just visiting my family. They would have been wasting their time.'

And now, a half-century after leaving, he still went back to Hungary every year, even though his parents had long since died. 'I find it hard to rationalize the affection I feel for that country. I'm seventy years old and I only spent ten of those years in Hungary, but it is still the place where I feel most at home. My biggest emotional connection. I suppose those ten years were at a very crucial stage in my life. And every year I go back to Palanka, now in Serbia, too, with a busload of others like me. I just walk around. If people ask me what I'm looking for, I'll just say history. Homesickness tourism, we call it.'

Now that he was retired, he organized a troupe of Danube Swabian dancers and musicians who went on tours of the Danube Swabian diaspora, particularly the 250,000 Danube Swabians who'd resettled in America and Brazil. In doing so he was preserving a satellite culture that had twice been uprooted from its origins and was now scattered to the winds. 'Which is why when you ask me what I am, I still say I am not a German, no matter what it says on my passport. No sir. I am an international Donau-Schwabe.'

Donauwörth and the After-Effects of War

The villagers in Battle of Blenheim country were raising their maypoles and preparing themselves for a day of heavy drinking. The first of May was just around the corner, and council elders were gathering in squares and summoning up others with their mobile phones. It was one of those rare occasions in the country diary where pure manpower was still required, and where the farmers held sway, because they had the knowledge and the equipment necessary for raising and decorating the maypoles. For the rest of the year agricultural workers railed at the inadequacy and the stupidity of the village's other menfolk, who were barely worthy of the title 'man' and yet who still had big houses and fine cars. Now it was their chance.

This was Bavaria – I'd left Baden-Württemberg behind at Ulm – and it was proving surprisingly rural. What with high-tech Munich, right-of-centre politics and the headquarters of Audi and BMW, I'd always assumed it to be a wealthy, sophisticated place, but along the cycle way I'd encountered genuine shepherds spending whole days with their sheep and moving them along the banks of the Danube through grazing that was still community-owned. With a combination of well-aimed stones and browbeaten dogs they kept their flocks gathered in tight bunches around them like rippling woollen skirts, decorated with blizzards of flies and perfumed with ewe's milk. These were scenes I was expecting to see in Hungary and Romania, but not in a land of high torque and robot production lines.

As for the maypoles, they were very low-tech, and the technique of hauling them upright hadn't changed for hundreds of years. They were giant fir trees, sometimes as much as 50 metres tall, stripped naked of any sideways branches and festooned with streamers, wreaths of flowers and bunches of tinsel. Carved figures of local tradesmen such as the carpenter, the bricklayer, the farmer, the notary, the blacksmith and the tailor were distributed up the pole. This whole confection would be towed into the village square by a farmer in a pork-pie hat, who would cast a critical eye over the mayor's deodorant-wearing assistants, mutter something disparaging to his dogs, and instantly take charge. He was, after all, the only person left in the community who still had his image carved on the pole; it is not so easy to represent, in wood, an assistant director of marketing services.

The process of raising the pole itself was laborious and longwinded. The first step was to slide the tree's base into a pre-prepared slot in the ground, rather as a pole-vaulter anchors his weapon before launching himself upwards. Then pairs of staves joined at the neck with rope, like giant chopsticks, were distributed through the groups of men, and as the tractor's mechanical forks did the initial lifting, so more and more of those staves were wedged between the trunk and the ground. Eventually thirty men were deployed, all under the supervision of the fat farmer in the pork-pie hat, three or four of them to each set of staves. They looked like Lilliputian figures in a Chinese restaurant, using chopsticks to stop a giant bling-covered noodle from falling on their heads.

Eventually the angle became such that the tractor could no longer do the main lifting, and it was down to manpower alone. Then it was a matter of hauling the staves down the trunk and repositioning the taller ones closer and closer to the base, until eventually, after a lot of shouting, gibing, sweating and swearing, the farmer adjudged it to be nearly upright. He filled the hole around the base with giant wooden wedges, thumped them into place with his tractor, and it was this wedge-hammering that finally brought the whole operation to the last vertical fullstop.

The maypole had taken thirty men over two hours to erect, and as a reward they gathered round a barrel of beer that one of the mayor's deodorant-wearing assistants unloaded from the back of his BMW, showing some usefulness at last. The fat farmer in the pork-pie hat was in the thick of the celebration, a man's man, the hero of the moment surrounded by wellwishers, and he was intent on forgetting all those solitary days in the fields, just him and his entombed asparagus. His tractor was unlikely to be moving again that day, unless his wife came out to tow him home.

For me, cycling from one village to the next became a join-the-maypoles experience. I could visualize my progress on the map, a little inky line linking the dots. I was doing the journey surprisingly quickly. It was an easy landscape, barely troubled by the slightest of slopes, and I'd just invested in some ludicrously expensive chain oil that worked like magic drops, curiously not on the chain, but on my legs, which just went faster and faster all day. Around me, the spires of churches and lines of poplars became the ingredients of a moving jigsaw that required creative assembly; what I needed to do was line them up with the shoulders of hills and corners of cornfields to compose the perfect picture. A tree here, a church there, a red roof, the glimpse of a river, the curve of a road, wait . . . wait, that's it! Kerrching! Cut and wrap. But then one element in the composition would elude me at the very last moment, the church spire would slide behind an unexpected factory, the road would smother the river, or a vulgar, puffed-up cherry-blossom tree would appear in the foreground shouting 'Look at me! Look at me!' My image would disintegrate, and I'd have to start again with a whole new set of ingredients. Just occasionally a perfect picture would come together by accident without my looking for it, but then as soon as I'd noticed it, I'd moved on, and it was gone. Transient art.

Now that we were no longer crowded together in a small valley I couldn't see a great deal of the Danube, but I could guess where it was thanks to the industry that had colonized its banks, elbowing the cyclepath out into the fields. I glowered at these installations. However gleaming they were at the front, I knew that they were pissing dirty stuff into the river out the back, and occasional patches of froth gave away their guilty secret. The river had behaved badly out of Donaueschingen, for sure, but it didn't deserve to be adulterated by man. At that stage I didn't realize I was nearing a stretch where it had swallowed up some 3,000 horsemen.

Other people might have been alert to the imminence of a big story as they approached Blindheim, but I didn't recognize the name. I'd been lulled into a semi-hypnotic state by the steady ticking-off of -*ingen*s across the plain. There was Offingen and Lauingen, Gundelfingen and Dillingen, like the tolling of bells, but then suddenly there was Blindheim – or Blenheim, as British historians prefer to call it – a real surprise in the midst of the Bavarian cornfields.

For me, the name Blenheim belongs to a country house in Oxfordshire, and I didn't begin to make the connection until I'd deciphered the inscription on a statue of two men shaking hands at Blindheim's crossroads. The inscription talked of the Herzog (aka Duke of) Marlborough, and how, for England, his victory in the fields around Blindheim in 1704 represented '*der Aufstieg der Weltmacht*', the rise of a world power.

My sense of history is pretty crap so I'm not usually disconcerted by discovering something I didn't know before, but the idea that British puissance had its origins in the cornfields of Bavaria was a new one on me. As I read on, I learned that the British Queen Anne had been so impressed by his victory that she had rewarded Marlborough with 'a very fine castle in Woostock [*sic*]' called Blenheim Palace. Was that misspelling of Woodstock revenge for our adulteration of Blindheim? If so, we deserved it, although you could forgive a British soldier for getting it a little bit wrong. After all, the Tommies couldn't handle the multisyllabled Mesopotamia (now Iraq) when they were stationed there in the 1950s, so they had rechristened it, endearingly, as 'Messpot', and Messpot it remains.

The battle of Blindheim, aka Blenheim or even Höchstädt (the name of the nearest big town is used in many European history books), was a turning point in the War of Spanish Succession, a war whose name has provoked volleys of yawns in schoolrooms across Europe. The details are long and complicated, but suffice it to say that this was one of the largest battles in European history, where the British were fighting with the Prussians, Austrians, Dutch and Danes in the so-called Grand Alliance. Their enemy was the old foe, France, under Louis XIV, who was threatening European domination. The Bavarians had come along for the ride.

The Franco-Bavarian army consisted of 56,000 men and ninety guns and was well used to victory; the Grand Alliance army had 52,000 men (a third were British) and sixty guns and its command was shared by Marlborough and Prince Eugene of Savoy, a colourful character in his own right who'd played a big part in the undoing of the Ottoman Empire. Prince Eugene was gay and slightly built, and a most unlikely figure for a military leader, then or now. Based partly on his appearance, and partly on his original inclination towards becoming a priest, he'd been refused a military commission in France, the country of his birth, and so he'd ended up joining the Austrians. Initially he'd defended Vienna, very successfully, against the Turks, and it must have given him considerable satisfaction to turn his leadership skills against France, the country which had behaved so dismissively towards him in the first place.

The Blindheim/Blenheim battlefield stretched for nearly 4 miles and I cycled right across it, listening to the birds sing. The extreme right flank of the Franco-Bavarian army had been protected by the Danube, and the extreme left flank touched the undulating pine-covered hills of the Swabian Jura. At the front of the French line ran a small stream, the Nebel, in ground that was soft and marshy and only fordable intermittently, and this stream flowed into the Danube at Blindheim. Between Blindheim and the next village of Oberglau the fields of wheat had been cut to stubble and were ideal for deploying troops. From Oberglau to the next hamlet of Lutzingen the terrain of ditches, thickets and brambles was potentially difficult ground.

Marlborough took 36,000 troops and attacked from the left, with the aim of capturing Blindheim, while Eugene was to lead 16,000 men from the right. For their part, the French weren't expecting an assault, although any attempt at surprise was negated by the lack of cover. 'I could see', wrote one of the French generals, 'the enemy advancing ever closer in nine great columns . . . filling the whole plain from the Danube to the woods on the horizon.'

For many hours it looked as if the result could go either way. In the late afternoon Marlborough had to rebuke a cavalry officer who was attempting to leave the field, 'Sir, you are under a mistake, the enemy lies that way . . .' Eventually, with one more weary charge, the Grand Alliance managed to rout the French cavalry. The remaining French infantry battalions fought with desperate valour, trying to form a defensive square, but they died to a man where they stood, right out in the open plain.

The majority of the retreating French headed for Höchstädt but most did not make the safety of the town, being brought up short by the Danube where those 3,000 horsemen drowned; others were cut down by the pursuing cavalry. Marlborough, still in the saddle conducting the pursuit of the broken enemy, managed to snatch a moment to scribble a note to his wife, Sarah, on the back of an old tavern bill. 'I have no time to say more but to beg you will give my duty to the Queen, and let her know her army has had a glorious victory.'

French losses were immense, with some 30,000 killed,

wounded and missing, and bodies turned up downriver for weeks to come. The myth of French invincibility had been destroyed overnight and French hopes for a bigger slice of Europe were postponed until the Bonaparte juggernaut started to move a hundred years later.

With the thanks of much of Europe ringing in his ears, the Duke of Marlborough returned to England. The Queen granted him Woodstock Park and promised a sum of £240,000 to build a suitable house, Blenheim Palace, as a gift from a grateful crown in recognition of his victory. If it hadn't been for Blindheim/Blenheim, say historians, all Europe might have been conquered by the French, with consequences that don't bear thinking about. Cricket might never have existed.

A couple of hours after leaving one battlefield I was cycling into another, equally unexpected. Germany's Romantic Road is a chocolate-box tourist route which runs 200 miles north–south from Würzburg to Füssen, and in the town of Donauwörth it intersects with the Danube cyclepath and the Jakobusweg. The latter is probably better known as the St James's Way, a pilgrimage route which starts in Oettingen and stumbles from one apostolic church to the next as it heads south and then west, joining other arterial routes which all eventually lead to the Spanish city of Santiago de Compostela.

It all sounded very spiritual and uplifting on paper, so I was surprised to come across the high-security airbase and manufacturing plant of Eurocopter, a helicopter specialist with significant military contracts (particularly in the Middle East) on Donauwörth's outer edge. These days Eurocopter is owned by EADS, the European Aeronautic Defence and Space Company, but once upon a time it was better known as Messerschmidt, which explains why Donauwörth ended up as a bomb target in the Second World War. I cycled around its barbed-wire perimeter, grinning up at all the security cameras and *Grüss Gott*ing at security men in suits, who watched me pass without comment. Even if big deals were not being made with governments and warlords behind that bullet-proof glass, I certainly got the impression that they were.

Donauwörth wasn't what it seemed, either. Despite the romantic image and the careful pastel configuration of the houses that lined its main street, most of the old-looking façades were facsimiles. Bombing had reduced the original town to rubble, and some of the houses had only been reconstructed as recently as the year 2000. The airborne pummelling had been compounded by the billeting of 12,000 ethnic German refugees from the Sudetenland on Donauwörth at the war's end, which had the effect of tripling the local population at a time when food and shelter was at a minimum.

Forcible resettlement of ethnic Germans from elsewhere had taken place all over Germany, which had had to absorb eight million refugees at a time when it was at its lowest ebb, being burdened with huge reparations whilst losing 27,000 square miles of its territory. Some of the refugees were farflung Danube Swabians like Franz Flock, and some were from distinct multicultural regions with large German minorities, like the Sudetenland and Silesia (the latter now in Poland). Many had been economic migrants in previous centuries, migrants whose big mistake was to retain their Germanic culture, and who were accordingly redefined as the enemy when the nationalistic tide turned against them. Like the Danube Swabians they'd suddenly found themselves *persona non grata* in their host nations. But nor did they find themselves welcome in their supposed fatherland, becoming a traumatized generation of the unwanted. Although it is little recorded and rarely discussed, hundreds of thousands of today's elderly Germans still feel they don't truly belong in the towns in which they have lived for over sixty years. My mother-in-law, born in Silesia, and now living near Bremen, is one of them.

This unwelcome swelling of the German population turned out to be one of the driving forces behind the post-war economic miracle, because as a labour force the incomers were very motivated to prove themselves, and, with no local roots to bog them down, they were willing to move to areas where manpower was most needed. So Donauwörth didn't remain Sudeten-dominated for long – or so I believed.

I found a room in a creaky, old-fashioned boarding house which belonged to a thin, elderly lady who was in a stage of life where everything becomes a source of worry. She was anxious about everything it was possible to be anxious about. About her hip, and whether it needed replacing. About her visitors, and whether more of them were suddenly going to arrive or not. About keys, and whether they were going to be lost. About bicycles, and whether they were safe in the outhouses. She tried to manage that anxiety through signage, all over the house. 'Please remove your shoes here.' 'Please close this door.' 'Please open window after you've used the bathroom.' 'Please leave this door open.' And the endearing 'This toilet roll is for using here, not for taking away,' which conjured up visions of all kinds of illegal employment of toilet roll elsewhere.

Those parts of the house that weren't for visitors had '*Privat*' labels stuck on them, even down to a flannel hook by the bathroom sink, which was also labelled '*Privat*', for the proprietor's flannel alone. I'm afraid that, for me, that was one sign too far; during my post-cycle shower I took advantage of that private hook to stop my socks getting wet.

All these signs made my host seem like a dictator, which she was not. She simply knew how things were best arranged, and she relied on her signs to be her lieutenants, always on guard against guest error. As I went to bed I imagined her sitting in her kitchen, listening, hoping that the signs were doing their duty, worrying that doors were being left open when they ought not to be, and concerned that shoes were being left inappropriately unremoved.

At breakfast time she seemed much more relaxed, possibly because I was the only guest. She told me about a pilgrim who'd stayed with her while doing the St James's Way.

'He was in a terrible state. Didn't speak a word of German or English, a bundle of nerves. He was crying, his skin was blistered and his hair was streaked and knotted with dirt. When I asked what the matter was, he explained that God was helping him, or at least that's what I think he was saying. Honestly, it didn't look like God was helping him very much.' She allowed herself a small smile. 'And I had another gentleman staying, you know what he said? He said "He doesn't need God, he needs suncream!"'

For a moment she looked as if she was about to laugh, then she checked herself. 'I'm sorry, are you religious? It wasn't me that said he didn't need God, you understand.'

'Don't worry,' I said. 'I take it that you're not religious either?'

She shook her head. 'My mother used to be.'

There was something in the way she said this that made me pursue it.

'And what happened?'

The landlady looked reluctant. 'The war happened.'

'Your father was killed?' It was an obvious conclusion.

She nodded. 'And then we had a lot of people. Come here.'

'Ah-hah. From Sudetenland. I read about that.'

She seemed relieved that the back-story didn't need explaining.

'How many?'

'In this house? At the worst time we had as many as twenty.' She started to clear the table. 'You cannot imagine. It was just me, my sister and my mother. My mother became very angry, her husband missing and now her house full of strangers. She hadn't wanted to go to war in the first place.'

There was a short pause while she disappeared to the kitchen with the dirty crockery, and when she returned she seemed to have made a decision to talk more.

'We only lived down here, this was our part of the house. The rest was theirs. Upstairs. Our house, but theirs, you can't imagine. And two of the families, they stayed here for six years.'

'Surely they became friends?'

She shuddered. 'We didn't talk to them. Never, not even in the street. My mother told us not to. I didn't even talk to them at school.'

Now I understood the origin of all the signs all over the house. 'So you wrote notes telling them what they could and couldn't do?'

She nodded. 'And when they left, my mother didn't want to move back upstairs. She started renting those rooms out. She used to say it was high time we made something out of our property for ourselves. She was very bitter.'

I said I understood.

'There was a lot of suffering in those days. It ruined my mother's life. She lived a long time, another forty years, and it never left her, that bitterness, particularly as she got old. But it is not something we talk about, we Germans. My sister and I, we knew why our mother was so difficult in those last years, and she was very, very difficult. There was nothing we could do. Or say. The doctors knew, the nurses knew, everyone knew, but no one ever spoke about it. It's like a disease you're too ashamed to mention. You can't talk about German suffering during or after the war, however huge it was, because of course it was all our fault.'

I sensed, with alarm, the nearness of tears, so I attempted a detour in the conversation.

'And today. Are there many Sudeten Germans left in town?'

'Of course. For my generation, Donauwörth is divided. I don't talk to them, for my mother's sake. But the younger people, they get on, which is how it should be; it wasn't their war. I suppose you could say that time is healing things, but it has taken more time than you can possibly imagine. And for people like my mother, it never healed.'

Half an hour later I was wheeling my bike out of her shed to resume my journey when my landlady emerged to ask if everything had been *'recht'*, a word that carried more weight than the usual 'I hope you enjoyed your stay.' She was asking whether it had been OK to talk about the forbidden – about German suffering during and after the war. So I said it had, it had been very *recht*. Besides, it meant I didn't have to 'fess up to the illegal use of a flannel hook.

From Donauwörth the road started to lollop away with consummate ease, but it is not so easy to lollop on a bicycle and 'consummate ease' is far easier to write than to achieve when there are hills in the equation. The landscape looked lazy, rising and falling like the chest of a sleeping giant, while the road samba'ed sideways, doing an off-the-shoulder number, too louche to go over the top. I rumba'ed over it as best I could, but all the saddle fitness I'd gained over the last ten days seemed to evaporate after the first hour. Some days were like that.

Still, there was plenty to look at and I was in no hurry. I was entering the valley of the Altmühl, another tributary diversion from the Danube, a land of glossy meadows and hidden biergartens, veined with little waterways tressed with bridges and muscled with birch and oak. Leggy hunters' watchtowers stood on stilts in the clearings, empty and hollow-eyed until the deer season started, when they'd once more spit lead. Birds of prey rose into the sky as the day warmed, circling upwards above ruined castles atop plugs of rock, where lizards were no doubt just starting to sun themselves, unaware of the danger overhead.

The ground here had a substantial chalk content so there was no chance of missing the cycle way, a clearly identifiable dribble of white ribbon that threaded between distant wheatfields. It was as if a country-loving road painter had recently passed this way on his holidays, and had been unable to move on without leaving his mark between carriageways of cereals. For much of the time the route stayed up on the valley sides, around the lower fringe of the trees, scared to get its feet wet in the valley floor. I found it an irritation, climbing unnecessarily only to descend again, but once in a while I was rewarded with a view of a patchwork landscape whose colours were beginning to separate out and become more complex as the season progressed beyond spring's pure and luminous green.

It was the weekend and the weather was fine, so the route began to be busy with others, mostly families with younger children or vigorous fifty-somethings whose offspring had left home. Long-distancers like me were few and far between, which was one reason why I'd first noticed the American cyclist in Ulm, and I now came across him again in the outskirts of Eichstätt, a baroque university town that could have been a chunk of Vienna airlifted into the valley. The other reason why he was unmissable was the music coming from his handlebars.

I never learned his name, the American, but there was no doubting his nationality. He wore baggy shorts, a Hawaiian shirt, garish sneakers, a reversed baseball cap and his handlebar-speaker was broadcasting a station called VoA, turned up loud. Most cyclists slipped through towns and villages virtually unnoticed, but wherever this man went people stopped what they were doing, stared and nudged each other. Even the cows stared. It is hard to radiate a mixture of indifference and aggression from a bicycle saddle, but he managed it.

I'd tracked him from a distance before the chance came for conversation as we both pushed our bikes over Eichstätt's un-cycleable cobbles. He must have been in his late thirties, although his style would have you believe him to be younger, and his manner suggested he was in a hurry, although his cycle speed was no more than average.

'Where are you from?'

'USA,' he said, quite unnecessarily, not looking up, but nodding to the beat coming from his speaker.

'I can tell that, but where in the USA?'

'Houston. You bin there?'

I said I'd once changed planes in the airport.

'Well I sure as hell am looking forward to getting back there, out of all this bullshit.'

'You're not having a good time?'

'Do I look like I am? Do I really look like I am?' He looked at me for the first time, and I could read the anger in his eyes.

At that moment there was a break in his music and he scowled at his handlebars.

'Is that Voice of America? Are they still broadcasting?' I asked.

He was hauling a mobile phone out of his pocket to check its screen display and I could see he'd wired it along the bike-frame to the speakers.

'Not *broad*casting,' he said, sarcastically, '*web*casting. You have heard of that where you're from?'

The music started again. Plainly, he was listening to Voice of America via his mobile phone. I couldn't pretend to myself that this was normal behaviour.

'Christ, isn't that a bit expensive on the phone bill?'

'Worth every cent,' he grunted. He looked at me again, suspiciously. 'You don't sound like a Kraut.'

I told him I was British.

'Hey.' His tone was suddenly conciliatory. 'Pleased to meet you, friend of America. You can't tell these days with them square-heads, some of them speak such good English.' He sounded resentful.

Sensing an opening, I suggested we stopped for an ice-cream at a small Italian café by the roadside, and surprisingly he agreed. Even more surprising was the good German in which he placed his order.

'Are you in the army here?' I asked. I knew it was the wrong explanation as soon as I said it. For one thing, his hair was far too long.

'Do I look like I am?'

'I just wondered, what with you speaking good German . . .'

'My parents,' he muttered, and then more quietly, 'always blame the parents.'

We ate our ices in silence. If truth were told, both of us were a bit surprised to find ourselves in each other's company. He'd unplugged his phone from the speaker, although I noticed that he'd not bothered to stop the download, so VoA continued to play companionably to itself in his pocket, a furtive umbilical cord to the motherland.

Eventually, he picked up where we'd left off. 'My parents, see, they were German.'

'Were? You mean they changed nationality?'

'Nope. They died. Four months back.'

I said I was sorry, but he shrugged my words away.

'Hey, they didn't want to live any more. They were old. Jeez, they were already old when they had me, and I think I was a mistake. Any road, they never brought me here, they never talked about family or Germany, the only thing they ever did that was German was to speak it to each other when they didn't want me to understand. Otherwise, nothing, nix, zilch.' His tone sounded accusatory.

'Didn't you ever want to find out why? Why they left?' I was beginning to wonder how his parents had died. Something lay behind all that anger.

'Hey, I was too busy being an all-American kid, mainly because my folks so plainly weren't. Not that they would have talked about it anyway. Leastways not to me.'

Feeling we were rapidly entering difficult territory, I thought it was safer to change tack.

'So you are here trying to trace family?'

He shook his head and sucked on his ice. 'Thing is, I don't think they were from Germany itself.'

'Ah, so probably from Sudetenland or Silesia or

somewhere. Refugees. Maybe even Danube Swabians,' I ventured, but none of the names seemed to register with him, so I continued: 'I know a little bit about this. They probably had a really hard time. Perhaps that's why they didn't want to talk about it.'

'You think?'

There was a silence during which he peered at me speculatively. Then he appeared to reach some decision, finished his ice-cream and placed some loose change on the table. 'Need to git going. See ya.'

And with that he returned to his bike and plugged in his phone, and once again the baroque cobbles of Eichstätt rang with the Voice of America.

6

Ingolstadt: a Shock En Route to the Forum

At this point of the journey I had another of those narrow escapes for which I should be more than truly thankful. It involved my two items of baggage – a shoulder bag which had all my valuables and notebooks in it, and the saddle-bags on the bike which had everything else.

I was on my way to Ingolstadt, riverside home of car manufacturer Audi and where I'd made an arrangement to tour the factory, but when the day of the factory tour dawned I was still 30 kilometres away so a short train journey was required. Accordingly I waited at a quiet country station, and having never put my bike on a German train before, I was feeling not a little apprehensive about getting everything aboard.

As it turned out everything went swimmingly, or so it seemed. German railways thoughtfully provide special on-board cycle zones, flagged by bicycle symbols on the outside of the relevant carriages. The train duly pulled in, I struggled aboard and I was just securing my bike, full of admiration for the facilities, when my world turned upside down. The bike was safe and sound, as were my dirty socks and T-shirts in the saddlebags, but everything of any real value was still in my shoulder bag – and that was still on the station platform, where I'd left it momentarily while lugging the bike over the threshold. And just as I realized what I'd done, the train started to move.

What followed was a moment of complete, utter horror, so strong that I could feel it in my knees. My guts fell through to my socks and my head churned with the sound of a room full of washing machines. Everything was in that bag. My money, my credit cards, my notebooks, my passport, my telephone, and even my train ticket. I could go nowhere, eat nothing, call no one, without it. Its loss would ruin the next week, for sure, and it could well endanger the whole of the rest of my project. And I had nobody to blame but myself. What a fool I was! Not just for leaving the thing on the platform, but for not foreseeing such an eventuality and at the very least dividing my money between my two elements of luggage so that I would have some kind of emergency supply. Stupid, stupid, stupid!

It's hard to keep your thoughts still in such circumstances. One of the first was 'If only I hadn't used that *"privat"* flannel hook!' Followed by 'Thank God I didn't transgress with the toilet roll.' Physically I virtually turned to stone, standing stock still in that moving train, but mentally I was all over the place, my thoughts scattering like a flock of newly released sheep without a sheepdog to shoo them, uncertain which way to go. What was I going to say to the ticket inspector when he found I'd boarded his train with no ticket or money? More importantly, what was I going to do when I got to the other end? How on earth do you extract yourself from a mess like this? I supposed I would have to go to the police.

By now the train had been fairly rattling along for some minutes, and it started to slow. Of course – the next stop! I was unaware of how much time had elapsed, how much of a stopping train it was, how far we had travelled, or whether we'd followed a road, but it wasn't miles and miles, and we hadn't crossed any cities or gone through any tunnels, of that I was sure. Furthermore I could visualize the bag, still sitting tidily on its station bench. All was not lost – I knew where it was, and all I had to do was get back to it!

I bundled my bike out as soon as the doors opened to find myself in a quiet agricultural village with no sign of any major road, but with half a dozen lanes snaking away across the fields in all directions. Scouring through the empty streets high on my pedals, trembling, adrenalin-fuelled, searching for a clue as to which route to choose, I met the eye of an old gentleman cutting his garden hedge. He listened to my question, clearly alerted by my strange accent and the urgency in my voice, and then he pointed out a track and explained how I should follow it, keeping left through several intersections until it met a road . . . it was 8 or 9 kilometres, he thought. As he spoke, I was reminded of another old gentleman whose eyes I'd met long ago, when my bag had been stolen on the island of Fuerteventura. Plainly, this was the Second Coming of my own personal representative on earth.

Then I was away, hollering my thanks into the wind, gravel spitting from under my tyres, giving thanks to all those days of accumulated cycle fitness that now produced both power and speed. That journey was a blur. The tracks were gravel, not easy cycling, and I prayed at each junction that I'd heard him aright and listened well. When I eventually arrived at tarmac, exactly as he'd said I would, I blessed his cotton socks, his halo and his messianic beard; his boilersuit became a cotton shift, his hedge-trimmer a shepherd's crook. From then on it was a matter of head down, pump hard, and pray that the phone in the bag didn't ring, attracting passerby attention. As I pedalled, I rehearsed several different scenarios: the bag was there, untouched (dream on, I told myself); the bag was there, empty (more likely); the bag was on someone else's shoulder (what would I say to them?); the bag was with the station controller (was there one? I think the station was unmanned); the bag was in someone's car (probably that car coming past me now).

I reckoned I had three things on my side. The first was the shortness of time that had elapsed, perhaps just twenty-five minutes, since I'd left it there. The second was the station's rural location, which would greatly reduce the numbers of passengers who'd stood on that platform, and the third was the infrequency of the trains. Plus, of course, God.

As I came storming down the final straight and swerved off the road into the station precinct, two things happened in quick succession. The first was that my rear tyre blew out with a bang as I hit a bump far too fast and too hard, and the second was that I saw the silhouette of my bag, exactly where I'd left it.

Thirty seconds later I'd sprinted through the tunnel and was on the platform, clutching the bag to my chest, making all sorts of mental promises about being a good boy from now on, being nice to children, donating to charity, not using private flannel hooks, etc., etc. And resolving henceforth to divide my worldly wealth between my different kinds of luggage.

Anyone watching this performance would have found it bizarre and possibly endearing, but there was absolutely no one there to witness it. The station was deserted, and no doubt it probably had been ever since my train departed. The birds continued to sing, the clouds continued to scud across the sky, a distant car made that straw-sucking-dregs-of-milkshake sound across distant tarmac, as if nothing had happened. It was only my own little world that had so nearly imploded, and even that wasn't such a big deal in the overall scheme of things.

Eventually, after many long minutes sitting cradling my bag as a mother would cradle a lost child, I uncurled myself from the edge of that bench and set about trying to mend the puncture. A small hole in a rubber tube was a very small price to pay.

After an experience like that everything becomes a bonus, at least until the adrenalin wears off. So when I eventually arrived in Ingolstadt, still just about in time for my tour, I was beaming idiotically. I presented myself at the Audi Forum after a gentle cycle through a city centre that was immaculately grouted by prosperity and Scotchguarded by wealth, where everyone smiled at each other. It all hung together so neatly and tidily that you could have turned the city upside down and shaken it and nothing would have fallen out.

Audi is the guardian angel that suffuses Ingolstadt with well-being. The company settled here in the 1950s, a refugee corporation which found itself homeless after the division of Germany had placed its main plant at Chemnitz well and truly behind the Iron Curtain. It now employed 31,000 people – a third of Ingolstadt's total population – turning out 2,200 cars a day, but you'd never have guessed anything was being made (apart from money) from the Audi Forum. This collection of glass pavilions felt like a living, walking architect's model for some kind of campus, with everything just so. It was populated by smartly dressed and smiling young urban professionals. Dozens of them stood in gossiping groups around playing fountains, slim, good-looking, as self-conscious as extras on a film set. At regular intervals the groups would break up and then re-form in another area of the courtyard, in the shade of young trees, as they'd been told to do by the director.

There was an unreality about the Forum. It didn't feel like a place of work, because no one seemed hurried; it wasn't a leisure attraction, because there were no families and no fee to pay; it wasn't a student campus, because everyone was far too well dressed; it wasn't a place of worship, because young urban professionals have little time for God. It could have been an advertisement for a high-class optician, or perhaps a dating agency for the cash-rich, time-poor. There was something Brave New World about it, largely because the figures on the set looked as if they'd all come from the same designer's hand. The Audi board must have said to the architect, after viewing all the drawings and animations, 'Yes, we'll take those giant, cantilevered, curved constructions to display our product in; we'll take the fountains, the courtyards and the young saplings for the spaces in between; and we particularly like the look of the people, we'll take lots of them. A couple of hundred, probably more, and dress them in shades of grey. When can you have them delivered?' So there they were, the Audi acolytes, strolling and smiling and feeling comfortable in the company of fellow disciples.

The Forum is Audi's contribution to the mythologizing of what American architect Frank O. Gehry has called 'cultural expressions of movement' (cars, to you and me). They've all done it, the German car manufacturers: BMW in Munich, VW in Wolfsburg, Mercedes in Stuttgart and

Audi in Ingolstadt; they've all opened flagship visitor centres that redefine the concept of a factory outlet. This is not retailing, it is a leisure-experience-cum-marketing-operation. A massive flag-waving exercise which is all about brand image, brand loyalty and raising the brand profile, and which must be working, because these centres are attracting more visitors than the local art galleries and museums. Mind you, the car makers have yet to get the ultimate accolade of actually appearing on a Bavarian maypole.

For customers already committed to the ideology, the likes of the Audi Forum must seem like glorious affirmation that they have made the right choice, which is why they smile, linger and stroll, enjoying the companionship of their community.

For the manufacturer, the Forum represents a chance to celebrate what they've done, and this celebration is something the Germans have not always been good at doing. In the half-century that followed the war they left it to their products to speak for themselves, fighting shy of the messy world of advertising. It is not that they have never had the creative gene; after all, this is the nation of Beethoven and Goethe, whose *Faust* is so dense you need two brains to read it, one to try to work out what the hell Goethe's on about and the other to keep your body alive while doing so. But the emphasis of the twentieth century has been on national resurrection through productivity, not individuality, of progress through organization and application, not through originality. Thoroughness and honest labour have been the touchstones of the German revival, and advertising, which dabbles in half-truths and exaggeration, is an uneasy bedfellow, particularly for a nation that had recently experienced the mass hysteria of the Nuremberg rallies. Put succinctly, Germans couldn't allow themselves to bullshit, and in the modern world that meant that they were underpowered as salespeople, so they relied on letting the products do the talking. Or hired an overseas agency to do the bullshitting for them.

A British architect working for a German partnership in Hamburg once explained this dichotomy to me. He saw his main task as to champion the talent within his firm, promoting it both within Germany and overseas. His fellow architects were producing great work, he said, but they didn't have the self-belief to take it out and show it to the world.

This lack of confidence is not just restricted to architecture, but to other creative industries. Lots of German design, advertising and brand consultancy is imported from overseas, much of it from the UK; we're doing their blagging for them. Many of their TV programmes have a foreign inspiration, and their comedy shows regularly commission British writers. Their favourite piece of television comedy, repeated year after year on New Year's Eve, on all channels and in all households, is a British end-of-the-pier sketch called *Dinner for One*, starring Freddie Frinton and May Warden, in the original version recorded back in 1963. Ask a German about *Dinner for One* and his eyes will light up, and he'll start to quote the whole script, in English.

So these palaces to automobility, these temples to vroom like the Audi Forum, are an important milestone for German society because they represent a change in mentality. They represent a nation starting to make some noise about what it's good at, having recognized that just making things, however well, is no longer good enough – they have to be able to sell them as well. Fluffy marketing campaigns in television, newspapers and magazines are not their style; they've gone for show and tell.

My Audi factory tour was led by a perfect corporate specimen in the true American mould, illustrative of the new generation bringing transatlantic marketing skills to German manufacturing. He was a young, ambitious man without a moment of self-doubt, who'd never encountered irony, and who delivered his message with a rather piercing insistence that what he said was the absolute truth and nothing but. He'd learned the gospel according to Audi, and he knew it inside out and back to front. Moreover, he gave it to us in our inner ear, via headsets that we all had to wear so we could hear him over the din of the factory floor. The voice of Audi inside our heads.

The guide ran through the factory's environmentally friendly credentials. He told us, with great earnestness, how 70 per cent of components arrived by train and 65 per cent of the end product left by train, which rather overlooked the fact that, no matter how they came and went, the whole purpose of the place was to make cars, and it is cars that are bringing the environment to its knees.

And then, as we entered the production lines themselves, he asked us to switch off our mobile phones on the grounds that they might operate on the same frequency as the production-line robots, with potentially interesting results. There were, he said, 900 robots assembling the 20,000 components that went into the Audi A3. That represented 98 per cent automation, and certainly it was an impressive sight. These robots looked more like giant lobster claws than imitation people, with tiny, gleaming, multicoloured lights for eyes. They operated behind metal grilles that suggested captive animals at the zoo. Their arms waved, paused, dived, delved and delivered streaks of sparks, juddering with effort, eyes flickering through different colours of pleasure and pain. And between choreographed routines they would stop occasionally, winking impassively as they considered their next move, humming '*Vorsprung durch Technik*' before zeroing in on a new panel to deliver another delicate stripe of green glue.

Up close, it was easy enough to see what they were doing, those robots, but further away they were just a sea of waving claws and it was impossible not to wonder what these angry beasts might really be up to over in the distance, away from the public eye. They could be making something for themselves in their spare time; they could be dismantling what their colleagues had just put together; or they could be stealthily dismembering one of the 31,000 workers who'd fallen into their hands. Perhaps the interdiction on the mobile phones was a serious mistake, and if we'd switched on we might have heard them plotting insurrection or planning their Saturday night out, how they were going to go to downtown Ingolstadt and hang out outside McDonald's. After all, for them transport wasn't a problem; they could knock together a suitable vehicle in a matter of minutes.

Towards the end of the production line the robots were increasingly supplemented by people, completing the last stages of assembly, with the cars moving slowly overhead and the workers standing underneath, wearing them like hats. Then came the symbolic moment, the 'marriage' between the body and the chassis, the moment which should have been accompanied by trumpets and bells, but which instead was witnessed in sterility by a group of white-coated men with clipboards, watching for tell-tale escapes of juices, who looked decidedly unmoved by the poetry of the moment. A couple of stages further down the line came the crucial point when the fuel went in the tank, the key went in the ignition and the engine turned over for the first time, demonstrating that the whole 20,000-piece jigsaw had been worth the effort. Those cars that didn't immediately burst into life – and there were one or two – were hand-hauled ignominiously out of the line to see the headmaster. After which they had to go round the last bit again until they got it right.

I'd read that Audi had quite an ageing workforce, and here was the evidence. For one particular function, installing some interior components, the company had devised a chair on a swinging arm so that the worker didn't have to stand and bend. It was, said the guide, so that productivity could be increased. Allowing workers to operate from a comfy chair meant they could contribute more with less effort, producing more cars per hour. And that was what the company needed to do: get more out of its people – a tricky task when they were all getting older. But if it didn't, then it might as well shift the whole operation to somewhere where it could get more people, younger and cheaper, but that would no longer be in Germany, with all the marketing implications that that would have for a 'German' car.

Half an hour later I was reunited with my low-Technik 20-euro set of wheels and making *Vorsprung durch* the Forum's car-delivery area. At the junction where Audi's private road met the public highway a woman had drawn up on the kerb, unable to wait any longer for her first oral fumigatory experience in her new cultural expression of movement. She was having a fag in her car.

7

Regensburg: the Pope and
the Punk Princess

For the next couple of days the weather deteriorated, having reminded itself it was still early in the year. The trees dripped down the back of my neck, the rain slid down my nose, and I found I could see my breath pasted on air that was thick with the smell of wet leaves. Even though it was May, I regretted not bringing gloves. For the first time in the journey I found myself cycling just to get to the other end.

Bad weather is mood-affecting, but not everything was unhappy. Beneath my wheels the transformation of the cyclepath on these cold, damp days was dramatic. It was as if someone in the hedgerows had fired a starting gun and all the slugs and snails of the neighbourhood had surged forth at the signal. They'd been waiting for days, hidden away, miserable in the dry heat, thinking how lovely and damp it looked over on the other side, but barred from crossing by horribly hot and dusty conditions. But now they were off to play in the road.

I whirred on, tyres slick with slime, lured onwards from one village to the next by the smell of local breweries, whose cloying, sweet steam lingered low in the damp conditions. Ingolstadt was the city that had witnessed the signing of Bavaria's much prized beer-purity law, the *Reinheitsgebot*, back in 1516, stipulating that beer must not contain anything other than water, malted barley, hops and yeast. And one of Bavaria's demands, on agreeing to join the new country called Germany in 1871, had been that the rest of the country should sign up to the beer law too, so the *Reinheitsgebot* has pretty much set the standard for this beer-drinking nation ever since, to the benefit of all mankind. You'd think that the result might be that every beer tastes the same, but I can assure you they don't, and the breweries of the Altmühl region were a welcome diversion on those damp days.

In particular I made a point of stopping and supping at the riverside monastery of Weltenburg, where the monks have run the oldest monastic brewery in the world since 1050 – nearly a thousand years. The brewery sat on one side of a giant interior courtyard filled with chestnut trees, just along from the church, providing a choice between praying and drinking. And to banish any uncertainty about the sanctity of the latter, hanging in the brewery window was a giant photograph of a Kloster Weltenburg beer-delivery lorry in front of the Vatican in Rome. If it was good enough for the Pope, then it was good enough for me, so I settled at one of the trestle tables under the chestnut trees, along with a boatload of daytrippers who'd come up the Danube from Kelheim.

The river here was the colour of spring cow-pats, and just below the gentle shingle at Weltenburg it ran fast and hard through a gorge of limestone cliffs bearded with greenery. It was particularly deep in this stretch, up to 20 metres in places, and there was no room for a towpath, which meant that early navigators had had to unhook their horses and hand-haul themselves and their boats upstream with the help of iron rings sunk into the gorge walls, until the river broadened out again by the monastery, where the horses were waiting to hitch up again. But there was no hurry; after all that effort a little legitimate intoxication provided by monks was the nearest thing to heaven.

In the broad Weltenburg courtyard the speciality dark beer was served by once-handsome middle-aged ladies in heavy boots, rough worsted waistcoats and green aprons, who looked as if they might well have been recruited a thousand years ago themselves. They were confident and earthy, not servile or spiritual, and I wondered what today's monks made of these worldly women, with their air of having seen it all before, in their midst. It was not as if there weren't monks around, because occasionally a black robe would emerge from one door, scurry along the side of the courtyard, and disappear into another. After a hard day at work in the heady air of the brewery they would surely represent a temptation, those waitresses. Some of the monks must have had cell windows looking down on their beer garden, and they'd be able to watch them as they waltzed between the tables, laughing and joking with the guests.

But not, it seemed, with me.

'Is the white sausage made by monks too?' I asked the waitress who stood over me while I surveyed the menu.

'Only the beer,' she said.

'And is the cappuccino made by a Capucin?'

'It's made by a Pole,' she said, dismissively. When you've been around and seen the world you know a plonker when you see one.

I turned this exchange over in my mind and by the time I'd guzzled most of my *Dunkelbier* I'd concluded my German must have been deficient in the white-sausage-monk association. Up above me in the chestnut tree a bird started singing an insistent note: 'Pissed. Pissed. Pissed.' I wasn't, not quite, but another beer magicked up by monks and I would be, so I stumbled off to the monastery church to admire its very theatrical baroque interior. Besides the usual extravaganza of ogees, pinnacles and pediments, there was a George slaying the dragon above the altar, framed in marble pillars with a finish like polished birds' eggs, while everything above and behind it was gilded and curlicued. The organ pipes were supported on two more pillars and looked ready to march down the nave and give good old roistering George a rousing chorus, while right above my head was a big oblong lantern whose ceiling was decorated with a frescoed sky and cherubs looking down at the congregation from the balcony edge. The lantern distributed daylight handsomely throughout the church, but at a price, because from the outside it was an ugly brute, and it gave the church the look of a baroque camper van with one of those cantilevered roofs that you raise when you want to go to bed.

By now I'd moved from a land of *-ingen*s into one of *-ing*s, lots of them. There was Töging, Essing, Sittling, Pförring. Most of which I was doing, I think. And then there was Marching, which I wasn't doing, Pissing, which I did sometimes, and Bad Gögging, which didn't sound like a good idea. I did get some Startling, too, when quite without warning an ICE, Germany's high-speed train, pierced the valley walls like a steel needle and thread and shuttled across in front of me in the blink of an eye. That train was the only straight line in a world full of curves, and it sliced across from one tunnel to the other so fast that I couldn't be absolutely sure it had existed. Certainly most of the passengers on board would have been oblivious to the world outside their window, but a few might have looked up from their Essing and Sittling and caught a glimpse of a figure on a bike in the Pissing rain, and wondered idly what it was like out there. By the time they'd finished reading the newspaper they'd have been approaching Munich, but I was still bumping my way across the tracks in my bid for Budapest, contemplating the incongruity of high-speed trains making guest appearances in a world of slugs, monks and Romans.

Eventually I came to Bad Gögging itself. It turned out to be a small spa town which had started life being called Limes Thermae by the Romans, whose ruined fort of Abusina was on the top of a nearby hill. In their day the Limes had been a line of Roman fortifications which had stretched all the way down the Danube to the Black Sea, marking the boundary of empire, and Abusina must have been one of the more comfortable postings. At the end of their guard duty the legionnaires could trundle downhill to flop into a choice of several thermal pools, all between 25 and 37 degrees, for post-guard-duty facials, armour-chafing body scrubs and waxing of centurion bikini lines.

The pools had since been enclosed in a big modern spa centre, where you could get, amongst other things, a paraffin bath and a hot chocolate massage, neither of which I found particularly tempting. It was clear from the posters and brochures that modern Bad Gögging was marketing itself as a place to roll back the years, to halt the ageing process without going under the knife. But it was lunchtime when I cycled through and not many people were on the streets, so I couldn't judge for myself whether its clientele were rejuvenated, happy, white-smiling sixty-somethings, or whether too much warm water only served to make them wrinklier than prunes. The only evident visitors were a couple of pre-teens kicking their heels in the infant playground of a local biergarten, looking as if they'd been deposited there by spa-obsessed grandparents who'd taken them away on a lovely bit of Bad Gögginging and couldn't understand why they looked so glum.

Beyond Gögging, past the Essings and the Sittlings, I found a room in the house of a dear old Bert in a village whose *Gasthof* advertised good '*bürgerliche*' cooking, and which to emphasize the point had a wall-fresco of burgers in hats looking like they thought everything was burgerlicking good. This Bert and his wife were my most eccentric hosts on the cycling stretch of the journey. He was a great talker and a great laugher, and he had a thick country accent which was made even thicker by the amount of alcohol he consumed, on what must have been an hourly basis. I suspect he'd been a farmer once upon a time, because his powerful shoulders and the way he held his arms slightly away from his body suggested a lifetime of hard labour. But he didn't seem unhappy with his new career as master of ceremonies, seeing it as his particular role to talk at his guests and, between sentences, to laugh his short bellowing laugh.

'Here comes the brains of the operation, hurr hurr,' he said, as I was clambering off my bike in his courtyard. From the street behind me emerged an elderly lady pushing a pram, and I naturally assumed he was introducing me to his wife.

'Only one year old, hurr hurr, but already she's got more brains than the rest of us put together, hurr hurr.'

I struggled to keep up with anything he ever said to me, and he said a lot. I barely got more than every third word, but he didn't notice. I don't think he even realized I was a foreigner; probably just thought I was unusually quiet for a Frankfurter. That evening I could hear him downstairs, growling and bellowing for hour after hour, but I couldn't hear anyone else. I assumed his wife probably left him to soliloquize at the TV, but in the morning they were both in the breakfast room, reading aloud to each other from the newspaper, looking up briefly to offer me tea or coffee. It was plainly their morning ritual, no matter whether anyone else was in the house. He'd read bits to her, she'd grunt, and she'd read bits to him and he'd laugh, hurr hurr. Then they'd swap sections and repeat the process, ending up reading the same stories to each other all over again, having plainly not listened at all the first time round. They'd found a way of co-existing, and they really didn't give a hoot about what anyone else thought.

Appropriately, I arrived in Regensburg with the *Regen*, rain. And despite the dour conditions it was clear that the former capital of Bavaria, once the hub of Charlemagne's empire and the seat of the Imperial Diet of the Holy Roman Empire, was a lovely old city, still essentially medieval in its layout. It was the first city I'd encountered on the river which had not been re-arranged by the RAF, and the result was 1,400 buildings of serious historical significance still standing, many of them more than five hundred years old. It would have been lovely on a sunny day.

Centuries as a trading crossroads, particularly for salt brought up the Danube, had imbued the city with a cosmopolitan spirit. In the narrow pedestrian lanes, lined with jewellers and antique traders, you could have been in the back streets of The Hague, where the main noise came from the pigeons settling around the gables overhead.

It was a city whose nationality was determined by the weather forecast. When the days were warm, it'd be like Italy, with tourists sitting around the terraces and piazzas eating ice-cream and shopkeepers at the doorways of their boutiques congratulating each other on the artistry of their window displays. When the sun was high it could be Nice or Marseilles, where shade is provided by tall buildings by the waterside and the siesta rules at midday. But in the rain it reverted to being decidedly German, with everyone going about their business resolute and grim.

Ecclesiastical buildings dominated the centre. Robed figures fluttered down pedestrian alleys, and I got a sense that Bible studies were breaking out all over, behind Dominican, Benedictine and Carmelite doors. It wasn't so long since Pope Benedict XVI had been here, soon after his elevation from plain old Cardinal Ratzinger, and it was here that he made that now infamous speech in which he quoted a declaration that the Prophet Mohammed was 'evil and inhuman' because of his command that faith should be spread by the sword. The Islamic world had reacted angrily, and the Pope had been forced to apologize, pointing out (rather disingenuously) that he'd only been quoting the view of a fourteenth-century emperor, not his own. Benedict/Ratzinger had taught theology in Regensburg back in the 1970s and still had a house in the city, so I could see how, back amongst unchanging, medieval cobbled streets surrounded by friends and former colleagues, the views of fourteenth-century emperors might have seemed of suitable interest. And I could see that, to someone who had dwelled amongst medievalism and academia, the impact that repeating those views made on the wider modern world might have come as a surprise. Anyway, Benedict returned to Rome rather chastened by the experience and hopefully resolved to be less naïve in his choice of words thereafter. Possibly he had also renewed his supply of Regensburger Karmelitengeist, an alcohol-based cure for flatulence which is made and sold by Regensburg's Carmelite monks from their monastery on the Alter Kornmarkt square. The formula contains twelve herbs, and only two monks know the magic mix that will prevent a Pope from losing his dignity during the quietly meditative passages of evening prayer.

Regensburg's biggest single attraction, and the reason for its historical importance in trade, religion and politics, was its bridge across the Danube. The Steinerne Brücke was built back in 1130 and for centuries was the only river-crossing between Ulm and Vienna. To my eye, it still looked in pretty good order, a hefty piece of stonework arching its back over giant slippered feet which thrust their toes into the fast-flowing river. As with practically every construction of such age, it had a legend attached, and one which was repeated by every tour leader whose group came to stand on the arch. They were told that story as they looked back at the medieval skyline studded with towers and the mullioned garret windows that dug their heels in to stop themselves sliding off steep roofs and spiking themselves on the eaves below. There were few straight lines in that cityscape, and with every building at a slightly different angle to its neighbour, it was hard to judge either distance or perspective. Sitting on the parapet, looking back at the soft yellows and ochres of old walls whose outlines were softened further by drizzle, turning it into a fading fresco on a riverbank, I listened to various accounts of the bridge legend. The basic story runs that the bridge-builder had made a bet with his rival the cathedral-builder that he could complete his project first, but in order to assure a win he had entered into a Faustian compact with the Devil. He'd enlisted Satan's help with the bridge construction, agreeing to Satan's terms that he could take possession of the first soul to cross to the other side. The bridge-builder duly triumphed over the cathedral-builder, and he tricked the Devil, too, because the first soul to cross the bridge had been a donkey. Or a dog, cat or chicken, depending on which group leader you believed.

Of the four or five accounts I overheard, only one narrator queried its authenticity. The problem with the story, she said, was that at the time of the bridge-building there was no cathedral in Regensburg, and nor would there be for another 150 years, which didn't make it much of a race. So even back in the Middle Ages there was no letting the truth get in the way of a good story.

As unmissable as the Steinerne Brücke, and built at much the same time, was Regensburg's Historic Sausage Kitchen, supposedly Germany's oldest restaurant, in a low stone cottage with a tall chimney on the city end of the bridge. Unmissable not because of its architecture – it looked like a Greek quayside taverna with trestle tables in front – but because of the all-pervasive smell of grilling *Wurst*, which wrapped itself alluringly around every street corner, triggering a Pavlovian response in every passerby. I felt some sympathy for the staff who stood around the grill inside, forever prodding, checking and turning. When you live with the smell of sausages, waking up with it, going to sleep with it, and existing with it every hour in between, you can have too much of a good thing. By the time they got home at night they must have been lacquered in sausage fat.

I ordered my 'six with sauerkraut', sat down and watched the tour guides pause en route to the bridge to run through the list of the Kitchen's celebrated customers. From my perspective, on a hard bench by a greasy quayside, it didn't seem Goethe's, Mozart's and Haydn's kind of place, but I daresay they were practically forced to try it, because in those days the best address in town had been the White Lamb Hotel directly behind the Sausage Kitchen, and its important guests must have been tormented by the smell drifting through their windows, morning, noon and night. '*Mein Gott*, I have to have a sausage,' Mozart would say to Haydn, pushing aside his half-finished oratorio. The British Saxe-Coburg-Gothas had recently had the same problem with itinerant *Wurst* sellers outside Buckingham Palace. I wondered whether they too had been so pestered by the smell that they'd eventually sent out a valet to buy some surreptitiously. '*Mein Gott*, I have to have a hot dog with onions.'

One of my purposes in coming to Regensburg was to add to my bag of encounters with high society, and the prospect of meeting Princess Gloria von Thurn und Taxis was more mouthwatering than the smell of grilling sausages or frying onions. The Thurn und Taxis family is one of Germany's richest, and Gloria's son, the young Prince Albert, in his early twenties and studying at Edinburgh University (another German aristocrat who values a British education), is the world's youngest billionaire, valued at $2 billion. I knew the prince was unlikely to be at home, but I'd been communicating with Gloria's staff and the princess hadn't said an outright 'no' to granting me an audience. In the mind of an optimistic travel writer, spending a lot of his day on a bicycle with plenty of time to speculate, that lack of a 'no' had mutated into a strong possibility that we would meet. But a couple of days before I finally broached the city walls, the message came through that Gloria would not be in town after all. Instead I was offered a complimentary palace tour.

It was a poor substitute for meeting the Lady Di of the German aristocracy. She'd married Johannes von Thurn und Taxis when she was twenty and he was fifty-four. Although she was titled – her mother had been one of the Hungarian Széchényis – she'd also been a modern day Cinderella working as a waitress. He, meanwhile, had spent most of his adult life having a good time, particularly with his own sex. There was plenty of gossip about the relationship, no doubt much of it instigated by those who would have liked to have married one of Europe's richest men and who considered themselves eminently more suitable for taking him in hand than Gloria. And it was, by all accounts, an unconventional marriage; when Johannes celebrated his sixtieth birthday, Gloria had had his cake decorated with sixty confectionery candles sculpted in the shape of penises. There were all manner of rumours about how the relationship worked, but aristocrats I spoke to further downriver were generally of the opinion that Johannes and Gloria had loved each other. They'd certainly managed to have three children in fairly quick succession.

Johannes had continued his extravagant lifestyle until his death in 1990, and the children grew up with parties attended by rock musicians and film stars. Meanwhile the glamorous Gloria had pretty much free rein in self-expression, altering her appearance and her hair colour with every breeze of fashion. Her exuberance and her appearance made her the darling of the gossip columns, which christened her the Punk Princess or Princess TNT, and she was forever being photographed out on the town, spending money.

On Johannes' death she'd shocked Germany's

aristocratic community by deciding to hold auctions of some of his possessions, including his Harley-Davidson – a decision which wasn't considered dignified. But since then she'd sobered up and proved herself a very astute manager of the family's immense wealth. Mind you, she continued to hold fairly outspoken views, famously declaring on a TV chat show in 2001 that AIDS had spread through Africa not because of lack of education about safe sex, but because 'the blacks like to *schnackseln* a lot'.

Much of Johannes' and the Princess TNT's fast living took place in a former monastery, St Emmeram Palace, close to the heart of the city. The Thurn und Taxis home is not just a palace: it's a town, with the outlying areas given over to museums, galleries, a brewery and restaurants. In the shop I stood in front of a rack of postcards of Gloria as she is today, with and without her good-looking children, thinking how elegant and competent she seemed, not in the least bit racy or unconventional. A few moments later I heard her voice inside my head (via a headset) 'cordially inviting' me into her home and asking me to try to keep to the carpets; she was the last person I'd expect to go round tut-tutting at dirty footprints.

The Emmeram Palace is one of the largest in Germany, with over five hundred rooms, more than Buckingham Palace. Between them these rooms amass 14,000 square metres of parquet flooring, several Gobelin tapestries and a crystal ballroom chandelier, which weighs more than a ton, above a photograph of the whole family sitting demurely with Cardinal Ratzinger before he was Benedicted. But despite the size and grandeur of their home, the Thurn und Taxis family does not have an immensely long tradition in Germany, with the current prince only the twelfth in the line. The family were originally Italians, the Thurn being a corruption of the Torrianis (towers), and the Taxis were the Thassis (badgers). Their wealth emanates from their status as postmasters for the Holy Roman Empire, which all came about because their own extended family was so widely spread back in the late fifteenth century – towers here, badgers there – that the head of the family devised a communication system to further their mutual business interests. He'd set up staging posts every 25 kilometres on key routes, each ready with its own horses, where approaching messengers would sound their horn so that the next horseman could be saddled up and ready to go. Using this method, messages could be sent from Innsbruck to Brussels in just over five days, which was unprecedented speed in those days, and the service quickly attracted other users. Thus the Thurn und Taxis became the CNN of their day, because whenever messages were carried, news travelled too. The family had a monopoly on the Holy Roman Empire's postal system for nearly four hundred years until Bismarck finally placed it under state control in 1867, and Deutsche Post still bears the symbol of the postmaster's horn.

The elevation of the Thurn und Taxis to the nobility, fairly late in the day, gave them responsibilities in which the Emmeram Palace played an essential part. They had to do their bit in entertaining the emperor and his ministers on a regular basis, which meant a suitable diet of music, dancing and dining in grand palace rooms – and providing a bed for Empress Maria Theresa, a bed that was suitably supported by gilded swans. The princess's own bedroom was rather less showy, but it did have a connecting staircase to the prince's chambers, and if the prince wanted to 'see' the princess he would send a manservant down with a poem and a rose. If the princess was willing to 'see' the prince, she'd send the man back with another poem, perhaps a rhyming couplet or two about the benefits of a good wash, and fifteen minutes later the prince would arrive, having given the princess time to empty the ashtray, turn off the TV and take her curlers out.

I couldn't imagine the whirlwind Princess TNT making assignations in such an old-fashioned way, but the sex life of nobility is always a source of fascination. These days Gloria appears to spend an awful lot of time with her best friend, an unmarried Italian princess, so she continues to keep the gossip columnists on the go. Gloria's reaction? In a magazine interview in 2006, she said this: 'If you tell people that you live in chastity they think you're crazy. I don't really care what people think, because I'm going to be Alessandra's best friend anyway. I would be terribly lonely otherwise.'

8

Passau: Learning the River's Rules

From Regensburg the Danube, which had hitherto shown every intention of making a break for the Baltic, changed tack as if somebody had whispered something alluring in its ear about the Black Sea. It swung its bows to point at Vienna and ran full-bellied before the wind. I had appointments to keep, so I put my head down and pedalled with it, grateful for the wind assistance, while around me the rain stopped and the sun came out, steam-cleaning the farmland, polishing the greens and turning dirt to dust for the hoovering breeze. The season seemed to speed up before my eyes. A cuckoo in the woods repeated its insistent note, 'Global-warming, my-arse; global-warming, my-arse.' Blunt lapwings mewed and chuntered as I cycled past, the bolder amongst them like mortar-boarded headmasters, heckling and scolding, and others screwing through the air like poorly made paper darts thrown repeatedly by some invisible hand.

The Danube plain was carpeted in young flannelette romper suits of corn, newly stencilled with tractor tracks, and it smelled freshly laundered. In a couple of months' time it would be wearing flowery prints of yellows and reds, heavily pregnant and perfumed, and two months later it'd be into another season of long skirts of ochres and russet greens, frayed at the edges, fruitily pungent and past its best. But for now the infant year was still bouncy, fresh and rosy-cheeked, and every now and then the wind would trail its invisible fingernails across the corn, rippling it this way and that, tickling its belly until it sighed with pleasure.

The builders were in at Walhalla, a giant Danubian Parthenon that jutted out of the hillside not far from Regensburg, and an unmissable monument for anyone moving along the Danube valley. That day the massive frowning forehead of stone was flanked by scaffolding which looked as if it was giving the pillars builderly acupuncture, and indeed billboards suggested the restoration was to 'make Walhalla better', which itself sounded like an oxymoron. The original Valhalla of Norse mythology had contained the statues of heroes gloriously slain in battle, but this one was a vast vault completed in 1842 at the behest of King Ludwig I to celebrate the great and the good of the German-speaking world, all the way from Friedrich Barbarossa, emperor, to W. A. Mozart, composer, and added to subsequently by committee. There were kaisers and writers, artists and composers, field marshals and scientists, all mixed in, not in any evident logical order. Accordingly Bismarck, Wagner and Bach looked very grumpy at being placed together, having long since exhausted all topics of bombastic conversation. Anton Bruckner looked vaguely stoned, Einstein was suppressing a chuckle, just having thought of something particularly interesting – that no one would ever know now that he was dead – and Schubert looked as if he'd had a good breakfast and was now looking forward to his lunch. Many of them were half turned towards the vast door, beyond which lay a fabulous view of the river basin, now stretching out luxuriantly under unaccustomed sun. But that door opened only once while I was there, to admit me, so they didn't get much of a view, and as I left I could have sworn I heard whispering and the rustle of paper darts as I closed the door behind me.

By now the Rhine-Main-Danube Canal had doubled the size of the river, and bridges no longer looked bridgey, up to their ankles in water, but had been reborn as giant stalking creatives of concrete. The flat blade of water they spanned wasn't so rivery, either, but it was no longer empty. The susurration of my tyres on tarmac and gravel was occasionally joined, in harmony, by the heavy bass of a pusher-tug or the clattering of a barge's old diesel engine, its pistons playing pingpong back and forth. I overhauled the *Buda*, a pusher from Hungary, heavily laden and easily overtaken, and exchanged waved salutations with a mechanic leaning over the rail. Poor devil, he was probably having a short break from a lifetime in the engine room with a grease gun.

Despite the link with the likes of Rotterdam and Hamburg provided by the Rhine-Main-Danube Canal, Danube traffic is a fraction of what it used to be. The exception are the river cruise ships, unseaworthy things whose bow and stern top-and-tail a medium-sized block of flats. I'd seen my first one tied up in Regensburg, and it only served to confirm that I'd made the right decision in opting to travel beside the river rather than on it. Cruise ships on the Danube have increased in quantity far more than any other form of shipping since the canal opened in 1992, but their clientele is mainly elderly, and their itineraries stick to the big cities, with on-board lectures and flower-arranging classes to fill the gaps between meals. I'd cycled past one alongside the quay at Regensburg, smelled the venison and chips, and seen the human cargo lingering on the threshold, halfway between ship and shore, uncertain whether it was worth stepping on to the land or whether it'd be better to stay aboard to be fattened up by more free food and wine in preparation for another hard day of watching cyclists slip astern.

These ships represented the latest evolution of river traffic that had started back in the tenth and eleventh centuries, when the Crusaders had used crude boats to travel downriver towards the Middle East. They in turn were followed by rafts that floated downstream carrying lime, charcoal, cut wood and building stone. At much the same time the Danube started to be used by salt-traders keen to connect mines in the northern Alps, near Salzburg, with lucrative markets to the south and west, and thus began the first serious traffic upriver, against the stream. At their peak in the eighteenth century these Danube salt convoys involved as many as forty horses hauling strings of five barges at a time. The first rider, at the head of the convoy, carried an axe, ensured the towpath was clear and shouted the commands. Then came the marshaller, in charge of 58-metre-long ropes, followed by the horses, with one rider for every two beasts, producing the power. Behind them walked two rope-handlers who made sure that the tows didn't get snagged unnecessarily on shore, and who were ready to tie off round any available rock or tree in the event of emergency. Out on the water, the first boat handled the tows and lined up the three barges behind it, and each of the latter had a steering oar and high prow manned with boathooks and poles to keep out of the shallows. The last of the barges carried horse-feed as well as salt, and at the tail of the procession came a small cook's boat, which also carried the fleet's quartermaster, whose job it was to record all the purchases of provisions and pay out for all work done in the course of the expedition. It was a whole village on the move.

Not surprisingly, this laborious and slow form of river transport lost out when the railways arrived, but it wasn't long before the technology used in steam locomotives was transferred to the water, bringing some of the trade back again. Paddlesteamers became a big force on the river from the 1830s and 1840s, initially powered by boilers built in Glasgow, a city which at that time was making steam engines for the furthest reaches of the British Empire. In fact it was two Englishmen, Andrews and Pritchard, who started the Danube's first major steamship company, the Erste Donau Dampfschifffahrts-Gesellschaft, or DDSG, which had seven seagoing and ten river ships in 1829. Fifty years later the fleet had grown to over two hundred vessels and given the German language its longest word: *Donaudampfschifffahrtsgesellschaftskapitänsmützenabzeichen*, which means the 'badge on the cap of a captain employed by the Danube Steam Navigation Co'. Badges, caps and uniforms were a matter of great pride on the river, and agents and captains all wore bow ties when attending meetings on shore.

As for their boats, they were living beasts, the old steamers. Sixty or 70 metres long and 20 metres wide at the paddles, they bounced, quivered and bumped their way upriver like giant sea lions crossing ice, paddles flapping, funnels belching. They had double windlasses in the bows, ever at the ready, so that some sort of foothold could be grabbed in the river if the beat of the engine should ever falter. The crew kitchen, complete with Aga, sat above one set of paddles, and its kettles were forever

The Danube rises in Donaueschingen, in
Germany's Black Forest, 2,480km
from the Black Sea.

The Danube cyclepath was delightful in the
spring sunshine, but I was sweaty and smelly
for my first encounter with Danube aristocracy,
the Hohenzollerns of Sigmaringen (*right*).

Blaubeuren, source of the river Blau, where
32,000 litres of blueness emerge every
second from a vertical cave.

(*Left*) Sigmaringen's Prince Karl-Friedrich Emich Meinrad Benedikt Fidelis Maria Michael Gerold von Hohenzollern, aka Charly, as in Charly and the Jivemates (*right*).

The Danube saunters through Regensburg, home to a pope, a princess, and Germany's oldest sausage kitchen.

Austria's Wachau, where picture postcards are made in heaven.

Princess Anita von Hohenburg with her daughter the Countess, on the terrace at Artstetten.

A splash of blue on the Danube: a floating swimming pool on Vienna's Danube Canal.

Budapest embraces the river while Bratislava's communist-era architecture (*below*) keeps its distance.

(*Above*) On the bridge at Esztergom, emulating Patrick Leigh Fermor.

(*Below*) Mark in his Budapest flat, his twenty-eighth address in thirty years.

Tamas tended the horses first, then the fire.

Laguna, the half-Lipizzaner who was scared of puddles.

The *Argo*, Serb-owned, a hundred years old and still going strong.

The Danube has been tamed by two massive dams – the Iron Gates – where it squirms through a gap in the Carpathian mountains.

Vlado, first mate (and best mate) on the *Argo*, although he did initially threaten to throw me overboard. The *Argo*'s toilet (*right*) required a special kind of agility.

being bounced off the hotplate on to the floor below. The smokestacks, built especially tall to minimize the potential rain of smuts and steam on to the deck, had to be mounted on giant pivots with balancing weights so they could be easily lowered to navigate the bridges. Down below, in a cacophonous ribcage of valves and ventilation, mechanics scurried about checking dials and pipes and surrounded by rushing water, some of it cold and some of it very hot, but all of it dangerous.

The steamship companies ran scheduled passenger services as well as freight. Of course they were slower than today's boats, but not that much slower. It would take a paddlesteamer two days to complete the 150-kilometre upriver journey from Passau to Regensburg, where today it takes one. But with average crews of twenty-five, the old steamers were very labour-intensive, so when technology moved on after the Second World War they were soon supplanted by diesel tugs trailing fleets of barges. Eventually that too proved too manpower-intensive, because each trailing barge required a crewman to watch over the steering oar, so now the latest evolution is the push-tug, where the barges are chained to the bows and controlled from the pusher's bridge. With this configuration, crews can be as small as four or six.

Given the power and the economy of these pusher-barges, with the largest shifting loads equivalent to a couple of hundred articulated lorries, it comes as a surprise to learn that the Danube runs at only a fraction of its freight capacity. One of the reasons for that under-performance was the very same stretch of river I cycled past that day, out of Regensburg, although I was unaware of it until I met up with Captain Josef Fenzl, *Hauptkommissar* of the River Police in Passau.

Captain Fenzl was a kindly, thorough, slight man whom

I reckoned to be in his early fifties. An administrator, a man who knew the rules and regulations, with none of the repartee and the street-smart swagger of a frontline policeman, he had fifteen officers to cover 55 kilometres of river. He knew his business back to front and inside out, and for every topic we discussed he had a box file full of documents, most of them yellowing with age.

We met in his office on the waterside just outside Passau, the last Danube city before Austria, on a blustery day of squally showers. The weather had deteriorated again. My hope had been to persuade him to take me out on patrol in one of his River Police cruisers, but Captain Fenzl regretted that his main boat was broken, and the temporary replacement was too small for bad weather. I was surprised at this news, which seemed rather ill prepared for a German police force, and my surprise must have registered in my expression.

'We do much of our policing on shore anyway,' the captain reassured me, offering me a chocolate liqueur from a fancy selection a doctor could have been given by a grateful patient, but which seemed rather frivolous for a police station at ten o'clock in the morning. 'If we want to go aboard a boat, we just ask the lock-keepers not to let him through. It is not as if a freight ship can easily get away.'

One of his main areas of interest was the level of water in the river. It wasn't something that had struck me as significant till now, although it was to become dramatically more so later on in my journey. He showed me an internet-based program that gave exact water levels, measured in *pegel*, every few kilometres through the whole German Danube system. The program was updated automatically, and drew attention to rising levels in tributaries and calculated resulting estimated future levels downstream. Clever stuff.

'Do all the captains have this?'

He nodded. 'Those that have the Internet. They need to know if the water's rising and whether they'll get under the bridges. And if it's low, they need to know if they're going to go aground. Sometimes they ask us, and if they give us their weight, draft, etc., we'll tell them if they need to get a move on or to wait.'

Trying to second-guess the water level played a big part in a captain's decision about how much to load. A barge captain taking on cargo at the docks in Rotterdam with a shipment bound for Austria or even further downriver had to take a punt on how much river depth was going to be available to him. Bigger loads produced more profit, but gave much less room for manoeuvre in the shallows. It could be a costly gamble.

'You can no longer rely on seasonal rain. These days, with climate change, it's hard to tell when the floods are going to come.'

I nodded. 'So what would happen if he got it wrong? If rain didn't come and the river level sank in the two weeks it took him to get down here from Rotterdam?'

'He must stop. If he goes aground, he has to face us. And to pay a fine, because it is illegal to travel when he knows he shouldn't. Otherwise, he waits until it rains, somewhere in the system. We had one last week, a Romanian with animal feed, 1.93 metres of draft but only 1.86 metres of river water. So he waited until the level rose. The alternative is for the company to send another barge to take off some of the load, but that costs money. And time.'

I had had no idea that freight ships were like salmon, waiting for a surge of fresh water before they moved.

'Isn't it worth dredging the shallows a bit deeper?' I ventured.

131

Captain Fenzl scratched behind his ear and explained that for most of the river the water level was controlled by hydroelectric dams, which effectively turned the Danube into a chain of long, thin lakes. There, the levels weren't usually a problem, but not in the stretch just upriver from Passau. 'Vilshofen to Straubing. In the last two years we have had sixty boats going aground here, and a few of them have lost all control, swinging out to block the main channel. Now that's a big problem. That's what makes the Danube so much harder than the Rhine.'

I remembered that scene I'd seen on Google Earth of the barges surrounded by stains of mud. It must have been on this stretch.

'So why don't they dredge it deeper?'

'The Greens. The Green lobby is very powerful in our government, and this section of river has been designated a nature reserve. It's pretty much the only piece of original, free-flowing Danube left in Bavaria.'

'Ah.' Now that I knew the reasoning I felt a great deal of sympathy for the Green point of view, but given that it made more work for Captain Fenzl, I didn't think I should voice it.

'So what do they think of you, the barge captains? Are they scared of you? Fining them and telling them not to move?' I said, with one eye on the liqueur chocolates.

'Not at all. Sometimes they rely on us to protect them from their bosses, who want them to continue even in low water. Most of them take great pride in doing what they do, and doing it properly. Particularly the Eastern Europeans. Although you wouldn't believe it if you listened to the Dutch and Belgians. Here, help yourself.'

Conversation turned to the other aspects of policing. Occasionally what he called the 'Danube telegraph' would tip him off about a vessel that shouldn't be on the water. 'Those older captains, they don't like to see a dangerous boat.'

His officers checked captains' log books to make sure the sailing hours were commensurate with the crew numbers and qualifications. 'To do twenty-four-hour working, they need at least four crew, and two captains with the right papers. The captains need to have the *Strecken* certificates for each stretch of water. If not, we keep them here until other crew arrive.'

It seemed very little, just four people in charge of the equivalent of two hundred articulated lorries, day and night.

'And what about stowaways, people-smuggling? East to West?'

He shook his head. 'Not one of our problems. There are too many controls on freight ships, at every border. And for the average stowaway, a freight ship is far too slow.'

Otherwise, his team verified the proper operation of bow-thrusting propellers, particularly important for boats about to enter the shallow stretch. They also checked the height of the cargo above deck. 'We had a Bulgarian with cargo piled so high it left just a narrow canyon for visibility down the middle. Crazy.'

'So do you get collisions?'

'Not often. Two German ships collided a while ago. It was one of the captains' birthdays, and he was down in the mess having a cup of coffee, so there was no one on the bridge. Except the autopilot.'

'And what about the passenger ships?'

Captain Fenzl said his team didn't have much to do with them. Most passengers were elderly Americans, unlikely to get up to much. Sometimes they reported a theft, but usually it hadn't happened in German waters, and mostly they were just after the insurance money anyway.

'Crew is a different matter, though.'

'Oh yes?'

'Particularly towards the end of the season. There are thirty to forty of them on most of the cruise boats, and all sorts of nationalities, Chinese, Eastern Europeans, Asians, with some prettier single girls amongst them. They've been going up and down the river without a break for months. It's like a prison camp on board. If truth were told, some of them go a bit mad. Cabin fever. You are with people who are not your friends, twenty-four hours a day, week after week, so there is bound to be friction. Hatreds grow, and there are lots of jealousies over the women.'

It sounded like hell on earth. Captain Fenzl went on to explain that these problems were usually for the captains to deal with, and that made the latter particularly frustrated because, unlike on freight barges, they hadn't recruited the troublemakers in the first place. So they felt they were untangling messes that were not of their making.

When all the chocolate liqueurs were finished, I said it was time to make a move. The captain gave me a lift in his police BMW up to the Veste Oberhaus castle so that he could show me where the Inn and the Danube met. The difference in colours was remarkable: the Inn a jade green because of the meltwaters it brought from the Alps, the Danube a dirty brown thanks to upriver slurry and factory outlets. Had he ever seen it blue, I asked?

'Very rarely. And only when the water is very low.'

I didn't find much to relish in Passau. It's a favourite of the cruise-ship companies and looks something of a baroque cruise ship itself, steaming downriver into the V between the Inn and the Danube, with Italianate belltowers, decked colonnades and steeples masquerading as masts, funnels and lifeboats. But the bishop's palaces and cathedrals of this Bavarian Venice were just empty scenery when I was there. Like some of the abbeys further downriver, they had no life of their own without tourists to rouge their cheeks, and it was midweek, early season and raining. Even the daily concert on the largest organ in the world, a 17,794-piper, seemed passionless and perfunctory, with the cathedral's interior flat and drab in leaky wet light. Amongst the tourists, you could easily pick out the couples off the cruise ships with their matching rainwear; the wet weather forced them to surrender their autonomy, welding them together at the hip under one umbrella and turning them into slow-moving, two-headed beasts that wheeled slowly and indecisively in Passau's pedestrian streets, never quite able to get both sets of eyes pointing in the same direction at the same time.

The biggest life force in Passau was in fact the Inn, not the Danube, and the confluence of the two rivers, at a point as sharp as a pencil, sounded like the *sotto voce* ripping of thousands of telephone directories. The river had at last become a proper highway, and lying in what amounted to a ship's cabin in a purpose-designed cyclists' hotel called a Rotel on the quayside, I could listen to the clattering of marine diesels as barges chewed their way upstream. There I waited for the forecast to change, and my clothes to dry, before crossing my first Danube border and shoving off into Austria.

9

Austria: Hitler's Home Ground

There's no great cultural leap on crossing from Germany into Austria. Street signs and car numberplates change, for sure, but the true differences are far harder to spot.

In the course of the last century the Germans have come to regard the Austrians as more backward cousins, and certainly there was something a bit more unkempt about the villages, although that also meant a few more wild flowers in the hedgerows. And yet Austria has had a far longer history of European domination than the Germans, having been the senior partner (with Hungary) in an empire that was far larger than the Holy Roman effort had ever been, a big Austro-Hungarian octopus that had managed to cling on to its territory for several hundred years in various configurations, stretching and shrinking, letting its tentacles have first more freedom, then less, depending on the danger. When threatened from the east, by Turkey, it was quite prepared to let Budapest go, and even to abandon Vienna if need be; when threatened from the west, by Napoleon, it temporarily abandoned

Vienna once more. The empire forged alliances and made concessions in ripples and waves, and was always ready to sacrifice some far-off territory in order to preserve the core, the aristocracy. Hierarchy and heredity were society's pillars, and etiquette was its moral code.

That aristocratic core has survived, right up to the present, in the small nation that still carries the 'Austria' name. This remains the country in Europe which most highly prizes status and titles, with the K&K (Kaiser und König) symbol of imperial monarchy still much in evidence. And back in the mid-twentieth century, while nations all around it were turning to communism, Austria stuck unswervingly to its hierarchical system, an island of tradition, a respecter of privilege. Accordingly I was to have more luck here with my aristo-hunting than I had had in Germany.

Austria's class-ridden society partly explains why it seems less accessible to the transient visitor. It is a closed, conservative community, with undercurrents and pecking orders that are hard to appreciate as an outsider, and it has a worrying recent history. There was, for example, a higher rate of Nazi Party membership here than in Germany itself; 99 per cent of the population said 'yes' to *Anschluss* (effectively annexation) with Nazi Germany; there was no partisan resistance during the war, and no government-in-exile, unlike in any other occupied country. It voluntarily provided more than the required 10 per cent of concentration-camp personnel, and after the war there was little in the way of internal de-Nazification. The only Austrians found guilty of war crimes at Nuremberg had committed those crimes outside Austria and even today there are strong right-wing Austrian movements which produce documents suggesting that there was no such thing as the Holocaust and that death camps never existed. No doubt the young generation of Austrians reading this will cast their eyes to the heavens at the reiteration of such old chestnuts, but as individuals the Austrians don't do much to change their image; they tend to be guarded and not particularly forthright, so you can never be absolutely sure what they're thinking. And then there are the Kampusches and the Fritzls, the secrets in the cellars, symbolic of a society that stays in its boxes.

The country is, however, extremely pretty and has two of the loveliest bits of the Danube. In Austria the river surges along, brimming with enthusiasm, dropping 150 metres in 300 kilometres. Once it gets to the other side it loses interest, taking a further 2,000 kilometres to drop 150 metres more.

The banks first close in at Burg Krämpelstein, originally the site of a Roman watchpost, perched right up on the cliff. According to legend, a poor but greedy tailor lived up here along with his goat. When the ageing goat started to produce less milk the tailor beat it; and when the goat didn't improve, he lost his temper and threw it off the cliff into the Danube. But as he did so the goat's horns got tangled in his braces and took him down too, so in the end it was the tailor who drowned while the goat swam safely to shore.

Stories like this one were being told and retold at lots of *Radlertreff* – bike meeting places – along the shore, big sunny courtyards where you could get coffee and cake at any time of the day, and most people helped it down with home-made schnapps. I had now entered on the most popular stretch of the Danube for cyclists, and although it couldn't be called busy this early in the year, there were plenty of organized groups on the route and many of them were doing more schnapping in *Treff*s than sitting on saddles. The bonhomie generated in these places intensified as the day wore on, often turning to song, and they would become quite intimidating for anyone not part of a group. On one occasion I was venturing into one such sunny courtyard when one of the group members shouted something by way of greeting, and all the others laughed, turning towards me expectantly for my reply. Unfortunately I hadn't understood – I was struggling with the Austrian accent – so all I could do was shrug, smile and ask for it to be repeated. 'Ach, a foreigner,' said another member of the group, and they all turned away as one, while someone else made another comment which I also didn't understand but which had everyone roaring with laughter again. Needless to say, I slunk away.

Thankfully the landscape and the exercise had their usual palliative effect. The rain had gone, and there were fruit trees and fishponds in the villages, clover and speedwort in the hedgerows, and river eddies with ducks, goslings and warblers. The steepening banks were clad in shaggy coats of deciduous and conifer trees. The conifers were dark, tall, military and sombre whatever the weather, while the deciduous were more frivolous and exuberant and far more responsive to changes in wind and sun. Aspen and birch in particular tossed their glossy heads like teenage girls, keen to catch the attention of passing youth. For me, a hoary old cyclist, pedalling through these woodland areas did no favours to my complexion; it was hard to pick up detail when moving from sunlight to shade, and time and again I plunged into pillars of insects swarming in the shade, emerging with skin like flypaper, lightly acned with gnats stuck on with perspiration.

Where the banks steepened and the valley narrowed, the river clenched its buttocks and thrust hard, accelerating with a sucking sound and forcing barges to labour upriver. Where the banks relaxed again, the river slowed, fattened and sprawled like a Swiss lake in the mountains and I knew there'd be a hydroelectric dam somewhere around the corner, propping it up. I found I could ascertain these changes in water speed by measuring my progress against the downriver boats, who given a good stream were usually a little faster than me. When the stream lessened, it was as if their keels were suddenly dragging through mud, and I found myself overtaking them again.

The most dramatic of the steepenings was the Schlögen Schlinge, a giant scything bend with a name that sounded like a speech impediment, where the river arched its back and thumped its tail and shook off all roads, railways and practically all houses, too. I found myself all alone in a great canyon of green, like a Scottish landscape that had been stripped of its austerity and garishly redecorated. For a while the north bank became virtually sheer into the water, and I was forced to catch a foot ferry across to the other shore, banging a metal sheet with a hammer to attract the attention of the ferryman – and of an outraged peacock somewhere further down the valley.

Some kilometres later the dappled corridor relaxed again and I crossed the river at Aschach, a true riverside resort with a proper riverside promenade. Guesthouses had terraces with fountains and flowerbeds, and lime trees provided shade to anyone who wanted to sit out on the prom with an ice-cream from the likes of the Gasthof zur Sonne or the Promenade Café Konditorei.

I stopped to read the town noticeboard.

'So, the Hot Pants Road Club is coming to town,' said a transatlantic voice from behind me; a cyclist in his mid-sixties was reading over my shoulder. 'I feel like I've got pretty hot pants myself.'

He turned out to be Canadian, and very pleased to bump into someone who spoke English. 'You travelling alone?'

I agreed I was.

He shook his head sadly. 'I don't know how you handle it.'

He explained how he had started the journey with his wife and their two best friends. 'I came here with my tennis buddy Jed three years ago and we had a great time, so this time we persuaded the girls to come too.'

'And they didn't like it?' I could see no tennis buddy, nor any 'girls'.

He grimaced. 'What a mess! I guess I should have known with all those discussions beforehand about how far we could go in a day. But everything was wrong, right from the start. The girls didn't like the hotels, didn't find them comfortable. They didn't like their bicycles, particularly the saddles. They had problems with everything.'

I said it wasn't everyone's idea of a holiday.

'But it turned sour. They clubbed together, the girls. They said we had no concern about our spouses. That they didn't belong on bicycles, at their age. That it wasn't dignified. And that they'd earned the right to a bit more comfort. So in the end they just refused. You know, to go on.'

'You mean they've gone home and left you here?'

'No, no, nothing like that. We hired a car and Jed and I are taking turns escorting them. It's not a good result, and I'm not sure what's worse, being in the car or on the bike. I am not going to pretend I am enjoying cycling by myself. I don't know how you manage. I mean, look at that lot,' he indicated another group of cyclists laughing heartily over glasses of schnapps. 'They're having a jolly time. Why couldn't we?'

I left him in Aschach, contemplating his disaster of a holiday. Jed was coming to pick him up, he said, and take him to that evening's four-star hotel for his rendezvous with 'the girls' in the hotel's spa. And although it was sad to meet someone who was so plainly not getting much pleasure from the Danube cyclepath, the encounter nevertheless made me feel good about travelling alone, free-willed and completely independent. The decisions I made were all mine, as were their consequences. No one had set my agenda, no one had to suffer my mistakes. I could start or stop wherever and whenever I pleased, and I could abandon the whole project and go home tomorrow if I wanted to, without having to justify the decision to anyone except myself. The success or failure of my journey was all mine; it was my own little work of art, my creation. Its motivation came from somewhere deep within me, it had assumed a momentum of its own, and it depended on no one else. Mind you, it could have been useful to have someone around at meal times, if just to warn me that I had food stuck to my face.

Crossing through strawberry fields and cherry orchards after Aschach I eventually reached a small and instantly likeable town called Ottensheim, and although it was still 10 kilometres short of Linz I immediately decided to stop overnight. The town had a wonderfully simple ecofriendly car ferry suspended from a cross-river cable that used the power of the current to push it sideways to and fro; the skipper spun the wheel, the ferry's nose poked out into the stream, and it was off, crabbing sideways along the cable, eventually settling against the pontoon on the opposite bank like a faithful dog returning to its master's leg. No engine required.

At the centre of the town was a market square no bigger than a football pitch which would have been swamped with cars had it not been for someone's innovative idea to dig out a car park directly underneath it, leaving the square free for restaurant terraces and extra stalls to set up for a big wine and cheese party on Friday evenings. There was also another Schwarzer Adler, this one rather more upmarket than Ulm's and run by a welcoming elderly couple who unfortunately hadn't passed on the knack of hospitality to their thirty-something children, who were in the process of taking over. And there was also, bizarrely, an international multi-lane rowing course tucked into a pocket at the side of the Danube.

Many of these initiatives were the work of a forward-thinking former mayor of Ottensheim called Walter Steiner. And it was Steiner who had seen the potential in the suggestion of a young regional tourism executive called Manfred Traunmüller of earmarking the defunct Danube towpath, once busy with those teams of horses hauling salt barges, for use by cyclists. The two of them erected home-made signs along a short section around Ottensheim on a Friday afternoon in 1981, and the first-ever long-distance cycle route in Europe was under way.

I met Traunmüller in his office in Linz, from where he now ran Donau Touristik, his own tour operator specializing in cycle holidays, which was offering twenty-eight different ways of doing the route between Passau and Vienna in various combinations of hotel grade, boat assistance and need for speed. He'd have probably had a men-on-bikes, girls-in-spas combo for the Canadians, if they'd only known. Despite a long association with cycling, he turned out to be a gnome-like, unathletic-looking man who bounced disconcertingly as he spoke, like a member of the Jedi Council, chiefly because he was sitting on a giant yoga ball instead of a chair. He recalled how he and Steiner had had to resist the objections of government in Vienna to the cycle route: 'So take us to court.' And how they had had to fund the first insurance cover themselves, in case anyone had an accident on the towpath and blamed them for it. Needless to say, government in Vienna now looks after that particular bill, now that many thousands use the cyclepath every year and it has become such a huge earner for the nation.

We ended up talking about Adolf Hitler, whose connection with Linz is deeply ingrained. He'd been born nearby and educated in the city, and Traunmüller knew someone who'd been in the same class at school. 'He was a loner even then. Not bright, but not stupid, and no friends. When it came to public speaking, though, he knew exactly what he wanted to say, even as a child.' Hitler had had great plans for Linz, seeing it as the city of his retirement years with Eva Braun. He'd wanted to build a grandiose metropolis, with giant pharaonic buildings, a front door on the Danube to rival Budapest. At its back door he'd initiated the giant Hermann Göring Reich Works that was to become the centre of the armaments industry during the Second World War, turning this city, too, into a major bombing target. It was the centre of Austrian industrialization thereafter, although you'd never guess such heavy industry existed in Linz today.

These days the Führer connection is not something the tourist office likes to dwell on, and the city has developed a strong arts and culture programme to bury bad memories under good. A big event in its cultural year is the Pflasterspektakel – a rotten name for an international festival. Hard to say and even harder to spell, it translates literally as 'cobblestone entertainment', and dates back to the time when all sorts of traders would gather in the market square. The giant Hauptplatz is still there, despite the bombing, and still surrounded by seventeenth- and eighteenth-century houses. It was designed back in the thirteenth century to be the biggest square in Austria, with the idea of turning Linz into a multinational trading crossroads on the Danube, and over a weekend in late July it looks as though the medieval traders have returned, as a very odd-looking collection of Belgians, Estonians, Slovaks, Bohemians, Spaniards, Britons et al. gather around the rococo central pillar. There they ply an age-old trade, a tradition of trying to please the mob in any way they can in return for a few tossed coins. And the mob plays its part, hissing, booing and cheering like medieval urchins.

The festival mechanics are simple, user-friendly and inexpensive. The town hall sends out invitations to street performers from all over the world – as many as five hundred of them – in advance. It tries to ensure that there are not too many clowns, for example, and that no one nationality dominates. It then subsidizes the artists' travel and accommodation and pays them a small daily allowance to make sure they turn up – because they're an unpredictable lot, street performers. Then, when they've checked in, a daily schedule is published distributing them around the venues, most of which are in the pedestrian heart of the city. Shows begin in the early afternoon and run on until 1 a.m., but there are no tickets sold, and there is no obligation to remain as part of any audience for any longer than the performer can keep your attention. The only financial pain comes if you are still amongst the audience at the end, when the performer passes his hat.

A typical afternoon's entertainment starts with a strange, gothic-looking group from Belgium who enact an odd parable of the search for a suitable bride for their make-believe king, using stilts, drums and a wheeled metal chariot, a sort of Boadicea meets Mad Max. Following them come two Hungarians dressed as bumblebees, but with old-fashioned bellows for wings. They run through a surreal selection of ballads, including 'Bara-bara-bara' (about 'the delight the shoemaker gets from smelling his leather') and another which they introduce as 'A lot of songs are about nothing – but this one really is about nothing,' and it comes complete with a groaning, yowling solo from a pair of yellow leather bellows.

Then there's an Indian magician who does rope tricks, a Slovakian jazzband, a balalaika band from Russia, bagpipers from Estonia and an Argentinian called Hugo who provokes howls of laughter when, after a seemingly accidental collision with an old lady making a determined beeline for a nearby church door, he reels away clutching a lacy black bra.

If they are good, the performers can earn well here, unlike in Britain, where street performance is regarded as a pastime for the work-shy, and barely a step up from begging. It doesn't seem very Austrian, either, and I suspect that Hitler might have taken an even more dismissive approach than the British. There would never have been a place for anarchic cobblestone artists in his perfect city.

I was haunted by Hitler's vision for Linz for some kilometres. It started with the docks, which once had the reputation as Austria's largest. They'd been developed after Austria–Hungary had been forced to give up its only seaport, Trieste (now in Italy), as a result of the First World War. Thereafter the Danube became the focus of the nation's shipping and the Linz shipyards became extremely busy with orders for rivergoing ships from the Soviet Union. These days they are boomingly, echoingly empty. The only vessel I saw was the lonely and forlorn

Schönbrunn, a 79-metre paddlesteamer which had been built in Budapest in 1912 and which still did occasional river trips.

And then the industrial district began, once the Hermann Göring Reich Works. Its chimneys were like a ragged piece of stitching on a raw, open wound between earth and sky, and amongst them I could see gasometers and what looked like a couple of pitheads, although I knew there were no collieries here. The chimneys came in all shapes and sizes, steaming, gently smoking, or emitting that distinctive piccolo wisp of wasp-coloured smoke that no one likes to see. It was easy to imagine them as a distant orchestra, those chimneys. A dirty steel band, playing a tune that wasn't meant for human ears, with reedy fluted chimneys, tall dark bassoon chimneys, short fat euphonium chimneys, and squirly multi-stopped horn chimneys. The string section was provided by the pylons: the small violin pylons, the larger cello pylons and the giant double bass pylons, using the wind as their bow. And every now and then one of the big fat chimneys would let loose a brassy note which was instantly visible as a great harrumph of smoke, making a huge mess on the stave. I could hear the percussion, the rattle of slag down chutes, the beat of cylinders, the thrum of spinning drums, because these were sounds that were within my register. But no doubt there was a lot more that I couldn't hear, particularly up at sparrow level, too high for my ear. An industrial descant inaudible to humans but which warned all other living creatures to stay well away. All I could get was a distant rumble, and an occasional tumbling clank followed by a screech, as if someone returning from a party early on a Sunday morning had stumbled into a blind dustbin alley and fallen over the neighbour's cat.

Hitler had developed his perfect city with forced

labour, and much of the stone for the building work came from the Wiener Graben quarry up in the hills to the east, where it had been quarried by inmates of the Mauthausen concentration camp. Today the camp rises out of the crown of a hill which has rolling views and high skylarks, looking from a distance like a reconstructed Roman fortress amongst innocent grasslands. This innocence is misleading. Originally built by inmates of Dachau, Mauthausen ultimately housed 200,000 prisoners, a mixture of ideological enemies of National Socialism (the majority of them Jews), plus Polish and Soviet prisoners of war. In the course of its seven-year existence 123,000 of them died here, either from execution or extreme physical or psychological abuse, and each morning would start with a new batch of dead prisoners stuck in the wires atop the perimeter walls, ragged with struggling, shredded like polythene bags blown in the wind.

The big task of Mauthausen's inmates was initially that quarry works in the Wiener Graben, adjacent to the camp, and then as the war developed the decision was taken to move Linz's armaments manufacturing underground, out of range of Allied bombers. So the prisoners were set to work in the surrounding countryside to create forty satellite sub-camps, digging a total of 7 kilometres of tunnels into the rock. Mauthausen became the central distribution point for these sub-camps, sorting out new batches of human moles and sending them out to where they were needed.

Although a large proportion of inmates' deaths were work-related, Mauthausen also had its gas chamber, tiled and lined with pipes to look like a shower room to alleviate the panic of those being herded in. The dead bodies would end up, ten at a time, in the cremation furnaces next door to the gas chamber, but only once they'd been through the dissecting room first to have their gold teeth removed.

Of those allowed to stay alive, the Russians in Block C had been treated particularly badly. They were only fed every third day with five spoonfuls of food, and if they dared ask for more they risked being beaten to death. There were no tables or beds in their block, so everyone slept on the floor, and in wet weather they were made to lie down on the ground so that the SS could walk over them without getting their boots dirty. The torment was unending. 'If there is a God, he'll have to beg my forgiveness,' one of them had scratched on the wall.

Most able-bodied camp members worked in the quarry, down a steep slope beyond where the modern monuments to the dead have been placed. In those days the descent to the quarry was rough and difficult, down steps of varying height. At the end of the day the workers were forced back up these steps carrying heavy stone blocks, and they were made to do so in tight formation. For the guards, it was a game; they would wait with amused anticipation for a weakened prisoner to stumble and fall, and when he did so he would invariably knock others down with him, creating an avalanche of people and stone. If the weight of falling co-prisoners didn't injure them, then the blocks would. And if nobody looked as if they were going to stumble of their own accord, then one of the guards would contrive to 'help'.

Occasionally the quarry was also used as a method of extermination for Jewish new arrivals, in order to terrorize the rest of the workforce. The SS forced them to push each other off the edge of what they called the 'Parachutists' Cliff' (an SS joke, because of course there were no parachutes) and they would come crashing headfirst down amongst other prisoners working in the quarry below. If they didn't die from the fall then they were left to drown in the quarry pond. Sometimes desperate prisoners who couldn't take the suffering any more chose the same escape route, cheating their jailers by jumping voluntarily from the Parachutists' Cliff on their way to or from the day's work.

The camp's multimedia archive narrates all of this, and has some particularly difficult eyewitness accounts. A local potato farmer described how he'd had to deliver potatoes to the camp every day and sign a document declaring he wouldn't repeat what he saw to anyone outside. Even when he did, he said, people didn't believe such inhumanity was possible: 'They thought I was drunk.' Apparently the Germans told the locals that Mauthausen was for dangerous criminals, which the locals were pleased to believe. And yet in one particular mass breakout, when five hundred got away, several were taken in and hidden by local families whose compassion overwhelmed their fear. One family described the anxiety of taking in one of these prisoners as stemming not from any danger of what he might do to them, but because their own son was out with the police searching for escapees. They'd had to live with this deception, at the heart of their own family, for many days until the escapee moved on.

As for the camp officers, there were some who were good husbands to their wives and good fathers to their children, and others who were plainly out of control. On one occasion a group of drunken SS officers had appeared in the middle of the night and demanded that the camp orchestra assemble and play for them until dawn. As a grand finale, after the performance, one of the officers strangled one of the musicians with his bare hands.

Mauthausen was the last concentration camp to be

liberated at the end of the war. In an almost unwatchable video, an ex-marine described what the US army had found when it arrived. 'We couldn't believe what had happened here. We couldn't believe that people could do that to each other,' and he stood in front of the camera and cried, emoting on behalf of all of us as he related how he and his colleagues had had to bury 1,200 people the first day and 300 a day for the succeeding three weeks, digging a trench and saying a few words over the bodies as they shovelled the soil.

Initially the liberators had kept the detainees in the camp to control disease and to restore their health until they were ready for freedom and family, but large numbers had elected never to go home. They chose instead to go for onward resettlement in Allied countries, leaving their families to believe they had died.

Some of that overseas resettlement was reflected in the nationalities in the visitors' book, which had the predictable 'never again' message in several languages and handwritings. But what most caught my eye was a simple entry from 'A survivor, with his daughter Judy' who'd been there the previous day, possibly the last visit of a long life. This survivor hadn't needed to add any words of his own to his daughter's simple entry. No doubt what everyone else had written seemed puny to his eyes, but perhaps he simply hadn't wanted even to come here at all until his daughter had insisted. I wondered whether he felt that guilt that survivors are meant to feel, believing that he should have died too, along with his colleagues. Or possibly he felt another form of guilt, because sometimes survival depended on something that survivors have never ever been able to mention to anyone: co-operation with the enemy. Hard to have to live with that.

*   *   *

For a while after Mauthausen the river crossed a flatland of fruit orchards and deer woodland until the hills of the Mostviertel came surging over the landscape, pushing a bow wave of forest ahead of them. By now the dandelions were shot and poppies were beginning to appear, the first hay crop had been cut and marshalled under a drying sun and farmers were bashing along back roads taking a shortcut to the next job, trying to keep a handbrake on spring. Up on the crests of each of the advancing hills stood either a church or a schloss, statuesque surfers of the slopes, and down by the river the shoulders of land flexed their muscles narcissistically at their reflection in the water and started to bully it again. The barge captains knew they were in for a slog because this was the Strudengau, a stretch of the Danube once infamous for whirlpools that could suck a small boat under, but whose bite had since been blunted by a downriver dam. Now its submerged rocks could only claw in frustration at passing barges like a cat trying to swat a fly from the wrong side of a windowpane.

In Grein I stopped to watch a local football match in the shadow of a boxy baroque schloss that had been given by Queen Victoria to the Saxe-Coburg-Gothas, the family of her husband Albert (and near enough her family too, because Albert's father had been her uncle). The local team lost, but it didn't seem to detract from the enjoyment of the occasion once a couple of the local bad losers had quickly left the pitch. It was a beatific evening, a relief after days of rain, and the cobbled Grein square was unchanged after several centuries, complete with an old-fashioned weather station with barometric gauges. Windowboxes were in bloom, a fresco on the *Apotheke* showed a team of horses pulling salt barges upriver, and swallows skeeting over the rooftops were enjoying a late hatch of insects rising from the gardens. A tiny shop selling books and cards had mounted its CCTV in the window, not for security purposes but so that passersby could see there was more inside. Young couples wandered through, glued to each other's hips, and an elderly couple followed, their hips distantly connected by the invisible elastic of years of marriage. This meant that whenever the wife stopped to peer over a fence, the husband kept going until the elastic stretched tight enough to haul her away. It was hard to believe that this was the same world where once there was poverty, terrorism and starvation.

Unfortunately I hadn't been able to give enough advance notice to catch the Saxe-Coburg-Gothas at home, and the housekeeper wasn't keen to speak to me without their permission. From their schloss (one of several they still occupy on a seasonal basis) it was clear they were immensely wealthy. The schloss was plain on the exterior but ornate inside, rather like a Muslim wife who wore a *chador* on the streets, but high fashion underneath. Inside its courtyard not a tile was out of place, and stags' heads lined the colonnades, each representing a forest domain.

It was frustrating to miss the Saxe-Coburgs, because they supplied the royal families of Britain, Bulgaria, Belgium and Portugal. But at least I'd met a Hohenzollern (royal families of Germany and Romania) and was on my way to have lunch with a Hohenburg and stay with a Habsburg, and there could hardly be a more potent name in European history than that.

10

Dinner with the Archduke, Lunch with the Princess

The Habsburgs started out from relatively inconspicuous beginnings in the eleventh century in a small castle in Switzerland. Whether it was due to a feisty granny, an inspirational schoolmaster, or just something in the water, they certainly did well for themselves thereafter. By the thirteenth century they'd moved east to become dukes in what was then called Austria, effectively a small portion of today's nation of that name. By the sixteenth century they'd become Holy Roman Emperors, as well as controlling Spain, much of Italy and the Netherlands, plus the territory that became known as Austria–Hungary – a massive area stretching right across to furthest Transylvania and incorporating bits of what are now the Ukraine, Poland, Slovakia, Serbia, the Czech Republic and even Italy. Over succeeding centuries they lost outlying Spanish, Italian and Dutch properties but they were still able to retain control over sprawling Austria–Hungary. Effectively that meant they controlled

Central and Eastern Europe from the sixteenth century until the denouement of the First World War.

As a dynasty the Habsburgs were old-fashioned imperialists through and through. They had a family code of allowing offspring to marry only into other royal households (on pain of being disinherited), which certainly helped keep them in the top slots. The lands they ruled were a collection of manorial estates more akin to a national park of feudalism than a state, and imperial borders varied according to local allegiances. As a rule they allowed the aristocracy to exploit the peasantry, and expected that aristocracy to support the monarchy in return. They handed out territory and titles as a reward for support, particularly when it came to pushing back the Turks, whose empire impinged on theirs to greater and lesser degrees over time, and who were their most persistent foe. Many of the big names in Hungarian nobility – the Esterhazys, Károlyis and Andrássys – were given their estates by the Habsburgs in return for military contributions to these campaigns, so when it came to internal politics even the powerful Hungarian families weren't going to rock the boat. The nobles had the land; the Jews did the business; the gypsies did the music; and the peasants did the work. That was the accepted order of things.

The lingua franca of Austro-Hungarian territories was German, particularly under Maria Theresa, who'd encouraged the spread of Danube Swabians like Franz Flock's family into some of the less populated parts of Central and Eastern Europe. And the cities were even more Germanic than the countryside, with early nineteenth-century Budapest being two-thirds German-speaking and having two daily newspapers in German but none in Hungarian – a remarkable state of affairs for the capital of Hungary. Even Count István Széchényi, regarded as the greatest Hungarian for his promotion of science, regulation of the Danube and reformation of feudalism, kept his diary in German. Over in Prague the situation was similar, with 50,000 Germans resident in the city but only 15,000 Czechs.

Then along came the nationalist movements of the mid-nineteenth century, at a time when the Habsburgs were struggling with feeble-minded Emperor Ferdinand on the throne. Ferdinand had the burden of many centuries of intermarriage behind him and is famous for one coherent command, which he probably never made: when told that his favourite apricot dumplings were unavailable (because apricots were out of season) he is said to have declared: 'I'm the Emperor, and I want dumplings!'

For a while the nineteenth-century nationalist movements were strong and Hungarian (or Magyar) was in the ascendancy in the eastern part of the empire. There, a language law was passed in 1844 barring German and Latin speakers from public office. Pragmatic Austrians who had property and power in Hungary didn't think twice about taking Hungarian names and addressing their staff in Hungarian so that they could keep their positions and estates. Then a student revolution in Vienna sent the Habsburgs scuttling away for the safety of Innsbruck, but they didn't need to stay away for long, having enlisted the help of the Russians, who marched up the Danube and put everything back where it was. The monarchy returned to Vienna and Germanization came galumphing back.

The empire was like that: it ebbed and flowed. It was mired in formality and protocol, slow to react, relying on old loyalties that were eventually being eroded, particularly in Hungary and Transylvania. In the end Emperor Franz Joseph reached a compromise with the nationalistic Hungarians, creating something called the Dual Monarchy, for the sake of an easy life. Effectively this meant that Austria and Greater Hungary became two separate countries, with two parliaments, but with the same king. However, with the same aristocracy ruling over most of the land, loyal to monarch rather than to nation, not a great deal changed in day-to-day living. Even today there are still high-society gatherings in twenty-first-century Budapest at which German, not Hungarian, is the dominant language.

All of this was orchestrated from the strange twilit world of the Habsburg court. Discussions would take place in the emperor's study over whether to become more centralist or more federalist, more gentle or more heavy-handed. The pros and the cons, the whys and the wherefores, were tossed to and fro across polished tables in shuttered rooms, while all about was dusty and formal. The court became particularly arcane and protocol-obsessed in the later decades of the everlasting Franz Joseph, Emperor of Austria from 1848 and King of Hungary from 1867. He started full of youth and vigour as successor to 'dumplings' Ferdinand, but 68 years later (in 1916) was still on the throne, lean, long-featured and whiskery, formal, inflexible, and finding his peoples particularly tiresome. I visualized him as a figure in a Roald Dahl story illustrated by Quentin Blake, brittle-boned and grumpy. In 1914 he had made the fatal decision to teach the upstart Serbs a thing or two after the assassination of his heir, Franz Ferdinand, while driving through the streets of Sarajevo. It didn't matter that he didn't much like Franz Ferdinand: he saw the assassination as the test for an old man's virility, and was determined not to be found wanting. As a result the whole imperial house of cards came tumbling down.

In the post-war world order the new Austrian government had confiscated all Habsburg holdings and would return them only if the family members renounced their claim to the throne, which most did. Which was why Archduke Alexander Habsburg-Lothringen was still in residence in the schloss at Persenbeug, where my finger was now pressing the buzzer. With the huge Habsburg back-story looming large over me, I had to admit to some trepidation as I waited for the gate to swing open. What kind of an archduke would Alex be? The I-want-my-dumplings sort? Or the whiskery, brittle-boned, inflexible sort? Happily, he was neither whiskers nor dumplings.

Persenbeug had once been one of the most important shipbuilding towns on the Danube, and its castle was another of those uncompromisingly solid baroque schlosses that sit imposingly next to the river, and where undoubtedly a toll would have been exacted from passing shipping in the old days. It dated from 1617, had been owned by the Habsburgs since the 1800s, and Emperor Karl I (Franz Joseph's successor to the throne) had started his short life here, eventually dying in exile in Madeira. Now it sat rather unphotogenically alongside Austria's first hydropower dam. The Habsburgs must have lost all political power by the time of the latter's construction, or else they'd never have tolerated such a provocative bit of engineering, right under their walls.

After my glimpses into Sigmaringen and Grein, the castle's interior was disappointingly understated. It had been divided up into sections, with subsidiary apartments used by staff from the estate and kept in camphor for other members of the family. Ancestor portraits and battle scenes hung on the walls and heavy wooden chests and suits of armour stood on check-tiled floors. It smelled of polish, leather, beeswax and oil-based preservatives, and if there were any great treasures or magnificent architectural flourishes, I didn't see them.

Archduke Alexander turned out to be in his late forties, sallow-cheeked, dark-haired, slightly stooped (which gave a false impression of being tall) and dressed in a light tan jacket and jeans. He was welcoming and hospitable but a touch distracted and hesitant in his manner in a way that nevertheless commanded your attention. He would have been hard to place if you'd met him on the street; a university professor, perhaps, or a caring hospital consultant weighed down by his sense of responsibility, who always had half a mind on the last patient he'd seen and the other half on the next. His wife, Marie-Gabrielle, Countess of Waldstein, was pretty, dreamy and winsome and I found it easy to imagine her in a fairytale world of princes and chandeliers.

Their lifestyle, however, was reassuringly down to earth. I found them sitting on a swing-seat in the small garden in the castle courtyard, with their three young children – no sailor suits or saluting – variously climbing over or on their parents or tearing off round the flowerbeds. They were interested in my bike and baggage, because they too were regular users of the Danube cyclepath, for family outings, just like any other family with young children living by the riverside. Nor was there any sign of staff (the archduke went to fetch me a can of beer himself) until a nanny appeared at around bedtime and whisked the children off.

That informality seemed to me a little at odds with Alex's title, but when I said so, he shrugged. 'Oh, there are lots of archdukes in the Habsburgs, so it's no big deal. Although not many still live in privately owned castles.' His English was faultless, and not as clipped and formal as Prince Hohenzollern's had been. 'The main advantage of the title is that you don't need to be introduced twice,' he continued. 'People tend to remember who you are.' Archduke Otto, the head of the Habsburgs, wasn't a close relative; he was from the Italian side of the family. 'They've always been comparatively poor inheritance-wise, Otto's side. Into politics and business, always wanting to feature on the world stage.'

'Does that mean that your side is not poor?'

He looked at me owlishly through circular glasses, measuring up his reply. 'We are wealthier than we were when your man came through seventy years ago.'

It turned out he'd read Patrick Leigh Fermor, and we had a conversation about whether an unnamed aristocrat that PLF had met at Persenbeug had been Alex's grandfather, who had sat tight in the schloss through the Second World War while the Nazis effectively commandeered all the family's land. Alex's grandfather had been no Nazi sympathizer, and when the Russians liberated the area they were happy to let him have everything back.

When PLF came through, the hydropower dam was just being constructed.

'All that talk in the book about the construction of the new power stations ruining the river's stock of fish, that sounds just like my grandfather – he was very concerned about the state of the river,' said Alex. Back in those days the run of salmon was so prolific that castle servants up and down the Danube specifically asked in their employment contracts not to have to eat the fish more than once a week. Now there are no salmon at all.

Alex himself had grown up locally and even attended the local school, where he hadn't felt any different to anyone else in the classroom. And now, with a team of seventy managers and foresters, he ran one of the biggest private forest estates in Austria, covering 14,000 hectares, or 54 square miles. It hadn't been what he'd set out to do, originally starting his career in brand marketing for IBM, but then the question of who would take over the management of the family hectares came up and his brother hadn't wanted to take it on.

'So what does he do instead, your brother?'

'If you mean what job, he doesn't really have one.'

I made some sweeping comment about how the unemployed generally struggle to find a role in life, but the archduke set me right.

'There are two types of people who don't work. Those who don't know what to do with their time and who are therefore rather unhappy. And those who read and travel and actually have rather a good time. My brother is the second sort. He reads everything.'

At this point in the conversation a man dressed head to toe in khaki with a rifle slung across his back emerged from one of the courtyard doors and walked past towards the main gate, greeting us as he went. I immediately assumed this to be a change in guard, or one of the archduke's personal protection squad on patrol, but I was wrong.

'One of our foresters,' said Alex when he'd gone. 'A Czech. Wrote to me out of the blue saying he wanted to work with us, and that doesn't happen very often in the forestry world. So I said come.'

'And the gun?'

'They're on a deer cull tonight. We need to kill four hundred a year. Personally I'm not a great fan of shooting.'

'I shoot,' Marie-Gabrielle chipped in. 'When I realized we were coming to live here I got my hunter's licence. I didn't just want to be a city girl that the locals would laugh at. So sometimes I go out with them. I've got some antlers and a good wild boar rug, but Alex won't have them in the house.' That didn't sound Habsburgian at all.

After dark we sat out on a balcony high up on the castle's outside wall overlooking the river, a balcony adjacent to the evening kitchen (as opposed to the breakfast kitchen) which the archduke had added to the schloss.

'Fortunately we added it before the National Trust registered the building as a national monument. We would never get planning permission for it now.'

'So is it costly to maintain? A castle like this?'

He shrugged. 'I don't want to turn it into a museum. There are Habsburg properties all over the place that are far more accessible than this. I don't see how we'd make any money out of it, and we'd have to be here seven days a week.'

Some distance beneath the balcony a slow procession of boats moved into the lock system of the dam that had been so disapproved of by Alex's grandfather. The passenger cruisers were pumping out light and sound; the freight barges were just dark, slow-moving metal slugs.

We talked about the children, and whether their upbringing was going to be any different to that of the previous generations. They were attending the local school, as he had.

'At this stage they're quite unaware of their family background, which is how it should be,' said the countess, who had a tendency to throw in whole sentences in German, peppering the conversation with '*das stimmt*' and '*genau*' depending on how much she agreed with what had just been said. 'They've got time enough afterwards to learn about the Habsburgs.'

The plan was for the children to attend the abbey school in Melk, just downriver, and then as for marriage partners, their parents had no preconceptions. 'If we prepared them to marry only a title then they might end up in a dysfunctional family all alone in some castle somewhere,' sighed the countess; I assumed she wasn't alluding to her own situation. 'I don't want that for my children.'

A Land Rover crunched up the castle drive under the balcony and stopped at an outhouse. Two men in khaki untied the carcass of a deer from the front bumper and lugged it inside. The archduke watched without comment, while I steered the conversation back to marriage partners. 'So you won't be staging big parties for the children and inviting the eligible and the suitable?' I explained how the Hohenzollerns had been preparing for just such an occasion at Sigmaringen.

Alex shook his head. 'I doubt it.'

His wife looked at him. 'But you will have to have a party for your fiftieth.' She turned to me. 'He's not very keen on the idea of parties, as you can see. He should have had one for his fortieth, but he had a good excuse.'

'My father died.'

'Would you invite Otto?'

'He wouldn't come,' declared the archduke.

The countess disagreed. 'He would.'

'He's too old. He's well over ninety.'

'You've got to invite him.'

I could see that she was the one who was going to make sure the family maintained its social connections.

Breakfast was at eight the following morning in a family kitchen in a different part of the building, and I found myself 'hullooing' down corridors feeling a bit like Pooh in the Hundred Acre Wood.

In the kitchen the archduke was making the coffee and the countess preparing the toast, surrounded by photos of the family. She was in a tracksuit, shortly departing for the gym, and he had his BlackBerry out, plainly already in work mode. His staff began at 7.30, in offices across the courtyard, and he said they'd start even earlier if they could.

'This is forestry. It's an old-fashioned country business.'

I found it hard to imagine him dealing in pulp and tonnages. He belonged on a bicycle on the wet cobbles of a university town on a darkening evening, where his mind would be on higher things.

'Do they call you "Your Highness"?'

The archduke admitted that they did. 'They prefer it that way.'

Twenty minutes later we'd all dispersed, he to his paper trees, she to her exercise machines, and me to my personal, mobile seat by the riverbank.

I didn't have far to go for my lunch appointment with Princess Anita von Hohenburg, so I took my time climbing up the 1,500 feet to Maria Taferl, one of Austria's most important pilgrimage destinations. The pilgrimage church was full of candles, so I lit one for my family, and then another for my journey. Then I thought that was selfish, so I lit one more for the happiness of people in general. And another for the state of the world, all the while thinking what an empty gesture it really was, lighting candles in a chapel on top of a hill.

Outside, I found a bench on the valley side of the village and settled to drink in the view, right across to a handful of low hills in the distance. If the Mostviertel had been the bow waves of ships, then these were the foreheads of swimmers making their way across the plain. In the middle distance regular scurrying red trains threaded their way, miraculously, through what looked like an unruly chaos of forest, field, tarmac and brick, but which must have had some kind of order to it after all. To the west was a small industrial town, but I found I could use a foreground tree as a big green eyepatch to block it out and the only sign it was there was the occasional shout, bark of a dog or rasp of a motorcycle that floated up the hill. Directly below me the 5-mile valley filled its arms with a bumper crop of Danubian water, on which barges moved like creeping arrowheads towards some as-yet hypothetical target.

From Maria Taferl it was a short, high-speed freewheel across to Artstetten, a far more romantic and castley-looking castle than the baroque box of Persenbeug had been. Artstetten had seven banded towers topped with copper onions and completed with dewdrop spikes, and was set in sloping parkland with rose arbours, fountains and mature trees. Two-thirds of it was open to the public, but its visitors didn't come here for the aesthetics; they came for the tomb of Franz Ferdinand and his wife Sophie, whose assassination had sparked the First World War.

Princess Anita was Franz Ferdinand's great-grand-daughter. A cheerful, energetic, bustling woman in middle age with a crop of straw-blonde hair, she had taken it upon herself to try to correct what she thought was a mistaken world view of her great-grandfather, who is portrayed in some history books as arrogant and reckless. The common view is that he provoked the assassination and thereby the war.

'He was hot-tempered, yes,' she said, as we walked through the castle to collect the keys. 'But he would always apologize afterwards. Here, look at this,' and she pointed out a cabinet of little china sheep. 'He'd give his wife one of these every time he lost his temper with her, to ask forgiveness. Sweet, don't you think? You see, unlike many of the other royal alliances at the time, he and Sophie were a real love match.' A far cry from those dynastic couples who'd got married without even being present at their own wedding.

As we descended into the crypt, she explained that Franz Ferdinand had never seen eye to eye with autocratic Emperor Franz Joseph. He had in fact only become heir by default when Franz Joseph's only son Rudolph killed himself in a bizarre and inexplicable suicide pact with his mistress at his hunting lodge at Mayerling, near Vienna – a suicide that Franz Joseph never acknowledged; it was always referred to as a 'hunting accident'. For a while afterwards Franz Ferdinand himself had been very ill with TB and had not been expected to survive; he felt betrayed by how much the rest of the court had ignored him during that illness, shifting their attention to the next in line. A particular defining moment came after his recovery when he married Sophie, a lady-in-waiting to the court, which greatly displeased the emperor and all around him. The marriage had had to be declared morganatic (of unequal status, and therefore their children would have no claim to the throne), given that the House of Habsburg's strictures allowed marriage only to members of other reigning royal houses. Franz Ferdinand had gone ahead with it, nevertheless.

And then there was the assassination itself, which stemmed from the unfortunate timing of his official visit to Sarajevo, on the anniversary of the Serbian defeat by the Turks at the battle of Kosovo Polje. Sarajevo had a large Serb minority, so the timing of a royal visit was insensitive, for sure, but Princess Anita was of the opinion that it wasn't deliberately so – at least not on her great-grandfather's part. The arrangement had been made by members of his household, and when told of the risk he ran by being there on that particular day, he had felt obliged to go ahead with it on the basis that he couldn't, as a future emperor, show cowardice.

As for the day itself, there'd been a first, unsuccessful assassination attack with a hand grenade that had bounced off the archduke's car and exploded under the vehicle behind, injuring some of the officers inside but not the royal couple. It was only later, after the day's formalities were done, that Franz Ferdinand and Sophie had taken to their car again, at the archduke's instigation, to go and visit those same wounded officers in hospital. It was on this compassionate journey that a Bosnian Serb student called Gavrilo Princip had found himself presented with a point-blank opportunity, and had taken it.

Franz Ferdinand and Sophie couldn't be buried with the rest of the imperial Habsburgs because of their morganatic marriage, so they'd had a crypt built at Artstetten. It was a relatively simple construction, dominated by the two main tombs, with a smaller plaque on the wall behind them.

'Yes, sad, that,' said the princess, seeing me looking. 'They had a stillborn child. They really loved their children, quite unlike other royal parents at the time.'

'Will you be buried in here?' I asked, looking at all the unallocated space.

'Probably not,' she said. 'I'll probably be buried with my second husband in Timişoara.'

We adjourned to the terrace to join Princess Anita's daughter, the gamine, vivacious Countess Alix, and the two women shared a cigarette before lunch.

'I know we shouldn't, but my mother smoked and she lived to a grand old age,' said the princess, but her next remark was cut short by a censorious gurgle from a gargoyle of a fountain-head set into the slope opposite. It started to vomit a mixture of brown water and leaves.

'Ah, that's Willibald.'

'The fountain has a name?'

'No no, Willibald is a wonderful old man who fixes everything and I asked him to investigate why it wasn't working. The fountain.'

So we sat down to pork and rice prepared by the countess, with Willibald putting his welly in somewhere up the hill.

'Alix comes to help me with running the house every summer,' said the princess, 'and a great help you are too, dear.'

'Nobody else wanted to do the job my mother is doing,' said Alix, addressing me. She was in her early twenties and (unlike her mother) both looked and sounded very French, which must have been either her education or her father's genetics, or both. 'There was a lot of family discussion about what to do with Artstetten and no one wanted to sell it, but neither did anyone want to take responsibility for running it as Mama does. It's hard for her. The house and the archive. A lot of work.'

Princess Anita smiled. 'My sister is jealous. I got the castle, she got the money, and she thinks I got the better deal.' She threw back her head and laughed. 'The very idea. She doesn't come here in the winter.'

'No central heating?'

'We've got an oil system, but it's very expensive. Besides, we've got a lot of wood to burn, and it's free. Did you not smell the log fires as we came through the house?'

I had.

'That's from last winter. At times of high pressure like today the air comes squeezing down the chimneys and we get to re-live last winter's log fires. I like it. It brings back memories of cosy nights.'

'Cosy?' Alix raised an eyebrow, sarcastically.

'The teachers at Alix's school used to complain,' explained her mother. 'They said I sent the children to school without enough clothes, but they were used to the cold from the house, you see.'

'What we didn't like was the dressing up in sailor suits.'

'Ah, yes,' the princess smiled guiltily. 'I did make you do that occasionally when rich Americans came to lunch. In those days I'd do anything to put the house on the map.'

'And we had to visit the Paris branch of the family and wear long dresses and sit in silence. Children did not speak.'

'Very proper, that family,' murmured the princess.

I knew that her first husband and the father of her three children had been French, and by all accounts a rather bumptious character. It sounded as if she was better off without him. Meanwhile her second husband spent most of his time in Romania, where he'd invested in a lot of agricultural land, so Artstetten had become her project alone.

We talked a bit about the aristocratic life, and I mentioned the archduke's brother, who chose not to get involved with business but to travel and read and generally have a good time while his brother managed the family's forestry business.

'Of course I know people who don't work,' said Countess Alix. 'I think a lot of them are very lonely, because who do they find like them? Not many people have so much time to sit around and discuss Proust. And if they do, they're usually strange.'

I asked what she herself was doing, and it turned out she was taking six months off from an unspecified job to go to New York and take in some sailing regattas, which sounded quite jet-setty to me.

'Not jet-setty,' corrected her mother. 'You should see the sort of person she sails with. They're all bears.'

Alix frowned but said nothing. This was a discussion she and her mother had had before.

'And do they call you "Countess", those bears?'

She wrinkled her nose and shook her head. 'Course not. But if people of my level send me a letter which doesn't have my proper title on it, then that irritates me. They should know better.'

When lunch was finished I asked the princess whether she had any official role in the local community.

'Certainly people come to me about local issues, which is no doubt why the mayor and I don't get on. Not at all. I mean, he bought a cow and called it Princess! I ask you! How obvious is that!' She laughed but I could see she was riled, and I could imagine that the mayor and she made a point of stepping on each other's toes on a regular basis. Princess Anita was not one for holding back.

'He has no liking for history, that one,' she was saying.

'And what about social life? Parties?'

'Oh yes, we have those. Sometimes for writers and artists. For the children. And once a year we have a big party, usually with five hundred invitees. We need to stay in touch.'

'So what will happen to Artstetten when you run out of energy?' I asked, as we cleared the table. The countess had disappeared inside to make coffee.

'Who knows,' shrugged Princess Anita. *'Après moi, le déluge.'*

11

The Wachau and the Vienna Woods

There's a stretch of the Danube in Austria where picture postcards are made in heaven. It's a stretch where the riverbanks rise up, studded with baroque churches and trellised with vineyards that were planted in the era of Charlemagne. A place where castles once sprouted from every riverside rock, showing their teeth and collecting their tolls. The Wachau.

I entered this hallowed stretch of waterway full of great expectations of a Narnia-like land flowing with milk and honey, but initially there was little change to the forest-and-cornfield combination that had escorted the Danube for the last couple of days. The first hint of change was at the small town of Aggsbach Markt, where a fresh milk machine had been placed in the main square for the benefit of walkers and cyclists; the good burghers of Aggsbach had plainly decided we were going to need some extra nourishment for what lay ahead.

The next village, Willendorf, was famous for its fertility symbol, a 30,000-year-old Venus in limestone, with heavy breasts and hips, who added serious weight to the theory that the Danube was the earliest corridor of civilization in Europe. The Willendorf Venus had been discovered back in 1908 during the laying of the local railway line. She's thought to have belonged to a nomadic hunter who would have been chasing mountain deer, bison, Arctic fox and wolverine through what was then a sub-Arctic world. She had no face, just braided hair all over her head, and no feet either, perhaps because the artist wasn't good at faces and feet, or because the lack of face made her more like a god than a person and her pointy legs made her more practical to stick into the ground.

The hunter would have kept her by his bedside as an ancestor image to ensure his hunting success; for me, sitting on the bench by the large Venus facsimile at the spot where she was discovered, I found her presence comfortingly maternal. She had the sort of silhouette you might see running an Italian pizzeria anywhere along the Adriatic coast, where she'd be laughing and shouting in equal measure. I'd been travelling a few weeks now, and I felt the need for someone to talk to. Encouraged by her comforting shape (and the absence of anyone else in the vicinity), I found myself telling her about my journey so far and asking for her blessing for what was to come, just as the hunter who'd owned her must have done. And confiding in that luscious-breasted presence gave me more heart than lighting a candle in the austere pilgrimage chapel at Maria Taferl.

After Willendorf the first vineyards began, but initially they had to compete for space with the more powerful fruit orchards, which batted the vines up on to ledges on the valley sides. There they rallied their troops and drew strength and vigour from the Loess soil under their feet, until from the town of Spitz onwards they had the confidence to mount a full-scale assault on the valley bottom, descending in tresses to smother the apricots and pears, and eventually to colonize every piece of available land with their massed battalions. Battle over, they were neatly drawn up for inspection by their vintners, in neat regimental order, turning landscape into maths.

Up close, they had a charm of their own. These vineyards were mostly small and family owned, worked by hand or possibly with the aid of a single old vintage tractor which would be lovingly polished by the farmer every day after work. Each farmer had a shed and a different theory about the lie of his land, so each patch of vineyard was slightly differently orientated from its neighbour, with the shed as its axis. The result was that, from afar, it looked as if the grande dames of Grüner Veltliner and the gentlemen of Müller-Thurgau were performing a stately quadrille around reluctant wooden partners.

The town of Spitz lay at the foot of the highly productive Tausendeimerberg, literally 'thousand bucket mountain', so-called because it could produce 55,000 litres, or one thousand 'pails' (an Austrian *Eimer* contains 55 litres), in a good year. Wine by the bucket doesn't sound like good marketing, but a lot of it never saw the end of the following year, because many of the Wachau's small vintners had their own improvised wine gardens where they sold their *heuriger*, or young wine, direct from the barrel, hanging a bunch of straw on their garden gates to indicate that the vintage was ready. Selling direct like this, without having to deal with the likes of retailers and bottling plants, was the only effective way that wine-making on such a small scale could ever be profitable.

I took a seat at a trestle table outside Konrad's, a long, low cottage under a spreading chestnut tree, where Grüner Veltliner was the bucket of the day. Konrad's menu was sparse, but the man himself was red-faced and cheery; would I like an *Achtel* or a *Viertel*? he asked. A *Viertel*, I said, without really thinking, and so a couple of minutes later found myself cradling a quarter-litre glass of wine, with some kilometres still to cycle.

I'm no great wine expert, but sometimes the sense of place adds immeasurably to the enjoyment of a drink, so I took great pleasure in Konrad's bucket, and great comfort from the fact that one of the other wine-makers turned up shortly after me and parked his tractor outside.

'You taking a break?' asked one of Konrad's other guests.

'Sure I am,' came the reply. 'I spent all morning making it, now I'm going to drink it,' and he disappeared inside.

The wine went quickly to my head so I ordered a 'fitness brot' from Konrad's menu (radishes, tomatoes and gherkins on buttered black bread) and watched the river traffic go by. In the foreground a couple of attentive ducks were shepherding their only surviving offspring round and round in an eddy, like a child in a playground, while behind them a Ukrainian push-tug struggled with one of the fastest-flowing stretches of the Danube. He had four barges of gravel lashed to his bows, deep in the water, and crabbed sideways around the corner, barely moving against the stream. Paradoxically, the very rain which gave him the depth to travel also made his progress tortuously hard.

The wine did the same for me, knocking all the power out of my legs and turning the slightest incline into a struggle against the rapids, but then this wasn't the place to be going fast. From Spitz onwards the valley was suffused with well-being and bathed in beauty. Strung with vineyards like a green harp, its music was the gentle clink of glasses in hidden terraces and the murmur of conversation. Gone was the coarse bonhomie of the schnapps-fuelled *Radlertreff.*

Eventually I arrived in Dürnstein, the honeypot of Wachau tourism, a primped and pretty place that raised itself high on a spit of land, forced a giant bend into the river, and commanded the main road to get down on its knees and kiss the hem of its skirt before disappearing into a tunnel underneath. Its houses were of painted plaster and stucco and daubed with geranium windowboxes, its new schloss was a five-star hotel and its main road was lined with *Gasthöfe*, art galleries and shops that sold local wine and everything you could ever make (and didn't know you even could) with apricots. Every hour or so a new cruise boat docked on the river below, sending a tidal wave of visitors up into Dürnstein's apricot-filled nooks and crannies. By evening they were gone, cradling their apricot-scented moisturizers, and the air became good enough to eat. Cooking smells mingled with grape must, woodsmoke and the perfumes of dressed-up dinner guests, and every hour the church bells set up a conversation with other hidden churches up and down the river, until eventually Dürnstein's Maria Himmelfahrt Abbey would join in lazily with its richer, deeper tone.

I was drawn to Maria Himmelfahrt's waterside bell-tower, which was painted blue and white and covered with statues and reliefs like a delicate piece of china. Starting with cherubs and magi dancing around the figure of Mary, it rose through sky-blue scrolls and saintly figures to obelisks topped with golden globes just below the belltower itself. It was so memorable I couldn't understand why the style hadn't caught on elsewhere. Plainly it had been built to impress passing river users at a time when paddlesteaming was all the rage, and it still did, because some weeks after sitting on the riverbank at Dürnstein I found that I shared my admiration for the Maria Himmelfahrt belltower with the piratical-looking first mate of a Serbian freight barge, while we were chugging past the war-damaged shoreline of Vukovar. A strange place to remember a belltower in the Wachau.

A destination like this needs a good story to provide the words for the brochure, and Dürnstein's was the tale of Richard the Lionheart and his faithful troubadour, Blondel. Despite his good press in children's history books, the King of England, Normandy, Anjou and Aquitaine was a bit of a loudmouth who made enemies wherever he went, and he had to return from his Third Crusade incognito through Austria, having deeply offended Habsburg Emperor Leopold by his loutish behaviour on the battlefield. Unfortunately for him, he was recognized, captured and imprisoned in Dürnstein castle. His loyal troubadour Blondel de Neale, realizing that something must have gone wrong when he didn't turn up at home, wandered through Europe singing his favourite ballads outside every castle, until Richard finally joined in.

A nice little history, but it says something about the popularity of the King of England, Normandy, Anjou and Aquitaine if, once he goes missing, the only person who goes looking for him is his fool. Not surprising, then, that it took a year before enough money was raised to pay the astronomical ransom for his release.

Today the castle is a ruin, for which the burghers of Dürnstein are no doubt very grateful. Once the stronghold of robber barons, built as it was on an exposed, steep set of rocks high above the village, it would have cost a king's ransom to maintain. As it is, its disreputable toothy wall-stubs flicked V-signs at the abbey cloisters and the diminutive cruise ships below, at the thousand-bucket mountain to the west, and at the distant hilltop monastery of Gottweig, the Austrian Montecassino, away to the east. A sojourn up here probably did the arrogant Lionheart no end of good.

Twenty-four hours later I was incarcerated in a monastery myself, in the heart of the Vienna Woods.

After Dürnstein, without the valley walls to shore everything up, the Wachau quickly unravelled. For a short stretch the vineyards were no longer charmingly mom-and-pop, but became disappointingly corporate and overalled men leaning on tractors talked to be-suited men leaning on Mercedes, representing opposite ends of the same organization. And then there was Krems, a handsome town where modern life snapped its fingers once again, dispelling the magical indolence of a vine-strung couple of days.

I ignored the glowering hilltop monastery at Gottweig and turned south, heading inland for the Wienerwald 'Vienna Woods', picked up by a following wind that had me longing for sails. But the Vienna Woods turned out to be growing on Viennese hills, so in the end I put my bike on a local train which took me to within pedalling range of Heiligenkreuz.

It was a diversion made with a purpose. Patrick Leigh Fermor had interspersed his staying in castles and under bushes ('There is much to recommend moving straight from straw to a four-poster, and then back again') with a couple of overnights in monasteries, so I was keen to try the same. The question was, who would have me? It's not as if there was a shortage of monasteries along the Danube, particularly in Austria, but several things had singled out Heiligenkreuz (Holy Cross) from those I'd cycled past over the last weeks. For a start it had a thriving population of eighty monks, whereas even the likes of the giant Benedictine abbey of Melk, despite being a much-visited, gloriously decorated building looming over the river, had a mere half-dozen. That made Heiligenkreuz the largest Cistercian monastery in Europe, bucking the trend of decline in most such institutions, and as a result it was about to receive a visit from the Pope. Moreover, its abbot was another aristocrat whose family had been much affected by war and whose nephew had just won an Oscar for a film about life in Stasi-dominated East Germany.

Stift Heiligenkreuz sat like a sprawling schloss at the heart of its own little village laid out in a series of courtyards, each less public than the last, with a theological college in one and a restaurant in another where you could order a healthy Holy Cross Salad, followed by more sinful desserts. The monastery buildings were more solid than they were massive, the copper gutters gleaming, the plain walls in the process of re-creaming, and the steep roof mottled with light and dark tiles and studded with the dormer windows of monks' cells. From one of them came the sound of a trumpet, played with skill.

Five giant plane trees stood in the central courtyard. Its western side was filled with the Romanesque abbey church, and its focal point was a highly ornamental baroque fountain topped with spouting eagles. Here I found Brother Samuel, a small, bearded, smiling, softly spoken monk who walked me to the guest quarters.

'I used to be a journalist too,' he confessed. 'On a motorcycle magazine.'

It sounded so unlikely that it had to be true.

'You didn't enjoy it?'

'I found it a struggle to stay alive,' said Brother Samuel,

still smiling. Somehow I knew he wasn't talking about the dangers of oncoming traffic.

'So this is . . . better?' I said lamely.

'Now I have no doubts,' he smiled even more broadly. 'My faith gets deeper and the experience becomes more intense every day.'

'Ah. I see.' I didn't, but nor did I want to seem at odds with my surroundings.

He showed me my room, which was equipped with leaflets about how to become a monk and had a supply of holy water by the door for anointing myself whenever I needed strength to go out and face the world. There he ran through the monastic routine and checked that I didn't need to speak to a priest, which I didn't (I couldn't say I'd had all my spiritual needs satisfied by a fat 30,000-year-old stone goddess).

I've not met many abbots, so I wasn't sure about the protocol: should I give him a high five or kneel to kiss his signet ring? Happily Abbot Gregor Ulrich von Henckel Donnersmarck turned out to be a calm, massive presence who would probably have taken either in his stride, but seemed content just to shake hands. He looked like a leaner Helmut Kohl, but for a slightly wandering eye which he would close in bright light, and he had a quiet decisiveness about him that would probably be very hard to resist in any walk of life. I found it easy to imagine him in the corporate office of an international freight forwarder, where I knew he had started his adult life.

'Ah yes,' he admitted. 'I am an abbot with an MBA. There are not many of us about.'

The Henckel Donnersmarcks had been members of the pre-war German aristocracy whose major landholdings had been in Silesia, one of those territories, like the Sudetenland, from where the German population had been evicted at the end of the war. Most of their property had been handed over to Poland in the post-war redrawing of borders. Gregor had been primed by his family for a life in business, but he'd also had a very Catholic upbringing, and the idea of taking holy orders at the age of thirty-four had come quite naturally to him. 'I liked being a forwarding agent, but it wasn't my vocation,' he said. I resisted a cheap joke about forwarding souls to God.

As we walked through the older parts of the monastery he agreed that his business experience had its uses. Heiligenkreuz had two hundred employees and owned several houses in Vienna, together with 20,000 hectares of forest (more than Archduke Alex) and one of the larger vineyards in Austria.

'Run by monks?' Cistercians, being a Benedictine order, believe in redemption through work.

'We try to do our best in all areas, but it is important to find the right people to work for us as managers.' In the end it wasn't too dissimilar to the sort of estate he might have been controlling if the family had held on in Silesia.

I asked whether the land-holdings were increasing or diminishing.

'In terms of hectares we have more than a hundred years ago, but in value, that's different. It is important to sell expensive land for development and buy other cheaper land for agriculture,' pronounced the abbot, wearing his business hat.

'And do you have an oversight of everything?'

'I attend meetings with the heads of my departments, but my main interest is in the spiritual life of the community.' I sensed he wanted to steer conversation away from all this talk of commerce, but I had one more question.

'Is it profitable?' It certainly looked to be so, judging by the condition of all the buildings.

'Let us just say that we don't have enough money to realize all the projects we'd like to do at the moment.'

And then, as if to emphasize the transience of the flesh, he made a point of stopping by the abbey's death chapel, where all the monks were eventually laid out amongst funereal baroque. 'I like to pass this and think that I will lie here one day.'

Heiligenkreuz was founded by French Cistercians back in the twelfth century, and was one of few monasteries in Austria with an unbroken history all the way through to the present. Accordingly its rather bland and stolid exterior hid a delicate Romanesque cloister, a sombre Chapter House and a lovely Fountain House with a sixteenth-century Roman fountain surrounded by stained glass.

'I take it you don't wash in here any longer?'

The abbot shook his head. 'These days everyone has their own facilities, en suite. I find it important to be clean.'

The Romanesque monastery church was a pleasure to an eye tired of all the florid baroque that lined the Upper Danube. It had a rough-hewn simplicity, with simple unornamented arches, stout columns, and no stained glass in the nave. Its softly lit, monochrome austerity could easily have belonged to a small late-Romanesque chapel in the foothills of the Pyrenees, not to a powerful and wealthy Austrian monastery in the Vienna Woods. Its simplicity was altogether more in keeping with my concept of how a monastic existence should be than all that sumptuous baroque, and I said so.

The abbot agreed. 'One of the reasons I am here is the spirituality of the medieval architecture,' he murmured. 'But we do have our baroque, too.'

And he showed me the Refectory. Ornamental in

the extreme, it was so rich and sweet that it looked like the interior of a Baked Alaska, although the meals themselves were more austere. Lunch and dinner were taken here in silence while someone read news from the Catholic world from the pulpit, after which one of the more senior monks would give a sign, and the community could talk.

'So you're not really silent at all?'

'Only at designated times.' The monks had radios, access to TV, the Internet, novels and newspapers. 'In fact I remember reading a review of this writer you are following in one of our newspapers,' said the abbot. 'What is his name?'

I gave him chapter and verse about PLF, and how the books had recently been translated into German. The abbot wrote the details into a notebook he produced from within the folds of his gown, and said he would make sure to head for a bookshop next time he was in town.

A distant bell tolling somewhere within the depths of the monastery reminded him of the next stage of the liturgical day, so I asked the abbot quickly about the Pope's forthcoming visit.

'Why here?'

'Because I invited him.'

I knew it wasn't as simple as that, and the abbot admitted, when pushed, that Heiligenkreuz's thriving monastic population probably had something to do with it, at a time when most European monasteries had a handful of increasingly elderly monks. He partly ascribed that success to the presence of the theological college on site, some of whose students elected for a meditative life over that of becoming a parish priest. But more controversially, Heiligenkreuz had also chosen to return to a Latin liturgy. It was said to have more spirituality and musicality than the German version, but I was aware it had also antagonized the Jewish world by its suggestion that Jews live in blindness and darkness, and that they need to be converted. These sentiments were not unrelated to Pope Benedict's own quotation of strong words about Islam. However, the liturgy was a subject unlikely to come up in any serious discussions during the Pope's visit, said the abbot, principally because of shortage of time. 'You will have to attend our services and decide for yourself.'

Over the next twenty-four hours I did just that. The monastic day began at 5 a.m., and there were seven celebrations in the abbey church spread through the next fifteen hours. I didn't attend them all, but for once it was good to have a timetable which was not of my own setting. It was hypnotic to sit in the congregation – there were rarely more than a handful of us – and witness the white-robed community file into the tall, carved-walnut choir stalls, like the ivories taking up their positions on a giant piano keyboard. There they tossed their cuffs as they opened their prayer books and rocked back and forth as they instinctively, without apparent leadership, filled the nave with sound. In that soft light, under those 900-year-old arches, their voices became a musical instrument that had its own separate existence, independent of their bodies. And in this way, seven times a day, they celebrated their unity, reaffirmed their spirituality and communicated all of that, and more, to their God. Even though I understood none of it (and wouldn't have related to much of it even if I had), it was impossible to sit in the stalls and not feel some of their inner peace.

That evening, out in the courtyard after Compline, long after the last candle had been extinguished and all the monks had filed away to their beds, I could still hear one of their number running through some of the liturgical harmonies alone in his dormer-windowed cell under the eaves. For him, celebrating his faith seven times a day and 365 days a year still wasn't enough.

12

Old Empires, New Nations:
Vienna to Esztergom

No matter what Johann Strauss may say, Vienna distrusts the Danube. The Austrian capital sits on a plain which used to flood regularly in winter, when the river would pioneer new branches and blunder at will across a region up to 6 kilometres wide. By the mid-nineteenth century the city fathers were fed up with this irresponsible behaviour, so they drew up a grand scheme that took twenty-five years and 100,000 workers to complete, thrusting the Danube into the straitjacket of two giant concrete channels that run through the northern suburbs. Shackling one of these channels is the Freudenau power station, a huge installation where 12 million litres of water per second pass through six turbines with a noise like a jumbo-jet convention.

Austria has nine hydropower stations sapping the Danube's power, of which Freudenau is the last and most recent, with a lock system the size of three football stadiums. When required it lights up half of Vienna, but at quieter times its excess electricity can't be easily stored, so late at night the surplus is used to pump water uphill to reservoirs high up in the mountains. There it can be released during peak periods, so that in theory one extra schoolchild returning home in late afternoon and turning on the Cartoon Network can trigger a giant waterfall in the Alps.

For me, on my bike, the river's banishment to the suburbs meant that there was no obvious route into the city centre. Instead I followed the Danube Canal, a lame, tame waterway that threaded under motorway arches where urban graffiti came out to meet me in slogans like 'Freedom for all children' and 'Nothing is certain', accompanied by white cats, yellow sharks and a man with an exploding head. The graffiti became increasingly apocalyptic as I progressed, with echoes of Meatloaf, Egon Schiele and the Simpsons, until under one arch there were two lads on a stepladder spray-painting an underwater scene. Art students, they said.

'Are you not worried about the police? Where I come from this is classified as vandalism.'

'They're not interested. Our teachers even suggest we come here. Unofficially of course,' said the one higher up the ladder. 'There's nowhere else we can get such a big surface.'

'But what about those people whose work you're covering up?'

'If you know who did it, then you don't cover it,' said the one below. He gestured around him. 'A lot of this was done by last year's students. And they've left. Too bad.'

As I cycled on I thought of two other artists who might have painted the motorway arches in their day.

The seventeen-year-old Adolf Hitler had come to Vienna

from Linz as a would-be art student, but had failed to get a place in the Arts Academy when his drawings of Linz – yes Linz – were rejected as an inadequate portfolio. Not wishing to return home a failure, he'd stayed on for five years, lodging in hostels and earning money from drawing postcards and from set-painting in the theatre. Interestingly, for someone who made a career out of war, he'd also been avoiding conscription, and indeed he eventually left for Germany because of the prison sentence that awaited him if he was caught, which is not something he mentions in *Mein Kampf*. At the time he wrote to a friend that 'I still believe that the world has lost a great deal by my not being able to go to the Academy and learn the craft of painting. Or did fate reserve me to some other purpose?' It's fair to say it did.

Twenty years later Patrick Leigh Fermor arrived in Vienna and ended up doing much the same thing, staying in hostels and earning money from his art, unaware that he was following in the footsteps of a draft-dodger who was about to start a war that would change the world. It was in a Viennese hostel that Leigh Fermor met a German called Konrad, one of the most striking characters in *A Time of Gifts*. Konrad had learned his English entirely from his reading of Shakespeare, and his talk was peopled with wanton wenches, lackeys and fardels. He called Leigh Fermor 'my dear young', and it was his idea that the author should go door to door in the prosperous Mariahilferstrasse district doing sketches of residents. That was how the young Leigh Fermor spent his next weeks.

I too headed for Mariahilferstrasse, but there were no Konrads in its Pension Esterhazy, which smelled like a sanatorium and looked like one too. In fact I barely saw another resident. Thus far I'd stayed in some pretty basic places, but this one had been stripped down to the absolute minimum and slathered all over with some plague-resistant, anti-fouling paint, the colour of dirty battleships. It had no pictures on the walls, no curtains on the showers and no seats on the toilets. And yet I still had to hand over my passport as a 'caution', so distrustful was the owner of his clientele. But at least it was outside the touristed city centre, beyond all those massively decorative palaces, galleries and museums that anchor the city so firmly in its imperialist past, stalked through by the whiskery ghost of Emperor Franz Joseph, his joints cracking, his ceremonial sword clanking by his side. These buildings turn Vienna into a weighty piece of scenery, an arcane, dusty place full of reminders of lost glories, where tourists go off in search of the Dorotheum, the Hof or the Belvedere, and are never entirely sure which one it is they've found. It is a city which forever missed out on a good sacking, burning or bombing, those invasive purgations which cleared the systems of many other European capitals and allowed them to leave one foot in the past while stepping forward to the present and into the future. As a result it wears its history on its sleeve, but little else.

On previous visits Vienna had struck me as a place of thickset middle-aged women with big hair and little dogs who murmured to each other in coffee shops. Of late middle-aged princesses who wore furs without a second thought, and of baggy-stockinged spinsters who were occasionally seen in public smoking a pipe. Even before Botox, decades of coiffure, skincare and avoiding too much emotion had set the expressions of the moneyed Viennese into masks, usually faintly disapproving, and their hairstyles were carved, not styled. From their mid-forties onwards they began to turn to stone.

In *The Glance of Countess Hahn-Hahn (down the Danube)* Peter Esterhazy says of Vienna that 'in a friendly little town, men's and women's gazes go scampering all over the place, but not here'. What constitutes normal behaviour elsewhere – simply forgetting to remove one's glance from another's face – is not the custom in the imperial city. As a result, he felt unnoticed and 'as grey as a concrete bunker . . . It is easier to join the dead in Vienna than talk to the living'.

But things had changed since I was last here and parts of the city had moved on, thanks to the newly enlarging Europe. For decades Vienna had played the role of the last outpost of capitalist civilization, almost completely surrounded by the Eastern Bloc, like a grand and glittering luxury cruise liner berthed in a port which the communist world could see, tantalizingly close, through the barbed-wire fence. The Viennese turned their backs on the grubby faces surrounding them, ate more *Sachertorte* and pretended they didn't exist, but in the years since 1989 the old customs and immigration restrictions had been steadily removed, boarding passes had been issued and now the luxury liner's decks rang with the footsteps of hundreds of thousands of incomers, whom the original passengers were still doing their best to ignore. This new subculture emerged particularly in the Internet cafés, where I spent a couple of days making my travel arrangements amongst fractured families Skypeing each other in a babel of voices and languages. Many of these places were run by Africans speaking a mixture of Arabic, French and English, with a clientele of Romanians, Poles, Czechs, Slovaks and Turks.

So where the inner *Gürtel* or ring road was lined with the monuments of old empire, filled with holidaying Western Europeans holding maps, the outer *Gürtel* had the newcomer encampment, the Internet cafés and girly bars, filled with the rest of the world making a new home. Occasionally the two worlds would overlap: in the inner *Gürtel*, a group of Turkish-origin breakdancers earned money from virtuoso displays outside St Stephen's Cathedral, its roof scaled like a reptile's skin, while in the outer *Gürtel* a tall man in a long coat and felt hat came striding through, looking neither to the left nor right of his long, cold nose, clicking the metal tip of his cane on the stone.

For a couple of days I hunkered down, sending filled notebooks home and receiving parcels of fresh socks in return. I had a meeting with the benevolent Danube Tourist Commission, who took one look at me and decided I needed a hot meal and a bath. I cycled out to look at the United Nations City, a clutch of bureaucratic office blocks that looked like a set of microchips printed on the sky, surrounded by a squatter town of doughnut shops, Irish pubs and cocktail bars. I tried, and failed, to attend a concert that included the Blue Danube waltz – although I did finally find a part of the Danube that was truly blue: a floating swimming pool.

I eventually tracked Strauss himself down to his eponymous museum behind a flaking façade above a McDonald's in an unappealing part of town. The museum was full of romantic portraits of the composer, forever in a tuxedo, with a fine bushy showman's moustache of which he was plainly very proud. Paintings depicted him at the piano, from where he dazzled a series of swooning, fanning ladies in ruffed dresses. But there was no recording of the tune he wrote in 1867 for a male choir, and to which an amateur lyricist supplied those clumsy words which have since become a national anthem for Austria:

Danube so blue
You flow straight through
The meadows and dales . . .

On my last afternoon in the city I pedalled down non-blue, non-meadowed, non-daled banks to the Cemetery of the Nameless, an obscure plot east of Vienna containing the graves of those who had chosen to end their lives in the river, and who as a result couldn't be buried in Catholic ground. No romantic end for them. No matter how heavily they'd weighed themselves down, the river currents used to bring their drowned corpses to the surface at this point, amongst old Hansa warehouses and barges with dangerous chemicals, a place where nobody would go of their own free will. Peter Esterhazy describes the Danube as a 'heavy eater', swallowing up Jews, Serbs, babies and Hungarian prisoners of war, but it seems that it wasn't so keen on swallowing up suicides. There must have been a couple of hundred buried here, all under the same metal cross with a silver Christ on a black crucifix, arms outstretched beseechingly, hungry for love. Most had the simple inscription '*Unbekannt*', unknown. People who, said a sign by the graveyard entrance, had 'fled from the world to where nobody could find them, and where there is no more pain'. Some had plastic lilies, but even more had old cuddly toys left on the graves, the Snoopies and teddies of compassionate children who sensed that some people had a greater need. And one, in a far corner right at the back, had a lit candle, suggesting a body that was by no means as '*unbekannt*' as the inscription suggested, but someone who had been, and still was, deeply loved, by one person at least, and whose story had never been told.

*　　*　　*

In the days of the Austro-Hungarian Empire Vienna had a diminutive neighbour called Pressburg, 60 kilometres away, to which it was connected by one of the longest tram rides in the world. That tram crossed what was later to become a buffer zone between East and West, between capitalism and communism, so the tracks were ripped up and watchtowers were posted there instead; they were the hooks on which the Iron Curtain was hung. The resulting no-man's-land helped to preserve the last vestiges of a true Danubian alluvial marsh, while everywhere else the river was being imprisoned in its progressive straitjacket of embankments and hydropower dams.

Wetlands like these are capable of absorbing and slow-releasing large quantities of water, thus removing the extreme highs and extreme lows of the river flow, and they are far better for the biodiversity of the EU's longest river. The canalization of the Danube, of which only around 30 per cent is truly free-flowing, has caused the loss of 80 per cent of the original floodplain, along with species like the moor frog and the black poplar. It has also had an impact on water quality, because those wetlands used to act as natural filters, cleaning the river water before sending it on its way. So now that the Danube is frogmarched through Europe, without looking to left or right, it carries its slop bucket with it from one country to the next and ultimately upsets the ecology of the Black Sea. From having been a reedy, marshy, wandering, wonderful, amorphous living thing, it has been rendered into straight lines, made far less interesting, and more dangerous, by the hand of man.

Certainly the communists weren't much bothered by environmental issues. On the far side of the Iron Curtain, the former marshlands on the southern shore of the city the Viennese still call Pressburg (but the rest of the

192

world knows better as Bratislava) had been drained and recarpeted in marching rows of brutalist apartments. Man's triumph over nature, never mind that they looked like school lavatory blocks from the 1960s.

Bratislava is the capital of one of the world's youngest countries, Slovakia, which was an integral part of Czechoslovakia until independence in 1993. In reality the city had never really been Slovak at all, but a largely German-speaking part of the Habsburg Empire, although technically it belonged to Hungary. In the rearrangements that followed the First World War it was handed over to the newly created nation of Czechoslovakia so that the latter could have a port on the Danube, and becoming the Slovak capital was the city's third rebranding in seventy years.

Border changes like this were settled by post-war treaties, which between them carved the rough outlines of Eastern Europe as we know it today. Besides the new nation of Czechoslovakia, these treaties created Yugoslavia, Poland, Estonia, Latvia and Lithuania out of what had been largely feudal territories with mixed populations ruled over by powerful landowners who took no account of people's needs, and who had been giving their allegiance to some empire or other in return for relative autonomy. In Western Europe we've had settled borders and a strong sense of nationality for hundreds of years, but most of Central and Eastern Europe didn't have single nationalities until the idea of the nation-state was thrust upon it by the treaty-makers.

Besides, apart from the Danube, there were no handy physical barriers that kept peoples boxed in, so all the ethnicities had freely intermingled. There were Magyars, Serbs, Saxons and Swabians all swilling around the same general area. Hungarians were widely spread in what is now Romania; Turks dominated whole swathes of what is now Bulgaria, former Yugoslavia and southern Hungary; Germans had big concentrations in what is now Poland and the Czech Republic, plus large regions of Hungary, Serbia and Romania, and they had settled in all the trading cities. And Slovaks were widely spread, the wild and woolly woodsmen of the East; but apart from the mountains, the Tatras and the Carpathians, they never really had a place they could call home.

The treaty-makers at Versailles and Trianon changed all this, drawing lines on the map and creating new names and nationalities just as they had done in the Middle East, with Syria, Iran, Iraq, Israel and Palestine. The driving idea was for self-determination – majority rule – but the new borders often trapped hundreds of thousands of one ethnicity in another ethnicity's country. Previously this had always been a region of comparatively free movement, so over the succeeding post-treaty decades millions of people took the remedy into their own hands, either crossing the new borders into lands where they were in the majority, or deciding to cut their losses and start again with a completely new life in the Americas. Thus Bratislava went from 60 per cent German in 1880 to 80 per cent Slovak in 1921, and thus, today, there are supposedly more Slovaks in Cleveland, Ohio than there are in Bratislava.

Thereafter communism clamped down on everything, preventing any further movement, incarcerating those who were thinking of moving in countries to which they'd never really belonged, and virtually halting all communication between families and ethnicities spread across borders.

Over the last two decades those restraints have been steadily removed, and now Central and Eastern

Europeans are crossing borders again. They're swilling around the whole continent, spilling over into the wider world, looking for a better place to settle, just as they did between the wars. Many – particularly those who belonged to a minority trapped in someone else's country – find it easy to leave. They've never really felt hefted to their own piece of soil, as a deer is to the scrap of mountain or moorland where it was born. So the Swabians in Hungary and Romania, the Saxons in Transylvania, the Hungarians in Slovakia and Croatia, and the Slovaks in Romania, they're all on the move. And leaving their homeland means that, wherever they end up, they never quite fit in. Not, at least, for this generation.

I found myself discussing these after-effects of war treaties with two kindly old gentlemen at the Association of European Journalists in central Bratislava, where I was welcomed with more deference than I deserved. Juraj and Peter were both good case histories in Trianon-created nationalities and in generational change. Peter was from the east of the country, and had grown up speaking Hungarian; Juraj, from the north, had a German grandfather and a Hungarian grandmother, and had grown up speaking German. Both had experienced multiple nationalities in their lifetimes – Hungarian, Austrian, Czechoslovakian – and both were now good Slovaks, proud of their country, and yet both had children who'd left Slovakia to pursue their careers overseas, though they hadn't gone as far as Cleveland.

In fact the Association was feeling pretty anti-American when I was there, with the membership still smarting from the release of the horror movie *Hostel*, produced by Quentin Tarantino, which told the story of two American college buddies who were lured to 'a Slovakian town' stocked with Eastern European women as desperate as they were gorgeous. Bewitched by the women, the Americans found themselves dragged into an increasingly sinister, graphic and gory underworld of organized crime, torture, human trafficking and sex tourism, against a backdrop that was recognizably Bratislavan. 'Why did they pick on us?' I was asked. 'Why choose our city?' I hadn't seen the film or even read about it, so I didn't feel qualified to answer, but I had to admit that there was probably some truth to the popular hypothesis that nobody cared about Slovakia, which was too far away from the United States and too small for anyone in the film's audience to know better. In response, I muttered something about Hollywood always needing to depict the world in black and white, in good and bad, and how the baddies had to come from somewhere, preferably somewhere that wouldn't object too vociferously. Slovakia had no political or economic muscle on the world stage, so it had been a soft target.

Certainly there was little sign on the streets of any kind of underworld. The capital city was no grander than many a Habsburg town I'd cycled through further upriver, but it had been ringed with suburbs and seriously smartened up in line with its new capital-city status. Its city centre had a feeling of wide-eyed innocence, of still being a new boy at the capital-city game, and its citizens were on their best behaviour in their new national front room, which was freshly decorated and awaiting visitors. 'How should I look in my capital? Am I wearing the right clothes for my capital? What should I do in my capital?'

And where in most capital cities there's a clear distinction between the local and the tourist – the former in a hurry and viewing the latter as a nuisance – here everyone was a tourist, even the locals. They seemed rather surprised, and elated, that their historic city centre was actually rather a nice place, certainly when compared to the buckled tarmac, cracked concrete and discoloured steel that had colonized the southern shore, where many of them lived. They were also very good speakers of English, which made me realize how Germanic my journey had been up to then. Here, English was deemed necessary either for a life overseas or for finding a job at home, and the former townhouses of aristocratic families like Palffy and Esterhazy were now occupied by international anglo-centric consultancies, come to teach these people how to become proper capitalists, for which they'd be charging a very fat fee.

There was, though, another kind of English on the streets that wasn't quite so welcome: stag parties. Party organizers had started to promote Bratislava as an alternative to Prague or Riga, and now there were a couple of herds of them moving from bar to bar, joshing each other loudly. I don't know whether or not Tarantino's *Hostel* had helped sell the city to these groups, but I saw nothing that would suggest to me they'd come to any harm here, unless they tripped and fell into the Danube after one Slivovica (cough medicine meets vodka up a dark alley) too many.

I left Bratislava over the Bridge of the National Slovak Uprising, better known as the UFO bridge, whose main suspension pylon is topped with a giant saucer-shaped viewing gallery, 85 metres up. This UFO Tower has become the unofficial emblem of the city, and locals joke that the only way to avoid seeing it is to climb up it, but secretly there's still some pride in its construction, which is internationally admired not for its aesthetics, but for its engineering. To my eye it looked less like a UFO and more like a giant jockey desperately hanging on to the reins of a tearaway bridge, bolting from the gruesome architecture creeping up on it from the southern shore.

Fortunately the cycle route skirted all that ugliness, sticking instead to the ridge of the embankments which braided the river's edge, and after fifteen minutes I found I'd snuck out of Bratislava the back way. I was back in countryside again, but this was an unreal countryside that was largely man-made, part of a giant communist-era project that had swallowed up more of the natural Danube marshland and riverbank and had caused considerable friction with neighbouring Hungary.

Slovakia's Gabčikovo dam had originally been planned as one of a pair, with the other to be at Nagymaros in Hungary, and between them they would have produced copious quantities of hydropower, to the glory of the communist ideal. But the Hungarians dragged their feet. Being more aware of ecological issues, and living in a more liberal state at that time (the 1980s) than the Slovaks, the people objected more vociferously to the Soviet-led project, particularly because the Nagymaros dam would be located on the Danube Bend, one of Hungary's traditional tourism destinations. So while the Slovaks embarked on their end of the operation like good boys, the Hungarian works faltered, and then stopped altogether with the fall of the Wall. By that time the Slovaks had gone too far to be able to stop, so they completed Gabčikovo, and in so doing massively altered the dimensions and ecology of the river where it entered Hungary, creating a point of contention between the two countries that, along with the minority Hungarian issue, still sours relations today.

Viewed from the bicycle saddle, the landscape sur-rounding the new reservoir certainly had a feeling of unreality to it: a golf course without any little white balls.

On the shore, it was smoothed and shaped, carpeted in grassland, stitched with drainage ditches and banded with tarmac that would be busy with roller-bladers at the weekend. Out on the water there were clumps of surviving grassland and the wreckage of flooded forest with corpses of trees keeled over on their sides, like an elephant's graveyard that had filled with water, water that slopped and wallowed, directionless and disorientated, not yet decided whether it was a river or a lake.

And as for the border between the two awkward neighbours, it wasn't easy to find either. When it got close, the cyclepath veered nervously away from Hungarian territory back into Slovakia, without so much as a sign, so I had to burrow inland on country roads to find an arterial road with a bored border guard who clambered out of his cabin to look at my passport. There was no question of any 'Welcome to Hungary'.

Two days later I was back on the border again, this time in a light-green cantilevered no-man's-land suspended between the two countries, right above the turbulent centre of the Danube. To my right the basilica of Esztergom rose domineeringly above the water from the first riverside hill since Bratislava, while to my left stood yet another set of incongruous Slovakian apartment blocks, making an unnecessarily urban statement in what was essentially just countryside. Beneath me the revitalized river sashayed onwards, wiggling with pleasure at the prospect of leaving the boring plain and eager to throw itself through the chicanes of the Danube Bend.

I was standing at the mid-point of Esztergom's Maria Valeria bridge, old in design but new in execution. There had long been a bridge here, but it had been blown up by the Germans as they retreated at the end of the Second

World War, and for the next sixty years the wreckage had remained, a forlorn pair of twisted stubs. Neither Hungary nor Slovakia would pay for it to be replaced. The recent rebuild, using the old design, was meant to epitomize the improving relationship between the two countries, but it was done at the EU's expense, with the Union acting as marriage-broker after neither nation would take the initiative on its own. Whether the reconstruction had helped repair cross-border relations was difficult to judge, because now, rather than gazing longingly across the river at their spiritual home, the population of 'Upper Hungary' – i.e. western Slovakia – could nip across for a bit of cultural reinforcement, potentially widening the cultural gap between themselves and the majority Slovaks back home.

Nor are the Hungarian Slovaks the only satellite community still looking across to the mother ship; there are hundreds of thousands of ethnic Hungarians in Romania, Serbia and to a lesser extent Croatia, trapped in the mesh of imposed border changes. Today's Hungary is a pale shadow of its former glorious self, having lost two-thirds of its body-mass after choosing the wrong side in the First World War. Over 100,000 square kilometres of Hungarian flesh – more than was left on the Hungarian bone – was sliced off and thrown to its hungry neighbours. Thus Upper Hungary became part of Slovakia, but most of that lost land was away to the east, in a place called Transylvania, which was handed wholesale to an emerging nation called Romania.

As a result Hungary, which had formerly been an equal partner in the sprawling Habsburg Empire, was reduced by Trianon to a nugget of Magyars surrounded by a sea of Slavs. The treaty-signing was regarded as a tragic day in Hungarian history; shops were shut and black flags flown as the nation mourned its losses. Hungarians saw themselves as the big victims of modern Europe, and it was Hitler's promise of giving most of this lost territory back which encouraged them to have a second go at war. Thus they joined, and lost, two world wars in a row, and they have been smarting from the consequences ever since.

In normal circumstances the dismemberment of a nation like this would have been sufficient trigger for a seething discontent which would eventually have erupted into ethnic strife the likes of which later ignited the Balkans. But strongly repressive communism put a heavy lid on the boiling pot, halting any serious thoughts of rebellion within Hungary. Even so, nearly a century later, the restoration of Greater Hungary is still a voter issue in domestic Hungarian politics, particularly amongst older people. And while the young may not speak out on the subject, there is a general feeling throughout society that the nation has been on the wrong end of some very harsh decisions taken by the big bullies of Europe.

That victim syndrome is reinforced by a national predilection for pessimism. Hungary has the highest suicide rate in Europe, and its celebrity self-killers include a couple of prime ministers (both of them from the Teleki dynasty) and a Miss Hungary, not long after her coronation. The nation's heroes are poets and playwrights who generally die tragically, one of whom famously penned a song called 'Gloomy Sunday', which became known as the Hungarian Suicide Song and the lyrics of which supposedly hypnotized the vulnerable into taking their own lives.

Sunday is gloomy, my hours are slumberless
Dearest, the shadows I live with are numberless,
   etc., etc.

Eventually the composer, Rezsö Seress, could stand his lyrics no longer and jumped to his own death.

But I hadn't come out to the middle of the Maria Valeria bridge to throw myself off; I had come because it was here that Patrick Leigh Fermor had stood, back in the very last years of the original river crossing. After a big diversion north to Prague he had returned to the river at this point, and here he had paused, dramatically, poised between two countries – and two books. He'd ended *A Time of Gifts* on the middle of the bridge, with a description of storks filing across the sky, before picking up his journey into Hungary in *Between the Woods and the Water*. So for me, standing out in the middle of that bridge was the literary equivalent of a reel change in the middle of an old-fashioned cinema film. Looking up, however, I could see no storks, only a Tesco's plastic bag rising steadily on an upward draft of hot air, drifting out to mid-river and then hitting a cooler airstream and plunging down, meeting the same fate as the Tailor of Ulm.

Reading Leigh Fermor's account of Esztergom was difficult for me. Where he had soared stork-like in an inspirational riff that covered several pages, I plunged down like that Tesco's bag into a metaphysical bath of cold water. The middle of the Maria Valeria did nothing for me, so I plodded back to shore feeling leaden-footed and glum.

In truth, I'd struggled with my first days in Hungary. Although it was one of the first countries to shake itself free of communism, it remains one of the least-understood, least-explored regions of Central Europe. For long centuries it had been buried under Turkish rule, swiftly followed by integration into the Austro-Hungarian imperial system, and the two of them had conspired to fossilize its social structure and exclude any whiff of the likes of the Renaissance, the Reformation or

Humanism. As a result it is where Europe changes gear – cuisine, clothes, brands, attitudes and alphabets – and becomes . . . different.

From the perspective of northern Europe, we haven't yet learned how to appreciate the aesthetics of the nations beyond Vienna. We haven't studied their history or their arts, and none of them were British colonial territory so they never come up at university. Their church architecture plops into the gap somewhere between onion-domed baroque and Byzantine, their languages don't figure on most Western curricula and their people never really had the wealth to indulge themselves in design flourishes inside or outside their dwellings. Accordingly they're not in the books; the artistic, cultural and touristic surveys of Europe have passed them by. And accordingly, while we can happily declare that the Dutch wear clogs, skate on frozen rivers and eat cheese, and that the Italians drive Vespas, argue a lot and eat spaghetti, we can't make any such platitudinous generalizations about our fellow EU members in the East.

When it comes to Hungary, we do have a semi-excuse, because the Hungarians are newcomers to Europe. Led by Attila the Hun, they poured into the vacuum left by the departing Romans in the fifth century AD. Originally a Finno-Ugric race, they supposedly came from the lands between the Volga and the Urals, and their closest European relatives are the Finns, who are almost as suicidal as them. The joke runs that when the original Finno-Ugric tribe first arrived in Europe they came across a signpost with two arrows; one pointed to Suomi (Finland) and the other had broken off. So those who could read went to Finland.

The Hungarian language itself is linguistically distinct from the rest of Europe, and for a traveller like me, familiar with Latin-based or Germanic idiom, it proved as slippery as a bar of soap. No matter how much I repeated a word learned one day, I would find it had escaped me again the next, with the result that whereas previously I'd felt myself to be inside the European aquarium, happily swimming downriver with the rest, now I felt separated from everyone by a pane of glass. I could see people's mouths moving in my direction, but what emerged was a river of liquid sounds, with no recognizable linguistic wreckage that I could cling to.

It didn't help that the cyclepath suddenly evaporated, depositing me in the hot slipstreams of lorries, where I had to hold on to my hat in the heat. Fellow long-distance cyclists had evaporated, too, and any cyclists I met were no longer lycra-clad, but farm workers carrying tools or elderly women in headscarves going very slowly to informal vegetable markets at the village crossroads. Their bicycles were not the shiny and whirring variety I'd been travelling with thus far, but rattling boneshakers with wrap-around handlebars and a basket at the front.

Meanwhile the landscape beyond the road edge had lost the organized neatness of mechanized farming, letting anarchy creep in at the edges. In places the poppies were rampant, streaking the fields with scarlet stripes as if God had slashed the land with his fingernail and drawn blood, just to show that he could. The hedgerows were pungent with flowering wild fruit, marsh reed, alder berries and dying lilac, and cycling through it was as rich as walking down the perfume aisle of a department store. The air was hung with feathery seeds, held aloft by the rising heat from the tarmac, praying for a puff of wind that would bring them to ground.

On my arrival in Hungary I'd crossed the flatlands of the Moroni Duna, a tributary of the Danube, home to tall purple spears of marsh orchids and more delicate, egg-shaped bee orchids. Thick bushes of marsh elder lined the paths, providing shade for marsh gentian, tiny specks of deep, deep blue. I knew there'd be March hares and black Siberian storks hereabouts, but all I saw was the occasional disruptive diggings of wild boar.

For long stretches the Danube's banks became practically inaccessible thanks to abandoned industrial installations surrounded by barbed-wire fencing. In these relics of a less happy era every window was smashed and the only sign of life was a couple of caretakers in dungarees picking away at a green scab of a vegetable patch in the midst of flaking pipes and rusting boilers.

I'd stopped for a night in Győr, a sometime baroque town with a strong connection to Bavaria's Ingolstadt, because this was where the engines for Audis were made. In contrast to the land around it, the city was flush with civic cash, recently pedestrianized, strung with flower baskets, and it was full of students, flirting and eating ice-cream. But that reinvigoration didn't extend to the grand old hotel I found by the railway station, too large and unwieldy for new enterprise cash. It was being run into the ground like an obsolete old gas-guzzler. Bits were rusty and falling off, the plastic fittings had turned brittle with age, and whenever I went up to my room I was preceded by a cranky fly, which hovered in the corridor, waiting for me, like a persistent porter who hadn't yet been given his tip. The showers in the communal bathroom had no shower heads and were lined up all in a row as at a rugby club, with no curtains, presumably on the basis that there was no need for modesty in a world where all men were created equal. Downstairs, the receptionist had been there since time immemorial, and had taken on the colour, and the immobility, of the hotel stone. Most of the time he was on a proscribed coffee or cigarette break in the back room, and guests had to wait until the stipulated time had elapsed before he would creak back into view to hand over a key. Too old and too set in his ways for a job in Györ's new industries, the Audi plant or the Nokia factory, he was serving out his time in the only slice of Györ's past that respected the old working practices, and there was nothing more annoying to him than guests.

And so, a day later, I had finally arrived in Esztergom with mixed feelings about Hungary, looking to find inspiration in the city which had impressed Leigh Fermor.

It was easy to see why the Romans had chosen to build a fortress here. Esztergom's Castle Hill sits in a great strategic location on a corner carved out by the Danube and its tributary the Kis-Duna (small Danube). Whoever held the hill controlled the river and extended his authority over miles of surrounding plains. So it was a natural place for one of those Finno-Ugric princes who hadn't turned right for Suomi to set up his court, back in the tenth century, elaborating on what the Romans had left behind. Here his son István, aka Stephen, had been born.

Stephen is regarded as the father of modern Hungary, and Esztergom accordingly became the capital for the nation's first 250 years. From the fortress, Stephen cajoled and bullied the other Magyar princes and landowners into coming together under one banner – his. He also drove out paganism and shamanism, forcing his subjects to accept Christianity, so it is as the mystical St Stephen rather than brutal King Stephen that he is remembered in the massive nineteenth-century basilica which has been raised on the top of Castle Hill.

Modelled on St Peter's in Rome, the basilica's main feature is a round tower topped with a giant, light-green copper dome. It exudes power and solidity, and was built to impress by sheer size, if not by grace. From 5 kilometres away it had looked pleasingly like an elevated musical box – I could imagine lifting the lid for it to play a tune – but now, up close, it had no such frivolity. The massive walls were intimidating, not graceful. Inside, the huge domed space was bare and severe, finished in grey shiny marble and dotted with Maltese crosses, and that immensity continued in the giant crypt below, as monumental as an Egyptian burial site, lined with the flamboyant tombs of former archbishops covered in sculpture. That afternoon it was practically empty, and its monumentalism left me cold.

I found the city centre a disappointment, too. Esztergom is still the seat of Roman Catholicism in Hungary, but its importance is only written in stone, not in any evident vitality or spirituality. Traffic piled through the main street, but off to the sides the quiet bishops' palaces, monasteries and libraries were deserted, and the tree-lined promenade along the prettily named Kis-Duna was spoiled by the pungent smell from the turgid green water that flowed between its banks. I sat down on one of the benches and thumbed through the first chapter of *Between the Woods and the Water*, seeking inspiration. But it didn't help. Leigh Fermor kicks off the book with his usual whirlwind of imagery, meeting Esztergom's mayor and attending an Easter celebration on Castle Hill, which he describes in a handful of heady, baroque pages. There was no mayoral meeting or pageantry for me, so, beginning to appreciate the Hungarian expression 'under a frog's arse down a coal mine' (i.e. at the lowest of the low), I bought a few beers and retreated to my pension, where I watched Liverpool lose the final of the Champion's League on TV.

It wasn't a good moment in the journey, that day in Esztergom, and that's not because I am a Liverpool fan. I was struggling with Hungary, with the change from compatible Western culture to the more challenging East. I was also struggling with loneliness, and it was at Esztergom that loneliness finally got the upper hand.

As a solo traveller, you have to be prepared for downbeat days, and I usually tell myself that there's a creative edge to misery. It is only through such moments of loneliness that you touch base with the essence of your personality – who you really are – and hopefully you'll also discover a resilience that helps you to bounce back. Just look at the world's artistic geniuses, I reassure myself, they are almost invariably miserable much of the time. Misery comes with the territory of creativity, and it applies to travel, too. If I was a person who took everything in my stride with perfect ease, then this book would read as blandly as a tourist brochure. Its light would have no shade. It is the emotional highs and lows, the physical discomforts and disasters, that make an experience worth reading about.

But that difficult day in Esztergom, infected by Hungarian gloom, was particularly personal because of the inevitable comparison I could draw with Leigh Fermor's experience of the same place. Esztergom represented a chance for me to measure myself up against him, and I came out of it pretty badly. I tried to be philosophical: he had his style, I had mine. Journeys are bound to have miserable days, and I knew I had good stuff to come. I remember thinking, before I fell asleep, that I'd had enough of the bicycle. I needed a change of scene, a change of cinema reel, a change of pace. I needed to get to Budapest.

13

Communists and Aristocrats in Budapest

Budapest is the only capital city which truly straddles the Danube. Vienna shoves the river into the suburbs, Bratislava regards it with suspicion from a safe distance from behind a parapet and Belgrade takes a squinting, sidelong view from the top of a hill, but Budapest, according to Peter Esterhazy, 'allows the Danube to slide between its breasts'. Mind you, it is quite flat-chested on the Pest side.

I slid unpornographically between these unequal bosoms on a tourist boat I'd picked up in Szentendre. It was nearly 40 degrees in the shade, and I didn't fancy trying to pedal-penetrate my way into a major city in that heat, so I'd joined the tourists who'd come upstream to buy lace parasols and wooden puzzles in Szentendre's pretty streets and then to sit in its riverside cafés until it was time to go home.

The boat passengers were very cosmopolitan and it was a pleasure to be able to eavesdrop on understandable conversations again. At least it was until I overheard a posh Englishman getting into an argument with one of the crew over a lost ticket. The Englishman was pedantic in the extreme, indignant at any suggestion of dishonesty, and equally determined not to pay again. For his part the crewman was large, fat and shiny-headed and had a packet of sunflower seeds in his pocket which he dipped into at regular intervals. His end of the conversation, therefore, was punctuated by spitting small blizzards of seed fragments over the rail, which only served to aggravate the Englishman even further. At the expression 'downright ill-mannered' (it had to come sometime) I moved a few rows away so I didn't have to hear more. To block out the argument I peered fixedly at the musculature of the tree roots where they were exposed by low water.

Initially, as the boat moved downstream, the thickly wooded banks were giving nothing away, a model of impassivity. And then we started to meet sculling boats and canoeists coming upriver, the city's single spies. They were followed by an island colonized by ramshackle glass-fronted villas on piles, like captains' bridges that had been severed from their motherships by a passing storm and spirited away to an isolated lump of land. It was the handiwork of an invisible, all-powerful captain's-bridge collector in the sky who wanted them, as a magpie does, for their glittery glass windows.

Then came a half-finished motorway arch and then another older bridge, this time with a rumbling yellow tram that temporarily drowned out all attempt at conversation on board. At this point the banks became follically challenged and concrete embankments stepped forward, followed reluctantly by shy apartment blocks.

Suddenly self-conscious, aware that he was entering the grandstand at the end of a long race, the blotchy-complexioned old gentleman sitting in front of me folded

210

away his German-language Viennese newspaper and started to talk to his neighbour in Hungarian, while the rest of the architecture of Budapest started to assemble on the riverbanks like a reluctant army of mismatched soldiery dribbling out on to the parade ground.

There was Margaret Island, busy with joggers and spa-visitors; and there were the Houses of Parliament, a 691-roomed giant crab with a spiky haircut that had taken a thousand labourers seventeen years to build. Next door to it on the embankment sat a statue of Jozsef Attila, another prolifically suicidal poet with eight attempts on his own life after the age of nine, gazing at the Danube's bulging and contracting waters, whose

Each single movement, each and every wave.
It rocked me like my mother for a time
And washed and washed the city's filth and grime.

Atilla's vision of filth and grime is contiguous with the present day, but amongst those things it had washed away, from just where Attila sat, were throngs of Jewish children aged between four and twelve, machine-gunned into the river in the latter days of the Second World War. A row of metal shoes lined the embankment edge where they disappeared.

The boat slowed and turned back into the current in the lee of Buda's biggest hill, Gellert, topped by the city's most adaptable monument, Lady Liberty, holding a palm frond aloft for all to see. Lady Liberty is a true survivor amongst Eastern European statuary. She's overcome the vicissitudes of Hungary's very difficult century, starting her career during the fascist period as a personal tribute to a dictator's son, riding out the communist period as a Liberation Monument thanking the Russians for their advance, and now she stood as a generic memorial for all those who had died for Hungarian independence. Adaptable and ambiguous, she'd managed to epitomize heroism for each new regime, although she'd required discreet remodelling at every regime change in order to escape being melted down into ship's propellers.

Below her, we nosed ashore just upstream of the Chain Bridge, where art nouveau merchants' houses spread in staccato clumps along both shores, demi-semiquavers on a stave. The bridge is Budapest's most photogenic and elderly crossing, a string-of-pearls suspension, a suspender belt across a svelte river which was briefly stockinged by a rifling breeze. It was constructed in 1849 at the instigation of Count Széchényi, after he had been forced to delay his father's funeral for eight days because the river was too high for him to cross. This was an inconvenience that he found intolerable, and he decided it was time the city had a more permanent crossing, so he contacted a British engineer who'd just created a Thames river-crossing at Marlow: 'I want one of those.' Back then in Hungary the aristocracy made everything happen, even big things like the building of bridges.

For the moment I didn't need to cross it, but my destination was close to its western end, and within twenty minutes of disembarking I'd wheeled my bicycle into the kitchen of a fourth-floor apartment block in Buda's riverside Taban district. There my well-travelled 20-euro set of wheels came to rest, five weeks after leaving Donaueschingen. I never rode it again.

The apartment belonged to an old friend, a lifelong socialist and a teacher at one of Budapest's universities. Despite thirty years of living in communist and post-communist countries there was something very British about Mark, with his passionate support of Wolverhampton Wanderers, his umbilical cord (via the Internet) to BBC Radio, his fascination with cricket and his enthusiasm for James Joyce. Stocky, energetic and crackling with enthusiasm, he had a craggy face which habitually crinkled at the corners when he smiled. He was fluent in German, Czech and Hungarian and could cope in Serbian, Croatian, French and Irish, but in his spoken English he clung tenaciously to his flat-vowelled Black Country accent. Although he was massively interested in everything, his teaching was always top of his list, and he was forever gathering material and exchanging emails with his students, for whom he was plainly a caring, inspirational figure.

Socialism ran in the family. His grandfather had been a post-war Labour MP at a time when the Labour Party was keen to forge links with the wider socialist world, and had travelled out to Budapest back in 1946 to meet the government. Mark, therefore, was to some extent following in his grandfather's bond-forming footsteps, although his own political activity quickly got him into trouble when he first moved out to live and work in East Germany in the early 1980s. Completely unintimidated by the system, he'd started to criticize the GDR's heavy-handed brand of socialism and to bring copies of seditious magazines like *New Musical Express*, *Woman's Own* and *Cosmopolitan* into his English Studies classes, which resulted in a reprimand from the head of faculty.

'I was told I didn't understand Marxism–Leninism properly, and that I was an anarchistic euro-communist. And I suppose I was a bit of an anarchist, that much was true. I used to run English evenings, staging a male beauty contest in one of them, and then I did a cabaret on a summer course which had the corpse of socialism in the GDR in it. They didn't like that, they didn't.'

There were other acts of provocation, too, including trying to take a dartboard through Checkpoint Charlie, which aroused a lot of interest amongst the border guards, as did the Solidarity leaflet the guards found in his back pocket. The Stasi pulled him in for interrogation, and when he continued to insist he was committed to the GDR, albeit to a more liberal version than what they'd so far achieved, they changed tack and tried to recruit him as a spy instead.

'It was a real cliché. A guy in a leather jacket came out to visit. You could tell straight away who he was because he had a Lada, while everyone else had a Trabant. He was a nice enough guy. Brought me cakes and newspaper articles from the British press with bits underlined for us to talk about. But there was no way I was going to start working for the secret police.' After three visits the agent gave up.

Nevertheless there was no denying the strength of Mark's convictions and those of the friends around him. He was such a strong socialist that when his grandmother left him a legacy of £20,000 he dared not mention it to any of his circle. 'I felt ashamed of it. I was even tempted to give it away, but at that stage I was living in East Berlin and the money was in a bank account in the UK, so it was easy enough to pretend it didn't exist.'

Two decades later that legacy came home to roost when it helped him to buy his own parquet-floored, high-ceilinged apartment in Budapest, filled with sunshine, books, good conversation and the sound of rumbling trams. After twenty-eight different addresses in thirty years it wasn't an ideological cop-out, buying the flat, he maintained; he didn't consider property ownership to be theft. 'But I suppose I've mellowed in my old age,' he conceded. 'I'm not as active politically as I was, which might well be something to do with enjoying being within my own four walls. I still believe in equality of opportunity, grants for education, free healthcare, etc. The difference is that now I suppose I try to find things I have in common with people rather than trying to change their views.'

He continued to travel widely in Eastern Europe, heading off for rock festivals, starting conversations with strangers on trains, and cutting a popular figure in English-teaching seminars all the way across former communist states. I'd get emails from unheard-of places, at unlikely times of the night, sleepless in Gdańsk.

But Hungary was where he'd settled, and he was suitably dismayed at the haste with which Budapest had abandoned its former socialist ideals and swung to the right, which we discussed over a bottle of Hungarian wine and a cold cherry soup prepared by his Hungarian girlfriend, Magdi. 'At the moment we've got Victorian capitalism here in its worst manifestation. Everyone's afraid of losing their jobs, corporate greed is good, and tax fraud is acceptable at the highest level because it encourages outside investors. Meanwhile lots of people are effectively destitute and the health service is in chaos. What a mess.'

I stayed with Mark for several days, sallying out solo while he was working, and then, when he'd finished, going together to the open-air spa on Margaret Island or to the sulphurous Turkish baths at Rudas Fürdö, where naked men gossiped in the gloom about football, mistresses and the poetry of Petöfi. In these places we discussed why communism hadn't worked, with me pointing to the animal kingdom's hierarchies. 'Do you know why bees have a queen? Because if they had a central committee, there would be no honey.'

'Ah, but we're rational beings, not animals,' countered

Mark. 'No, the idea was fundamentally good, but the problem was Soviet control.'

From there we moved on to the challenges of democracy, Britain's cricketing failures, the parenting skills of mutual friends and how to tell your Zwack from your Tokaji.

Mark took my book-research seriously, and one day he came home excited at having made contact with Vajda Miklós, the literary editor of the *Hungarian Quarterly* who'd translated Leigh Fermor into Hungarian, so we climbed aboard a tram and went out to pay him a visit. Miklós turned out to be an elderly, heavily built, hesitant, softly spoken intellectual who lived in a small new apartment crammed with books, including several copies of his own translation of *Between the Woods and the Water*. It turned out he had a closer relationship to the book than we realized, because his aunt, Xenia, appeared in it under the pseudonym 'Angela', the married woman whom Leigh Fermor had met in Hungary and with whom he'd subsequently had a passionate affair while dashing around Transylvania. According to Miklós, his aunt had been a raven-haired beauty with an appetite for men, and Leigh Fermor had not been the first. Unfortunately, some time after her cameo appearance in his story, her life had gone badly wrong. She'd always had a difficult temper, and her divorce and the subsequent poverty had made it worse. Eventually she'd moved to Budapest and had ended up strangling her neighbour in a fit of rage. She'd spent many years in prison.

Miklós hadn't had an easy time of it, either. His family came from Arad, long since swallowed up into Romania thanks to Trianon. His father had been a well-known lawyer who'd died young, and his mother had ended up in prison on trumped-up political charges, so Miklós was brought up by his godmother, a famous actress, but he'd always struggled to find work.

'My parents were classified as "class aliens", so I had a document that followed me everywhere, although I never saw it, that made me practically unemployable.' He found bits and pieces of work as a freelance translator, and then, during the liberalizing 1960s, the *Hungarian Quarterly* finally gave him a job. It was to become his niche for the next forty years, and even though he had since retired, it was still effectively the family he'd never had.

His mother's supposed crime had centred on her free-enterprise espresso kiosk, where she'd worked long hours to try to support her son, and hers had been a show trial intended to frighten the middle classes during the early years of communism. According to the prosecution, the kiosk had become the venue for dissident talk and the focal point for an attempt to devalue the forint, and although Miklós said neither charge was true it certainly wouldn't have been the first time revolutionary talk had fomented in Budapest's coffee-houses. Which is why the communists effectively closed them all down.

Back at the start of the twentieth century there were six hundred of these places in Budapest, and although they'd be described these days as 'Viennese-style', many of them harked back (as do the spas) to the days of Ottoman occupation. (It was the Turks who'd introduced coffee to Vienna, too, although you'd be hard-pressed to find much acknowledgement for it in that city's archives.) Budapest's coffee-houses varied from smoky back-street hideaways to elaborate, ornamental palaces and many became second homes to writers, poets and politicians. In those days you could tell which political party and which social class a Budapester belonged to by which coffee-house his post was forwarded to. The coffee-house culture became a symbol of independence of mind and the setting for scintillating conversation, and we may yet look back on our own Starbucked era as enlightened, too, now that we're once again picking up our mail in coffee-shops, albeit digitally. Anyway, the communists certainly didn't approve. They had no time for the idle recreation, not to mention the idle speculation, that these places represented, so they swept them away.

Recent years have seen many of them restored to something approaching their former glory, and one of the most supremely serene is the New York Café, ridiculously over the top, extravagantly neo-baroque, with curving marble pillars rising to gilded niches and ceilings covered in frescos and statuettes. Pulling up a red velvet chair to a chrome-edged glass table in here, behind windows as tall as double-deckers, I read that Hungarian playwright Ferenc Molnár was so impressed when the café opened, back in 1894, that he threw its front-door keys into the Danube in order that it should never close. In the modern high street that sort of behaviour would get you banned from all Starbucks for life, but back then it turned the New York Café into a legend, and for a while it became the leading literary café of its day. Its writerly clientele would be provided with free paper and a basic, inexpensive writer's lunch of bread and cheese.

Alas, neither tradition has been maintained in the recently re-opened café. I couldn't see anyone who looked like a writer until I caught sight of myself in a mirror, and that was a shock. What with my notebook, my slightly dishevelled appearance and my half-moon reading glasses (a sad concession to age), I realized that I had reached the stage of life where people either look like their dogs or their jobs, and I don't have a dog. For much of my writing career I'd dismissed my appearance as distinctly unwriterly; I'd habitually describe myself as a pig farmer in chinos, waiting for the moment when I'd be weeded out of the literary world and sent back to shovel muck and mend fences. Now, seeing myself in the mirrors of the New York Café, I reckoned I finally looked the part. Besides, I was stuck with it, having passed the point where anyone would employ me in anything that had a pension attached.

I hadn't, however, chosen the right coffee-house to blend in, at least not according to Count Peter Bolza when I met him in the Muvesz – the Artist – later in the week. The New York, he said, was a fantasy, designed for tourists. The Muvesz, on Andrássy Út, was a much more likely place to find a true writer. Certainly it was surging with customers, gossip and cake.

The corduroyed, cufflinked count was another friend of Count Kalnoky, the Hungarian-Romanian aristocrat who'd helped me out with the contents of his address book during the planning of my journey. Count Peter was in his mid-forties, and he told me how he had been one of a select band of younger-generation aristocrats (along with Kalnoky) who'd returned to Budapest shortly after the end of communist rule. Up till then his family had been living in an apartment in Austria, and he remembered the day when a little fat man with a goose under his arm appeared framed in the glass of the apartment's outside door. 'We all called him uncle, although I'm not sure he was a relative at all. Anyway, he'd come to tell us that the long wait had come to an end. That it was OK to go back home.'

For a few heady years in the 1990s Budapest became the party city of Central Europe, and young Westerners – particularly Americans – gathered here to enjoy the celebratory after-shocks of liberty. Amongst them were around thirty aristocratic returnees like Peter Bolza with family names which would have meant instant dispossession under communism, and for a while they'd had a whirlwind social life, a magical time with dinner, discussion and dancing virtually every day. Eventually many of them paired up, got married, had children and in some cases relocated to a country life – I was to meet more of them later – but Count Bolza had remained in town, where he had forged himself a career as the interface between overseas companies and the local business community. That was where returnees like him had something to offer, he said; he had the necessary language skills and the cross-cultural understanding to make a bridge between the investor and the invested.

The count was a natural coffee-house demagogue. He was one of those people for whom conversation involved setting in motion long and ponderous trains of thought, and his interlocutor had to wait until the last carriage had cleared the platform before attempting a response. For him the return to Hungary had been, he said, like coming back into a family, restoring a sense of belonging, slotting all the pieces of a globally scattered jigsaw puzzle of uncles and cousins back into a defined shape that finally made sense. He acknowledged that it wasn't to everyone's taste, coming back, and probably 90 per cent of the escapees and their descendants had chosen not to. His own brother was amongst the dissenters, and had only set foot in Hungary once, and even then only because his father had specifically asked him to.

The story of his parents' original flight sounded like a chapter from *The Sound of Music*. They'd climbed a fence into Austria in the dead of night, with their only asset a gold watch which they'd sewed into the stomach of his sister's doll. And once in Austria his father, who'd been a high-ranking cavalry officer in the Hussars, had had to swallow his pride and make a living as a bicycle salesman. Of course those who hadn't left had fared far worse. Count Bolza told me of a fellow count who'd married a gypsy and was living in a run-down communist apartment block, and I'd heard talk of another who was squatting in a disused shipping container on Csepel, Budapest's industrial island. These were the ones who didn't get away.

But there were also returnees who were back ensconced within the family's four walls, as was Count László Károlyi, whom I'd arranged to go out to see at the Károlyi Palace at Fót, a short suburban train ride to the north-east of the city.

The Károlyis, along with the Andrássys, Széchényis and the Telekis, had been one of Hungary's most famous and powerful families, and their ranks included several prime ministers. They had been so rich, goes the story, that they didn't know the full extent of their own holdings. For example, in the mid-nineteenth century a head of the family had been making for Vienna to negotiate with the Habsburgs when his train had been stopped by a snowdrift. His staff informed him that he had a house nearby, so the whole contingent decamped from the train into a manor house that was heated, lit, staffed and with food ready-prepared every evening just in case the family should ever turn up. A house which the head of the family didn't even know existed.

It would have been hard to forget the palace at Fót, a classically colonnaded nineteenth-century chateau with over a hundred rooms, where the whiskery Emperor Franz Joseph had been a regular guest. It was set in parkland planted with rare trees, and every room had its own unique parquet flooring. This had been the family seat to some of the most prominent Károlyis, and Count László was proud of being the only Hungarian aristocrat to have been invited to return to his family property by the government. Mind you, that sounds grander than it was; the count and countess turned out to be lodged in a flat in a small corner of the building, while the remainder was being wound down as a government-run children's home. The home had been established as a direct consequence of the catastrophic 1956 Revolution, to mop up the offspring of fractured families whose parents had been killed, who had fled, committed murder or been declared insane. It had been a brutal time to be in Budapest, and those same palace rooms where lace-covered ladies had once flirted and danced had filled with 1,800 children who'd witnessed things that no child should ever see.

The Károlyis' apartment had its own entrance with a staircase that led up to a high-ceilinged set of rooms cluttered with family antiquities. Chief amongst them was the count himself, the apogee of an English pipe-smoking gentleman. Tall, distinguished, animated, interested and very generous with the gin, he was a good three decades older than the Bolza generation of new returnees. His wife, the countess, had flashing eyes, dangly jewellery, a tight skirt and had been a debutante in Vienna, although she was from a Transylvanian family. Plainly younger, it was not easy to tell by how much.

'I'm really terribly sorry we can't show you the rest of the palace,' said the count. 'It isn't ours to show. A blessing, really. As much as one would awfully, awfully like to have one's property back, the cost of restoration would amount to seven or eight million dollars.'

Count László's apparent Englishness was far more than just skin deep. He'd left Hungary right at the end of the Second World War, fleeing the Russian advance.

'The morning we left I'd been out beagling somewhere in the palace grounds. When I came back I was told we were leaving immediately, and I was to pack a rucksack. I was thirteen.' He paused to work at his pipe. 'We left in the family car, and we only just managed to cross the Danube in time. The bridge went up, boom, lit up the sky, minutes after we'd reached the other side. The roads were chaos, of course. The car was confiscated at the border, so we had to continue in a military truck.'

The family had had some money squirreled away in Switzerland, where he'd eventually completed his schooling, but at the age of seventeen he'd emigrated to Argentina with just $50 in his pocket, courtesy of the International Refugee Organization.

The count's pipe was proving obstinate so he gave it his full attention for a moment or two. 'I started as a construction worker, handing bricks to the bricklayer,' he continued, labouring away at the bowl. 'Then I moved to Peru and worked on a coffee plantation for twelve years, until coffee crashed. So then it was London. In 1965.' Puff puff. But while he'd been happy enough in every adopted country he'd lived in, he'd always felt Hungarian 'in spirit'.

In England he'd set up his own export consultancy, helping businesses to break into difficult markets, and that in turn had developed into an enterprise exporting medical equipment to further-flung corners of the world, particularly Iraq. Eventually it was the war in the latter, coupled with seismic shifts in Hungarian politics, that had finally persuaded him to return to Fót. The children's home had a new manager and wanted to rebrand itself as the Károlyi Children's Centre with the count as its patron, so they'd asked him whether he'd like to come back.

'It was very touching to see how we were welcomed

by everyone. You see, the Károlyis had always been on the liberal side of the political spectrum. We looked after people, we provided social security for the elderly because there were no state pensions back then. Personally I don't much like the term "aristocrat"; we were not educated to make money, but to serve God and country.'

I mentioned that I'd read about his relative Mihály Károlyi, the last Hungarian prime minister before the First World War, who'd been so liberal that he'd turned socialist, giving land and privileges away, much to the disgust of his fellow aristocrats.

'That was your uncle?'

'The red Károlyis. We don't talk about him. He did a lot of damage.' The count nodded, keeping the rest of that thought to himself.

His own father hadn't concerned himself with politics. He'd had more than enough to do with the palace and its 45,000 hectare estate – although that in itself had been massively reduced from the 200,000 hectares they'd had back in the nineteenth century.

'In fact the life I remember at Fót was rather austere, Calvinistic if you like. We weren't having a good time at the expense of serfs, as some of the history books like to suggest. There was the occasional ball, certainly, but we only lived in the smaller-roomed parts of the palace and the family maintained twenty-five social institutions for the poor and underprivileged. Personally, I don't like to cry after past fortunes, so I'm not in favour of recreating the aristocracy. I try to tell the young people it wasn't like it is portrayed in books, but then we have the occasional busload of old ladies from the countryside who come through – the municipality asks us to host them – and you overhear them saying to each other "You see, they got everything back."'

A knock on the door, and the count went to deal with something to do with parking; a film crew was using parts of the building to create a docu-drama about the Revolution that had created all those tormented children. When he returned, he told how he'd been involved in the previous year's marches in central Budapest – a commemoration of that same 1956 Revolution which had itself turned violent.

'The policemen hit me with their shields. It was just aggression, pure aggression.' He puffed on his pipe, which was co-operating at last. 'Then somebody I'd never seen before jumped out from the crowd and pulled me out from the middle of it all. "Mr Count, Mr Count, come quickly, come quickly." I think he thought there were people who would have loved the chance to take a pop at the aristocracy. And there may well have been. So it was probably wise.'

The count had got to the age where he didn't really care what people thought of him, so as we drank more gin, conversation became more scurrilous. We moved away from politics to the wider reaches of family connections in Hungary and abroad. 'Not every aristocrat is our friend just because he's an aristocrat. Aristocracy is a state of mind, nothing to do with money. Mind you, some of these locals, they can be so boring, sitting here talking about healthcare and haircuts.' His pronouncements began to swirl around in the ether, becoming more and more English as the gin tightened its grip, and the truly English combination of irony, humour and sangfroid meant it was hard to pinpoint his own personal opinion in the haze. But on Archduke Georg Habsburg, the son that Archduke Otto had posted to Hungary, he was unequivocal. 'When I meet him I'll tell him what I think of him, in the politest possible way.'

225

And on the subject of Hungary's relationship with its neighbour to the east he had strong words, too. 'Frankly, Romania is not a nationality, it's an occupation.'

Not every aristocrat had escaped, or had wanted to escape, the closing of the Iron Curtain. A few of them, including Count László's wayward uncle, prime minister Mihály Károlyi, had seen the communist point of view. Mihály's circle had included a certain Count George Paloczi-Horvath, a name that Count László didn't appear to recognize when I brought it up, but by that point in the evening we were flying along on a magic carpet of gin. In his book *The Undefeated*, Paloczi-Horvath described his Hungarian family as being top-heavy with representatives of the old feudal times, painting a picture of red-faced gentlemen with Gargantuan appetites and of thin-lipped matrons who peered out into the confusing world beyond the estate boundaries with expressions of total bewilderment. In his childhood, Paloczi-Horvath's elderly uncles had talked more Latin (a mark of class) than German or Hungarian and regarded non-nobles as a kind of subspecies of humanity, and yet families like his had relied on free peasant labour to keep them afloat. It was considered undignified for a noble actually to work, so their lives were essentially idle, apart from parties, banquets and horses. As for Paloczi-Horvath himself, 'my heart ached for Hungarian peasants'. Mind you, it couldn't have ached too much, because during the war years and after he had seized the opportunity to retreat to London and move in society circles with other political exiles, including ex-Prime Minister Károlyi.

He did, however, make his sympathy for the peasantry widely known, and eventually he was invited back to Budapest by the Soviet-appointed government to edit a new weekly magazine. Describing himself as 'in love with communism' and therefore blind to all its faults, he'd accepted the Party as one would accept a wise and severe father. It seemed to him to be the best insurance against the return of fascism, and a high-minded way in which to build a world without wars and poverty. By now thoroughly indoctrinated and promoted to control the media output, he 'thought, talked and felt in clichés'. But the Party was never comfortable with his aristocratic origins and his overseas contacts with that émigré society back in London, so eventually the AVO – the secret police – came for him during one of its systematic purges.

That evening in September 1949 he'd been listening to music with his girlfriend when they knocked at his door. They'd taken him to AVO headquarters at 60 Andrássy Avenue, which today lives on as the House of Terror museum. Its liftshaft is papered with pictures of executed *kulaks* (upper- and middle-class landowners) like him, some of whom had probably been in the building at the same time as he was. The cells are still in the basement, and it is easy to visualize how he had had to lie so that his wrists could be seen from the spyhole, because 'in this building we do the killing, nobody else'. He'd been made to type his life story repeatedly, and not allowed to sleep, for three weeks, while around him the basement filled with groans, whimpers, shrill shouts, screaming and sobbing, sounds you can still hear (simulated) in the House of Terror today. At one point his interrogators had made him stand facing the wall for days on end watching 'prisoner cinema', a state of starved hallucination where the grain of the wall started to move of its own accord, acting out scenes from his past. Then came the proper torture, with piercing pain for week after week, punctuated briefly by a visit to the sanatorium to prevent actual death. The biggest danger was insanity, so he occupied himself by re-living his life, backwards, forwards and any which way he could. The only indication of the passing of the seasons was when his guards grew either more suntanned, or less.

Eventually he was moved out of Andrássy Avenue into the brutal Gyujtofoghaz jail. Here the punishment of choice was the short iron, where the prisoner's body was contorted as far as possible and then manacled to an iron bar. The first scream was one of surprise that something so simple could hurt so unbearably. Then came the groaning and sobbing, then the piercing cries expressing utter terror and agony, shriller and thinner as the guard shortened the manacle and jumped on the prisoner's back. Eventually those listening for the first time wouldn't have identified the final cries as coming from a human being at all.

Many didn't survive the short iron. The elderly would suffer incurable injuries at once, and others had heart attacks. And yet it was a punishment meted out for the simplest of offences: taking your cap off too slowly when passing a guard or dropping your bowl while waiting in line for food. The worst of it was that these people suffering like this had never done anything wrong in the first place.

Along with his cellmates, Paloczi-Horvath tried to work out where communism had left the rails. Many of his fellow prisoners had been great leaders from the early days, idealists and supreme thinkers. Now they were having to deal with the fact that the whole edifice of their ideology, the grand cathedral of their faith, had collapsed on their heads. The system that they'd created had destroyed the individual, his internal integrity, his self-respect, honesty and correctness.

In prison, they tried to hang on to what they had been passionate about, debating how to fix it and how to make it work again. They realized that leaders cared only for power, that 'dictatorship of the proletariat' had become just a smokescreen to hide dictatorship of the Party bosses, that communism had been pure only when it had been in opposition. The Communist Party in power was neither communist nor a party; instead it was an apparatus in the hands of dictators whose power was based on the secret police, and if those dictators wanted to retain their power they needed to strike first, to terrorize any potential rivals.

Eventually, in the early 1950s, the system had begun to liberalize as the Soviets became distracted by America. The prisoners were allowed to write to their families and to have two visits a year, their first contact with the outside world. Mostly both parties had aged so fast and become so emaciated as to be physically unrecognizable, and the guards had to introduce spouses to each other – 'This is your husband.' 'This is your wife.' Both would then spend the rest of the visit clutching the wire netting that separated them and weeping, silently, having failed to find any suitable words.

Paloczi-Horvath was finally released in September 1954. For the next two years the system continued to liberalize, with writers beginning to be bold and getting away with it. It seemed that anything could be written, everything discussed, and those who had once been hanged as arch-criminals were being disinterred and reburied as heroes. Then came the mass marches of the 1956 Revolution, the fighting, the brief ecstatic victory, and the brutal Soviet return, ushering in a new, stricter inquisitional regime in a violated city where there was no food, no money and no hope.

During those difficult days there were only three types of people: those who had been in jail, those who were in jail, and those who were about to be in jail. Paloczi-Horvath escaped. He didn't want to be in jail again, and once over the Austrian border he got on a train for England with hundreds of others. Thereafter he joined the ranks of postcard-writers whose cards make a colourful collage on the Terror House wall in 60 Andrássy Avenue. All he could do was look on from a distance and send his friends and family his best wishes, written on the back of a card showing a red double-decker bus and sunny skies.

The Terror House apart, I could still detect a frisson of communism in the Budapest air. Buildings were still pockmarked with gunfire if you looked above street level. Streets were still underlit at night, heavy with the dust of history, and shops still fought shy of overly ostentatious window displays. Men with bushy eyebrows still stared distrustfully out from the hatches of pavement kiosks, wordlessly handing you your change, and there was still that burly leather-jacketed individual at the railway station who stood alone, scanning the passengers with the sort of intimidatory self-confidence that could only be born out of some secret power.

Of course a great deal has changed. The Liberty statue may have stayed, but four hundred streets have been renamed in two decades, and most of communism's mighty statuary has either been destroyed or is rusting away ignominiously in a field to the south-west of the city. Some of the street-renaming and statue-felling went hand in hand: the Stalin statue in Dózsa György út was pulled down on the first day of the 1956 Revolution, leaving just his boots in place, and for years afterwards Dózsa György út became known as 'Boots Square'.

Those very boots are now out at that south-western field, aka Statue Park, along with figures of Marx, Engels and dozens of others. Here they still strain every sinew in exhortation, addressing imaginary crowds across a scrubby patch of land. They raise massive clenched fists on muscular forearms in mid-exaltation, shouting across each other. Where once they'd addressed hundreds of thousands of Party faithfuls, now their only regular audience was composed of uninterested rabbits. Yet their power hadn't quite left them: one (unidentifiable) figure in this stertorous silence was wrapped in green plastic, still too potent, even in bronze, to be released back into the community.

While the size and frozen dynamism of many of the bigger pieces still had an unmistakable power, I found others on a more human scale, leaders whose names I didn't recognize but who were now marooned on the turf, behind whom I could creep up and mutter things like 'Ah well, better luck next time.'

By the exit stood a little gift shop where you could buy a mug with the legend 'coffee & communism = coffunism', a tin containing the 'last breath of communism', and a selection of revolutionary socks. I decided against carrying the last breath of communism with me, fearful of letting it escape by mistake in deepest Romania, with unpredictable consequences. And on my way out I caught the eye of Lenin, who stood over the entrance. Unlike all the others inside, he didn't look stern or demanding. In fact, if he hadn't been made of metal, I'd have said there was a twinkle in his eye. I got the distinct impression that it had all been a bit of a joke, really, this communism lark, and that he'd been surprised that so many people had taken him so seriously.

14

On Laguna to the Drava

Five days later I was on horseback, moving southwards across Hungary towards the Croatian border. I'd like to say I was flying along on a fleet-footed mare, but my rising trot was off-kilter to lessen the impact on assorted sores in sensitive places, and the reluctant Laguna, despite her water-friendly name, was goosestepping erratically to avoid stepping in puddles. We did not make a graceful pair.

I'm no horseman, but Patrick Leigh Fermor had left Budapest on horseback to cross the Hungarian plain on a horse supplied by yet another of his aristocratic contacts, so I'd wanted to do the same. And I'm pleased to say that my puddle-swerving people-carrier also had noble connections.

After making enquiries in all the right places, I'd come west from Budapest by train to meet up with Count József Hunyady on the shores of Lake Balaton, Hungary's inland sea. The count was another of that younger set of aristocrats who'd returned to Budapest in the 1990s, and there he'd met and married a fellow returnee of equal pedigree – Countess Katalin Almásy – and the two had set up home back where the Hunyadys had once been big landowners. There they'd restarted the family vineyard, opened an upmarket B&B, and helped establish a long-distance riding business that took advantage of 150 miles of green corridor that stretched between Balaton and the Drava river. It wasn't exactly along the banks of the Danube, but it would have to do.

Long-distance horseback travel has all but vanished from modern Europe since Leigh Fermor's day, now that roads are given over to cars and now that wayside hotels have turned their paddocks into swimming pools and stables into spas. But horses are to Hungary what paprika is to goulash, and have been ever since Attila the Hun and the Magyar tribesmen arrived on horseback from the Asian steppes. This is, after all, the nation that invented 'Hussar!', the flamboyant cavalryman and drinking cry which derives from the word *huszadik*, meaning twentieth; traditionally every twentieth man in the village was pressed into military service for the empire.

These days the cavalrymen are gone, although Hungarian schoolchildren are still encouraged to 'sit up straight like a Hussar'. Hungarian horsemen still go through the motions for tourists, particularly the herdsmen or *csikós* of the *puszta*, the Hungarian plain, whose horseback skills date back to when they were semi-nomadic outlaws making a living from rustling other people's livestock and then evading their pursuers. On the flatness of the *puszta*, with very little cover, that usually involved training their horses to lie down at the crack of a giant whip.

The climax of these tourist shows is usually the Puszta Five, named after a romantic painting by an Austrian artist in which the rider stands on the backs of two horses, holding the reins to a further three, ostensibly as an express way of delivering the post. But the Puszta Five is a fantasy: five horses don't go faster than one, and the painting didn't explain where the post itself was meant to go, unless it was under the herdsman's hat.

Happily, I didn't have to do any virtuoso manoeuvres on Laguna. My experience of horses is that they are dangerous at both ends and uncomfortable in the middle, and are principally used by well-to-do mothers as a diversionary tactic to stop their teenage daughters discovering boys and getting pregnant. But knowing that I wanted a horseback element to this journey, I'd taken four riding lessons in London before setting out, at a cost that made me blanch. The riding school declared that I would need around twenty lessons to get to the level required for a journey of several days with galloping included, but that was just avarice disguised as health and safety. By the end of my four lessons I can't say I was confident, but I knew the basics I had to do in order to survive.

Count József had picked me up from the station in an ageing white Opel with a child seat in the back. A mild-mannered, unassuming, reticent, academic-looking man in his mid-forties, he spoke English and German to his guests, French to his wife, Italian to his daughter and Hungarian to his neighbours. He knew the Leigh Fermor books well, he said, and although there was a Hunyady mentioned in them, it was not his branch of the family. It was János Hunyadi, the fifteenth-century warrior hero who'd routed the Turks outside Belgrade and was proclaimed the saviour of Christendom. His son, Matthias Corvinus, had presided over a real purple patch in Hungarian history, creating the Hussars, with and without exclamation marks, along the way.

To his credit, József didn't claim any reflected Hunyady glory, and had no lordly airs or graces. His family had been big landowners whose life in the 1930s had been busy with guests and horses. The original eighteenth-century family manor house, the size of a decent French chateau, was now a sanatorium for the mentally ill, and the security guard at the gateway gave no sign of recognizing the count as we drew up alongside. I'd been anticipating a passage in *The Glance of Countess Hahn-Hahn (down the Danube)* in which Peter Esterhazy described revisiting his family's castle and encountering grey gatekeepers who did so little work that dust sifted from their faces when they looked up. When Esterhazy had made his identity known 'all three of them sprung to attention as if possessed, clicking their heels like in some film and staring at me with their chins slightly raised . . . the most senior among them kept repeating, with tears in his eyes: "Your Excellency, Your dear, dear Excellency". And he stroked the top of my head.'

Sadly, none of this happened for us. Maybe it was the ageing car and the child seat, or maybe the self-effacing count didn't even drop his name into the conversation. However, he was persuasive enough to get us through the gate, despite the gatekeeper's anxiety that the director of the sanatorium was due and our presence would get him into trouble. We could go up the drive, he said, but not get out of the car. So we sat for a while in the white Opel in front of Hunyady's decaying family pile. It was half burned down, and its once-formal gardens were over-grown and full of wandering lost souls in nylon track-suits, rocking, jerking, mouthing and staring into space. Seeing the car and the people in it, one of them came and stared at us from right up close to the windscreen, clutch-ing a transistor radio to his ear.

As we left, Count József explained how his family had started to lose their property in the land reforms of the 1920s, and the manor house had finally been expropriated in 1944. From then on his father had led a wildly improbable and romantic life, despite a very difficult start being pulled out of the rubble from beside the body of his dead mother during the bombing of Budapest. In 1945 he'd been spirited away to relatives in Austria where he'd found work as a farmhand and primitive accommodation in a ruined castle, eventually becoming a showjumper and member of the Austrian Olympic team. From Austria he'd gone to Egypt to be the tutor to the Albanian royal family, who were living there in exile. In the 1950s he'd arrived in England, in pursuit of an English girl he'd met in Egypt, and became a stablehand in racing stables in Newmarket. A couple of years later he was in France, buying and selling racehorses, where he met an Italian girl, fell in love and moved to run a racehorse stable in Italy, where József was born and grew up.

An extraordinary life-itinerary like this was by no means unusual amongst former aristocracy, for whom the world became a post-war pinball machine. They came careering out of Eastern Europe pursued by the Russian bear, bounced from nation to nation, profession to profession, until finally many of them disappeared from sight into the world's furthest pockets. Only a few hit the trigger of 1989, to come rocketing back into the jaws of their own land and collect a hereditary bonus. Count József was one of them.

'I'd had no exposure at all to Hungary for a very long time,' he declared, once he'd completed his father's whirlwind CV. 'I don't even remember him talking about it. He had no desire for his children to go back. That chapter was finished in his life, he'd started again. He didn't even find it useful for us to remain in contact with the wider family.'

But then, after 1989, word started to spread of people getting their property back, and József, who by this time was working for a wine-importing company in Italy, visited the land of his ancestry for the first time. The feeling of affinity was instantaneous. 'I liked it very much. I was conservation-minded, and I saw how unspoiled it was, how affordable. I saw the potential.'

At the time, post-communist land restitution in Hungary was based on a voucher system. The state's defunct co-operative farms had been divided in half, with one half distributed to their former employees and the other half auctioned off to local villagers. Ex-landowning families like the Hunyadys who could prove their lineage were given vouchers which they then used in these local auctions.

With vouchers to the value of £13,000 plus his own personal savings, József had painstakingly assembled around 2,000 acres of land, section by section, auction by auction. Few other former landowners had his dedication. Mostly they came back briefly, claimed what they could and then sold it to the highest bidder before returning as quickly as they could to their bright, shiny new lives overseas, thus confirming the locals' low opinion of the aristocracy as money-grubbing wasters who only had their own interests at heart.

But József persisted, despite the lack of interest of the rest of his family and the suspicion of his neighbours. Amongst his new acquisitions was an old farm complex just outside the small town of Keleviz. Here he rebuilt the old farmhouse into Lehner Manor, and although it was diminutive compared to the property his family had lost, nevertheless its lofty ceilings, tribe of dogs, books, oil paintings and Biedermeier furniture all contributed to a sense of old-fashioned country living. There were riding boots by the back door, saddles on the banister and stables across the fields. *Between the Woods and the Water* was on his bookshelf, next to biographies of Lenin, poetry anthologies, bird books and a treatise on the consequences of American economic policy; the reverential way he talked about Leigh Fermor suggested that he saw the books as a record of how life had once been lived and a (partial) blueprint of how it should be.

At dinner with his wife Katalin, who was tall, raw-boned and seemed rather tense, we discussed how one of her distant relatives had entered popular mythology as the hero of *The English Patient*. The film's portrait of Count László de Almásy as a badly burned war hero trying to make sense of his life turned out to have been very overromanticized. In reality the count had been a spy who'd worked for anyone who'd paid him, and given that he was rampantly homosexual, he would have had no interest whatever in Kristin Scott Thomas.

'Oh, I can understand that,' I muttered. 'But to have no interest in Juliette Binoche, now that's criminal.'

Somewhere outside, an owl hooted. József saw me flinch and smiled thinly.

'It makes strange sounds. Sometimes I don't know if it is my daughter in great pain.'

Katalin, too, looked uncomfortable. 'Here it is dreadful in winter,' she murmured. 'You can't go outside for more than twenty minutes, it gets so cold. I'd so much rather be in Budapest.'

The stables where I first met Laguna were attached to a nearby manor house that had been converted into a sock factory during the communist era and was now tenanted by a nature conservation organization. The count was president of this Green Corridor Association, which looked after the horses and paid the guides. My guide was Tamas, an elfin-faced, ponytailed young man riding a frisky and elegant Arab stallion called Sandor, of whom he was very proud. Tamas was composed, not particularly expressive and probably a touch solitary in character, communicating better with his horses than with people. When I expressed my doubts about Laguna, who seemed stout and small, he leapt to the horse's defence. Laguna was half Lipizzaner, he said, and very tough, despite her seventeen years, which in horse terms is practically bus-pass. He did, however, give me his riding crop, and made sure he was standing in front of Laguna when he did so.

'She knows you've got it. So now you won't have to use it,' he said.

We'd started at the lakeshore at a bird-ringing station where a stunningly beautiful girl with graceful long fingers kept a daylight vigil over a filigree net that snaked out into the shallows through a corridor of reeds. When she wasn't picking frantic little feathered bundles out of her net and clipping tiny tags around their legs, cooing reassuring words, she sat on the doorstep of a little stone house by the water's edge and sang sad songs to a stork called Gunter, who patrolled up and down outside. She'd nursed the fledgling Gunter back to health after he'd been injured by gunshot, and now the stork was very protective of her in return, and more than willing to attack any man or beast who approached the cottage threshold. Something in his small storkly brain had clearly latched on to the fact that his mistress was both attractive and potentially vulnerable, and it was his duty to play the part of the protective male.

The first bridlepath we followed led away from the

lakeshore through verges of hollyhocks and cornflowers into small woodlands of dappled acacia, oak and pine. Tamas, who wasn't generally talkative unless it was on the subject of horses, confessed to feeling 'quite second-hand', by which I assumed he meant hungover, so he said we wouldn't be going fast. 'You will have time to create a partnership with your horse.'

Personally, I'd been thinking along the lines of a dictatorship, but Laguna was sublimely indifferent to my presence, stomping along in Sandor's wake, which gave me plenty of opportunity to think about getting my riding right in between ducking overhanging branches. It was all very well spending an hour in the saddle in Richmond Park, but five days on the hoof was a different prospect, so I ran myself through the key points, trying to direct my weight right down into my heels and timing my rising trot to Laguna's short stride. On the occasions I got it wrong and came crashing down on to her back I mentally apologized to the poor creature. Tamas had warned me that when he unsaddled the horses in the evenings he would be looking for sores and breaks in the skin. If Laguna looked to be suffering through my inept riding, we would have a serious problem on our hands.

Alongside us, amongst the trees, lurked the occasional fencepost, wild vine and overgrown cemetery, indicating where forest villages had once stood. The communists hadn't liked forest dwellers because they'd been too independent-minded, self-sustaining and hard to control, so they'd forced them to move out into bigger villages on proper roads where they'd be integrated into the mainstream.

These resettlement villages all tended to follow a similar pattern. There'd be a crucifix at the village entry, marking the beginning of a thin metalled road which had yet to be widened for traffic (because there wasn't any), and which deteriorated to rutted track again once it reached the village limits. On either side of it ran a wide green sward with benches in the shade and the occasional ancient Trabant becalmed in a rising tide of floribunda. Most of the houses were squat and square, with shuttered windows, gardens full of roses, vines above the terrace, chickens out the back, and doves, swallows and wood pigeons in the fruit trees. The main street would invariably be called Petöfi utca or Kossuth utca after Hungary's national heroes, and the big event of the day was the early minibus to town and the mid-morning visit of the gas-cylinder man or the haberdasher's van, when women in housecoats would emerge to exchange the news in mid-street. 'These women,' said Tamas, 'if you do something tomorrow, they know about it today.'

There was also usually a single village shop, identifiable more by the open door and the crates of empty beer bottles than by any sign or window display, with a cavernous drinking den next door, probably called a Büfe or possibly, more pretentiously, an Etterem, which might also have sandwiches and crisps in case the beer drinkers forgot to eat. And somewhere along the road's length would be the village hall, identifiable by the little flag sticking out from the wall and the big-bellied old gent sitting outside, staring at passersby and staying close to the seat of power, in case the mayor needed his advice. The mayors in these places were key figures, democratically elected, and a good mayor adept at securing government (and now EU) grants could make the difference between a flourishing community and one that was dying on its feet.

We'd been going a couple of hours when Tamas, who always rode up ahead, turned in his saddle and asked whether I was willing to try a canter. Whether I was ready or not turned out to be immaterial, because no sooner had he said the word than Laguna was off, at buttock-pummelling speed. 'Give her long reins, let her run,' called Tamas over his shoulder, but it was all I could do to hold myself on with my knees, let alone think about any form of horse control. The fact that I was on top and she was underneath was more a matter of historical precedent than expertise, and I thought it sensible to try to keep it that way. I couldn't hope to try to steer as well as keep my feet in the stirrups, but Laguna really didn't need me to do anything, even when it came to stopping, because when Tamas held up his hand after a couple of minutes she slowed instantly to a walk again. I was trembling from head to toe, but at least I hadn't fallen off.

In Gyötapuszta we had lunch of brown bread and *körözött* (a mixture of cottage cheese, sour cream, paprika, garlic and onion), a delicacy that indelicately repeated on me for much of the rest of the afternoon, especially during the rising trots. We pushed on further, trying a couple more canters through woodland where the sunlight danced from tree to tree, but all I could think about was the pain in my knees, the ache up my spine and the damage that I was undoubtedly doing to Laguna's back. By the time we'd reached our first overnight stop, in a hunting lodge near Somogyfajsz, I was truly concerned about my ability to continue. The distance we'd covered had been little more than 25 kilometres, and much of it at a walking pace, but we'd have to do far more cantering and even galloping in order to complete some of the longer days that lay ahead. I wasn't sure I could.

Lying thinking about it that night, I saw myself jogging the remaining 125 kilometres, with Laguna as a pack pony by my side. Next morning, sore in all sorts of unfamiliar ways and feeling far worse than Tamas' 'quite second-hand', I resolved to make some changes. I'd been to see Laguna the previous evening and noticed that Tamas had sprayed bits of her back with a green dye. Over breakfast he confirmed that this was what I thought it was: antiseptic, to stop her wounds becoming infected.

'Can we go on?'

Tamas shrugged. He wasn't giving much away. 'I think so.'

I told him my plan. I was abandoning the American-style, sit-deep-in-the-saddle cantering that I'd been taught at scandalous expense in Richmond Park, and instead planned to stand up in the stirrups over the horse's neck, like jockeys do. Tamas seemed to approve, although with him it was hard to tell.

We started out slowly, across open grazing with a herd of grey, long-horned cattle to our left and traditional *racka* sheep to our right. There was a cowherd with the cattle and a shepherd with the sheep, and as we came abreast of them these two men were standing in the no-man's-land between the two herds, shouting at each other. They included Tamas in their heated debate.

'So what was all that?' I asked when we'd ambled on out of earshot.

'The shepherd had fallen asleep and his sheep had moved into the cattle's land, so the cowherd had brought them back.'

'That's kind of him.' I wasn't sure why it was such a cause for concern.

'That cowherd knows lots of bad words,' mused Tamas. With a bit of further prodding it turned out he knew these men, who were out every day in the same pastures. The shepherd had a reputation as a heavy drinker.

'When he sees a glass of wine, he drinks it. And in our pubs we have very cheap wine, some of it not even made with grapes.' Tamas shuddered, but didn't elaborate. Anyway, it turned out the cowherd always took the moral high ground and was forever complaining about the shepherd's drunken state, but the latter, during his waking and sober moments, was a good herdsman and the sheep were in good condition. It would not be easy to find a good replacement.

Another hour further on we watered the horses at a sweep-well, a cross between a nodding donkey and a medieval siege machine with a giant counterbalanced beam that was surprisingly easy to handle once you'd got the general idea. And shortly afterwards we came across more old technology in the form of a rusty Soviet-made 4x4 waiting at a crossroads of sandy tracks. The driver leant out of the window and said something surly to Tamas which I could tell wasn't good news.

'Ah.' Tamas turned to me with an awkward grin. 'We need to go fast now or they'll shoot us.' My heart skipped a beat; was this the Cold War come alive again?

'They're hunting here,' he continued. 'And they don't always shoot straight. In any case, my horse is faster than a bullet. But Laguna might need the stick.' I think that was a joke, but he'd careered off before I had a chance to check.

For an hour he pushed the pace hard. Whereas before we'd been mainly walking with the occasional canter and trot, now we were mainly cantering with the occasional walk. Laguna pushed on doggedly, trying hard to keep up with Sandor, and I hung on grimly, holding hard to her mane in my new position with my head just behind her ears, as I'd seen it done at the races. Initially this new stance felt perilously unsafe (where exactly were we connected?) but gradually I also began to feel more at one with what the horse was doing, and I found myself whispering imprecations – mainly to myself to get it right – into her ear. I had no idea what sort of landscape we passed through in that hour; each canter felt like it started in one country and ended in another. Each time Laguna kicked ahead I felt as if I was entering another tunnel, with daylight a long way away, but each time was also very slightly easier than the last.

Eventually we reached another sandy crossroads and Tamas slackened off. 'That's it,' he said, 'we're clear of it now. You OK?'

When I got my breath back I said I was. I even ventured to suggest that I thought I might be getting better, not doing so much damage to rider or horse. Tamas nodded gravely. He'd been looking back regularly to make sure Laguna and I weren't too far behind, and he seemed to approve. 'We couldn't have done that yesterday.' It was tantamount to praise.

At the edge of the woodland were rows of shooting platforms on stilts, designed not as hides but to get the hunters substantially higher than their quarry. That way, if a bullet missed its target, it thudded harmlessly into the ground and not into one of the distant beaters or gamekeepers. Nevertheless every year brought its casualties. 'These hunters have money, big cars and run big international companies, so they don't obey the rules we Hungarians set for them,' said Tamas. He added that, in Germany, Hungary is promoted as 'the country where you can go to do what you like'. Including wounding gamekeepers.

'Besides, many of the clients are old and their eyesight is not so good.'

Irresponsible though these hunters' behaviour may be, the forest couldn't exist without them. If it wasn't for their revenue the trees would have to be chopped down for

245

timber and the land turned to fields. The luxury hunting lodges provided welcome employment, and even the local deer farms prospered from the hunting business.

'How so?'

'The hunting companies order extra animals from the farms and release them into the woods a month before the season starts.'

'Doesn't that make them a bit of a pushover?'

Tamas grinned. 'When you've paid all that money you need to kill something. You don't ask where it was brought up.'

That evening we stopped at the fish station at Boronka, a series of artificial lakes where carp were netted once a year and then trucked off to the fish-eaters of Italy and Spain. From the primitive fisherman's cottage, colder inside than out, you could look out over a layered pondscape with flatlands of lilypads in the foreground rising through reed grasslands via foothills of alder bushes to mountains of Scots pine behind. Tamas scythed a barrowful of grass for the horses, lit a fire to keep the mosquitoes away, and we listened to the frog chorus start with the sound of someone swinging on an old rusty gate. They were still singing away deep into the night as I struggled to find a position in my sleeping bag which allowed me to forget my suppliant, supplicant, suppurating butt.

By the third day the sky was rag-rolled, the reeds sibilant and the lake scurrying endlessly northwards, carrying messages for the wind. The good news was that the wounds on Laguna's back were not deteriorating, for which I whispered my thanks in her ear. Not being either of us in the first flush of youth, we both found it hard to get started in the morning, and she was easily distracted by potential snacks in the hedgerows, for which I couldn't really blame her. Those grassed forest tracks were an eternal temptation for a horse, a bit like asking a hungry teenager to march up and down the biscuit aisle at Tesco's.

As we were leaving Boronka Tamas pointed out a big dip in the ground by the last lake.

'Couple of years ago we dug some sand there to re-inforce the embankment, and found dead Germans. Seventeen of them.'

It had been part of the Eastern front. In the last months of the Second World War the Axis powers had made a futile last-ditch stand here against the advancing Russians, and in the hole the diggers had found bones, badges, tags, helmets, guns and grenades, all mixed together. One of the helmets had a small entry hole where the bullet had hit and a large exit hole where it had departed, and after a little searching they'd found the skull that had a similar small entry wound and large exit displacement. From the tags they could tell that the dead soldier had been only seventeen years old.

'What did you do with them all?'

'There's an organization. We called them and they came and did all the proper things. They seemed pleased at what we'd found. Those dead soldiers, they had brothers and sisters who never knew what happened to them, so now they had their answers.'

For a while our route followed the visible line of the trenches, which twisted and turned amongst the trees, slowly drowning in vegetation. I imagined the tree roots growing downwards through the debris of war, through bones, shrapnel, belt buckles, bits of water bottle and broken families, never to be reunited. I wondered whether the father of that woman I'd stayed with in Donauwörth, all those weeks before, was somewhere down there in the

247

cold earth – a fate you wouldn't wish on anyone, whatever uniform they were wearing.

'We didn't have a good war,' said Tamas, reflectively, after we'd been clipping along in silence for half an hour. 'Very few people around this part of Europe did. The Russians freed us from the Germans, but they also freed us from everything else we had.'

An hour later the vegetation changed again and we were amongst clean-limbed tall aspens with grass snakes on the path. Then the trees fell back and we emerged on to a large area of open grassland carpeted with daisies and adorned with red-and-black butterflies. I knew what was coming.

'So,' said Tamas, grinning at me over his shoulder. 'Now we see how fast Laguna can go.'

The rain started in the afternoon and continued for much of the next twenty-four hours in waves of thunderstorms, each one greeted by a chorus of enthusiastic treefrogs. Fortunately we'd already done the day's travel by the time it started, covering the ground much more quickly now that I had the confidence to gallop. So we hunkered down in the reed-thatched hall at the Petesmalom Reserve, another complex of fishponds, and I unrolled my sleeping bag on a mattress in the loft. I took advantage of the rain to read and rest, treating my sores with arnica cream. Meanwhile Tamas put on a wide-brimmed hat, stuck a big piece of deer liver on a giant fishhook and hurled it out into the middle of one of the ponds to try to catch a monster. Around him the sleeting rain drained all colour away from the landscape, leaving him just another tree stump in a two-dimensional world of silhouettes.

By the morning of the fourth day the skies had cleared and there was a new freshness in the air, but back in the saddle again it didn't feel as if I'd had a day of rest at all. My body ached all over, and the very first trot immediately undid any slight healing process that might have taken place. Laguna, on the other hand, felt frisky, at least by a plodder's standards.

This was the day I discovered her aversion to puddles. Previously we'd been travelling on dry, mostly sandy, tracks, but now the surface was liberally spattered with water and she would do anything to avoid getting her feet wet, even at a canter. Two days previously I wouldn't have survived these leaps and swerves, but now I clung on, with Tamas looking back on the corners like an engine driver's assistant checking the last coach was still attached to the train. I *was* still attached, even though I wasn't yet good enough to be Laguna's driver and force her to go straight.

The rain released the smell of wet acorns and dung, mixed with the musk of sweating horse. There were deer aplenty in the oakwoods, leaping away down the forest corridors, and I realized that I was now managing to notice my surroundings. At about midday we came upon a family of gypsies, collecting wood, but they didn't look up at us, and we in turn said nothing to them as we passed. Tamas was reluctant to talk about them, aware that Westerners are far more sympathetic to the general idea of gypsies than the people who actually live with them. He did say, however, that the communists hadn't wanted them wandering about and had forced them to settle in villages in order to absorb them into the system. In those days you were a threat to society if you were not working.

Despite the puddles we made good progress, reaching our next overnight stop, an empty schoolhouse in an abandoned village near Csokonyaviszonta, in the early afternoon. The village had grown up around an extensive farm once owned by the Széchényi family, but when the family went, the villagers had had to leave too. The grand farm buildings, plus a distillery that had manufactured vodka from potatoes, were all still there, but many of them were roofless and overgrown, a palace complex half hidden in shrubbery, an Angkor Wat of middle-European farming. Trees, instead of children, grew up inside the walls of farmworkers' cottages. Inside the stable blocks the symmetrical arches of muscular brickwork repeated over and over into the gloom, now home only to bats and owls. The factory walls had gaping holes in them where the old copper stills had been removed, complete, for their scrap-metal value, and only blackened patches on the walls remained from where the furnaces had once stood. I could imagine the Széchényis – possibly even Count István himself, he who'd put the Chain Bridge across the Danube – striding around these massive buildings on a tour of inspection. But what the aristocrats had built, the communists had left to rot.

Maybe it had been left to stand as a symbol of aristocratic exploitation, a brickwork embodiment of the popular sentiment expressed by national poet Petöfi that the nobility had built their wealth on the back of serfdom, as in the refrain of his scathing 'Song of a Magyar Nobleman': 'Peasants work until they die/A Magyar nobleman am I!' It was a sentiment echoed by my old friend George Palóczi-Horvath, whose graphic account of peasant life at the turn of the century described endless drudgery in appalling conditions for the benefit of morally corrupt landlords. Tenants were treated like animals, masters were legally allowed to hit servants between the ages of eleven and eighteen 'in such a way as does not cause a wound which does not heal within eight days', and unmarried girls were fair game for estate managers and the idle sons of the manor. In the latter part of the nineteenth century, when the peasantry had started to talk about rights and freedom, they had had their villages razed to the ground and had been asked to leave on a scale which far outnumbered the Highland Clearances. Around 1.5 million emigrated to America in the two decades between 1890 and 1914.

It seemed appropriate, therefore, that we slept out in the open that night, although the real reason had less to do with a display of solidarity with evicted peasantry and more to do with the dank, mouse-filled interior of the schoolroom. We found a couple of bedsteads which we dragged out to the fire, and we took it in turns to keep the latter going, all night long, both for its warmth and its deterrent effect on large mammals and mosquitoes. In the early morning there was still enough heat to brew a cup of coffee by placing a mug directly on the embers.

It was my last day on Laguna, and it was quickly over after that early start. We crossed a couple of railway lines and plunged into the overgrown border zone between Hungary and Croatia along the banks of the Drava river, a territory so remote as to be, in Hungarian terminology, 'beyond the back of God'. By the state of the wisp of a path it was plainly out of bounds for the usual forestry, hunting and wood-gathering activities. Eventually, after ducking through unkempt woodland and pushing through chest-high nettles, we were decanted on to a sandy spit of shore by the Drava itself, a surging, empty sheet of water, forested on either side as far as the eye could see, with no sign of either houses or boats.

'Funny how you always expect other countries to look instantly different,' I mused, out loud, looking at the far bank.

'Ah, but it *is* different,' said Tamas. 'Over there, ten years ago, they had a war.'

In celebration of our arrival he took Sandor off for a gallop through the Drava's shallows, but Laguna wasn't having any. She hadn't come all this way without getting her feet wet in order to surrender herself at the end. Tamas suggested I give her a bit of clip round the rump with the stick, but I demurred. I hadn't hit her once the whole week, and I wasn't about to start now. She had, after all, completed her part of the bargain. She'd carried an incompetent horseman across half the country without losing him once, which was a pretty good result. I feared that forcing her into the water might have pushed her good nature a step too far, and that if I so much as suggested it, then I would have been the one who ended up splashing around unwillingly in the shallows. I was under no illusions, because even after all those days in the saddle I was not, and never had been, anything more than a passenger.

15

Serbia: the Argo Gets New Crew

Antar and Marko were watching *Who Wants to Be a Millionaire?* on a foggy TV screen when the storm rolled over. It hit the steel decking over our heads with the sound of a thousand rebellious schoolchildren drumming their heels at going-home time, and zapped the would-be millionaires into a zillion green dots.

'Ach, there it goes again,' said Marko, slapping a meaty palm on the table with a chuckle. 'It'll be back in a minute. Serves us right for watching Croatian TV. Coffee? It's Turkish.'

I nodded, rose from the bench seat and climbed the steps to poke my head out into the deluge beyond the cabin door, into a scene that was straight out of Joseph Conrad's *Heart of Darkness*. It was dark, way past midnight, but still hot and humid. I was on a de-commissioned lighter that dated back to the early 1900s, chained to pilings on the Serbian side of the surging Danube. The river itself, churned with rain and the colour of greasy caramel, was only visible where it appeared in the yellow light cast from the cabin window. Apart from the empty flit boat moored alongside the lighter, we were all alone on the water. Gloomy shadows of trees crowded the bank in either direction above us, tossing restlessly under a relentless assault from the darkness above. But beyond that I could see nothing; the rain had effectively isolated the lighter in its own little world. Or it had until a fork of lightning illuminated the distant Croatian shore and revealed just how much river there was out there.

My eye was pulled back to the bank above me by the flickering arc of a spent cigarette butt as it glowed briefly and died. I knew there was a border policeman sitting up there, in a windowless watchhouse between the trees. If I listened hard I could just about hear the jingle of his transistor radio above the surge of rain. Apart from his cigarettes, it was the only entertainment he had to last him through the night.

I pulled my head in and climbed back down the stairs, returning to a welcoming fug of hot gas, sweet coffee, nicotine and unwashed men.

'Nothing.'

Antar grinned a chipped grin that spoke of a boisterous past. 'Be patient, my friend. Another hour, mebbe two. You need to learn how to wait on the Danube. You're lucky it's Attila, he's fast. Wid a Ukrainain, you could be three or four hours more.'

'Ah-ha!' interrupted Marko, triumphantly. He'd been working on the TV set, and now a green, ghostly image of *Who Wants to Be a Millionaire?* was beginning to reappear as the old valves staged a recovery.

'Dey summer storms,' explained Antar, 'dey only last few minutes.' And it was true, the outside noise was already beginning to relent.

I told myself to relax. After all, twelve hours earlier I had plodded into Serbia with only a vague idea what might happen next, and now here I was with a long boat journey within my grasp. Antar was right, I had been very lucky. Again.

I had always wanted to do part of my journey on the water, but I'd long since abandoned the idea of having my own boat. After what I'd seen of them upriver, I'd also discounted joining one of the passenger cruisers which worked the Danube, fattening their human cargo for the grave. So the only other option was to hitch a ride on a freight barge, and with that in mind I'd called up a few companies who ran barge fleets, but my explanations had usually been interrupted mid-flow as the person on the other end hung up. I couldn't blame them. What earthly benefit could it be to a freight-barge company to have a travel writer on board?

But then one German ship-owner made a suggestion. I should wait at a downriver customs point, he said, where all boats have to do their cross-border paperwork, and speak to the captains directly, because it would be their decision whether or not to take on a passenger. And it was he who suggested I do it in Serbia, on the basis that it was outside the EU, cowboy country, and 'anything could happen there'.

And so I'd left Tamas and Laguna waiting by the Drava for a horsebox to take them home, and headed east to cross the Danube into this 'cowboy country', walking into it across one of the most godforsaken no-man's-lands in Europe. This was the frontier between southern Hungary and the part of Serbia called Vojvodina, one of two troublesome provinces (the other being Kosovo) of the former Yugoslavia. It was midday, but the heat was already so intense that the air above the road rippled and swirled, and by the time I came abreast of the border guard in his cabin I was lacquered with sweat.

He took his time leafing through my passport. Border crossings were infrequent here, crossings on foot were rare, and British passports practically extinct. All three together were plainly worthy of special consideration.

'Where are you going?'

'Bezdan.'

His eyebrows climbed towards his hairline and he jerked his thumb over his shoulder. '*Bezdan?*'

I agreed, not sure whether to be dismayed at his intonation or grateful that he made it sound so close. He shrugged and handed my passport back. There was no reason to detain me any longer, despite the unlikely destination. As I walked on into Serbia I remembered back to Ulm and to Franz Flock's description of how he and his family had been forced to camp out, at the end of the Second World War, after border guards refused to let them back into the country of their birth. It had been this very same crossing, and it hadn't got much friendlier.

During the break up of Yugoslavia, Vojvodina had come to be regarded as a potential liability by Belgrade. Its ethnic mix, with six official languages (Serbian, Hungarian, Romanian, Slovak, Croatian and Macedonian) was a hangover from the days before empire was split into nations, and its uneasy relationship with the rest of Serbia meant that it was a prime candidate for secession. Large numbers of Serbian troops had been garrisoned here to stamp on any separatist tendencies.

Belgrade had good reason to want to hang on to it, because the province is hugely fertile country, so fertile that Empress Maria Theresa – she who'd initiated that Swabian migration from Ulm – had ordered the construction of a massive canal system for easier access to its grain fields, a canal system that had been part designed by Gustav Eiffel's office in Paris. In more recent years, before the Balkan war, the Danube riverbank in Vojvodina had been a place where Serbs would come to stay in holiday cottages, eat fish paprika soup and muck about in boats on the canals. But now those canals were sadly dilapidated, massively overgrown and largely unnavigable, with broken lock gates, defunct shipyards and crumbled wharves. It was a green, watery ruin that would have had great tourism potential if it had been almost anywhere else in Europe, but here it had been left to rot.

A shipping agent called Branko who spoke good German had picked me up from the village and taken me down to the shore, pointing out the careless damage the Serb tanks had done to the shoreline tracks and buildings. They'd knocked corners off houses, destroyed trees and churned up hardcore tracks like badly behaved joyriders. There was no money to fix any of it, even if there'd been any official desire to do so, so it all remained just as the army had left it, with only nature trying to cover the worst of the scars.

Bezdan's 'port' comprised a solitary pier with the old lighter attached, a half-ruined policeman's watchhouse and the brick-built customs house, which had started life as a pumping station for the canals. In theory there was a twenty-four-hour shop and twenty-four-hour petrol supply here, too, but all had closed at the start of the war and not reopened. Now you couldn't even get fresh water.

'Captains get what they want at Mohács,' shrugged Branko, the Yugo-agent. 'They have to wait there anyway.' Branko chain-smoked, looked as if he hadn't slept for days and had a big scab at the centre of his forehead.

I didn't dare ask him what he'd done to himself, but from his demeanour it looked as if it was still giving him a splitting headache.

Mohács was the customs port upriver, on the Hungarian side of the border. By all accounts it was a log-jam of a place for freight barges, where pompous customs officers enforced the letter of EU law to the minutest degree, aware that they were the new defenders of the European Community. During the break-up of Yugoslavia, Mohács customs had gone through boats with a fine-tooth comb to check that nothing was on board that broke the sanctions imposed on Serbia, a process called, innocently, REVISION. The name had stuck, and now Bezdan called its process REVISION too, although it was nothing like the Mohács operation. Captains hated the bureaucracy and the delay of the Hungarian port, said Branko, so he and his team did their best to make Bezdan's REVISION a far more pleasant experience.

When I described my own uncomfortable crossing of the border, he frowned. 'I am a Hungarian. When I was a child this area was all Hungarian and German. The Germans, of course, have gone and now I need a visa to go to Hungary, even though I'm Hungarian. It's crazy. And when I go, the Hungarians treat me like shit because they think I want to live there. I don't. Why should I? I am happy here.' He didn't make it sound very convincing.

He had all sorts of plans for the port at Bezdan. He wanted to create a restaurant, a café and a food shop for all those yachts that would be coming downriver now that Europe was becoming one continent again. But by the time skippers had finally completed the infuriating paperwork at Mohács they were champing at the bit to get on, and all they wanted from Bezdan was an official stamp and a pat on the back to send them on their way, as quickly as possible.

'Do the skippers' logs get checked?' I asked, remembering Captain Fenzl's talk of safety and the need to regulate a captain's hours.

Branko flicked his cigarette away and shook his head. 'A captain is responsible for his own safety,' he growled. 'It's no business of ours.'

'And do you think one would take me on?'

'In Serbia everything is possible. We'll have to speak to them for you. But you must be patient. Sometimes we have no ships for hours and hours. In this business, there is a lot of sitting around.'

Which was how I had ended up with Antar and Marko on the lighter. They were Branko's flit-boat crew, and nearing the end of a two-day shift they were high on sleep deprivation, Turkish coffee and strong cigarettes. Their job was to listen in on radio exchanges between river traffic and the harbourmaster and then sally out on the flit boat to meet incoming vessels to expedite the whole customs procedure in return for an agent's fee. I'd watched them do a couple of runs during the afternoon, followed by the stately procession of uniformed officials – the harbourmaster, the customs officer and the border policeman – who'd troop aboard the subject boat, disappear below and then reappear half an hour later clutching carrier bags, their REVISION complete.

'A present,' said Antar, vaguely, in answer to my question about the carrier bags. 'Everybody gives presents on the Danube.'

Branko had reappeared again after dark. I'd seen him a couple of times in the course of the day and each time he'd shaken his head wearily, asking me to be patient. But now he had news, and it was good.

'Attila is coming. Attila Munkas on the *Argo*. He's my friend, he says he will take you. Come, we need to get you some food.'

And he'd taken me into Bezdan where I'd bought armfuls of pasta and a bottle of brandy. So now I was waiting with Antar and Marko, and trying to be patient.

Not that it was dull on the old lighter. The two Serbs were almost as excited at the prospect of my long river journey as I was, and they'd set out to be entertaining, trying to translate some of the questions on *Who Wants to be a Millionaire?* for my benefit.

Antar was the most unlikely of flit-boat captains, despite looking the part with a chest like a barrel and hands like meatsafes. He crackled with energy, speaking an eccentric colloquial English which he said he'd learned in the 'arts undieworld' when he was trying to be a 'jetset music-man'. He winked at me. 'Busking,' he whispered. He was a chain-smoking vegetarian, and when he got fed up with the TV he would turn it off with a flourish of disgust, sit up on the bench in the cabin in the lotus position and describe the recipe for the 'happy bean stew' he was going to make when he got home. He queried me on my favourite rock guitarist, the age I liked my women ('I prefer dem at three hundred months') and even tried to initiate a conversation about religion. Not going to church meant nothing, he said.

'I believe in God. God know what I do. I don't need to go his house to tell him so. No?'

He had a son at medical school in Belgrade and was keen that he should stay in Serbia when he'd qualified. In his view the European Union was just a dictatorship with more rules and regulations than communism had ever had, and as such its continued spread needed to be resisted. Serbia wasn't bothered at being left on the outside, he claimed. For once the country was feeling good about itself, having just won the Eurovision Song Contest. 'You know who give us max point? Croatia! Good old Cro-a-ti-a, how about! Our friends across da water! And now our tennis men are going to win Wimbly-don, you watch!'

He too knew Attila Munkas, whom he said was a Hungarian Serb, coincidentally from this very village, and an excellent captain on a river that got increasingly difficult to navigate. It was my lucky day that Attila had happened along.

Towards three o'clock in the morning the *Argo* finally loomed out of the darkness. She was a long, low barge typical of any European waterway, high in the prow, low in the water and with bridge and passenger accommodation right at the stern. She was carrying china clay, reported Antar, listening in to the radio talk, 1,359 tons of it, headed for Ruse, Bulgaria. 'Dat mean in Bulgaria dey will be making shit-load of toilets! No?'

The *Argo* clanged alongside but I was instructed to sit tight in the cabin of the lighter while voices and footsteps moved around above my head. Eventually a tall, tired-looking, casually dressed man in his late thirties stooped into the light of the cabin doorway and beckoned. 'I am Captain Attila, please come,' he said in German.

As we crossed to the customs house I tried to stammer out my gratitude.

'Can you cook?' interrupted the captain, briskly. 'I'm dying for some proper food.'

For the next half-hour he left me alone in the dark customs-house hallway while he disappeared into the police office with my passport. When he eventually emerged he looked even more haggard. REVISION didn't look like a pat on the back. 'I will keep this,' he said, slipping the passport into his briefcase. 'We can't take passengers. You are crew now.'

It was with a great surge of light-headedness that I followed him back towards the river. I hadn't dared to allow myself really to celebrate my good fortune until it was all sorted, and now I was on my way to Bulgaria, by barge! That was over 1,000 kilometres of river! I was steeling myself to ask how long it would take when the harbourmaster appeared in the doorway to the customs house and called the captain back. Attila cursed under his breath as he swivelled on his heel, but a minute later he was back holding a carrier bag of something heavy, looking pleased.

'The harbourmaster caught us some fish.'

A day later and the *Argo*'s new deckhand had yet to do anything more onerous than make infrequent cups of coffee and do the occasional bit of washing-up.

Coming aboard in the dark, the barge had looked to be reassuringly well equipped. In the main accommodation block beneath the bridge the neat Formica-finished galley with stove and basin opened out into a generous sitting room, which had doorways to the captain's and first mate's cabins. The sitting room's main features were a TV and two leather-effect sofas freshly purchased from Ikea in Rotterdam, with the labels still attached, vouchsafing their authenticity, and there was a bathroom across the hallway from the galley.

My cabin was an 80-metre walk forward to the bows, in a room next to the engineer's. It contained a (non-Ikea) sofa for me to sleep on, the crew washing machine and several boxed garden swing-seats, also Ikea. The engineer and I shared the forward bathroom, although it proved unusable. The bath had a tell-tale inch of water in it that refused to go away, but the *pièce de résistance* was the toilet, impossibly mounted on a waist-high cabinet and with such limited clearance above it that urinating required mountaineering skills, tenacity and the ability to piss at an angle. If you wanted to do something more serious and sit on it you could only do so by clambering up and reversing backwards in a crouched position until your shoulders wedged under the ceiling. It certainly gave you something to push against.

The toilet's extra height was designed to make sure that drainage would continue to be effective even when the barge was sitting low in the water, as now, but the toilet was blocked anyway, no doubt because of the extreme duress one's sphincters were put under by that unaccustomed crouched position. It was impossible to sit up there, shoulderblades against the ceiling, and have a delicate shit, just as it is impossible to take a full tube of toothpaste, stamp on it, remove the lid and avoid a substantial and immediate evacuation.

All was not quite shipshape elsewhere in the crew accommodation, either, nor in the debris of rubbish, wires and broken winches stacked behind the bridge. Apparently it had been far, far worse at the start of the journey, and as we waited for new crew at Bezdan, Attila explained that the *Argo* was a recent purchase by a Serb shipping company from a Dutch owner-skipper who'd gutted it of everything, but who'd left carpets deeply ingrained with the smell of his old, fat, nearly dead Alsatians. In Rotterdam, where Attila had loaded the china clay, he had torn out the carpets and invested in several cans of cloyingly sweet air-freshener, but now, three weeks later, the smell of decaying dog was still all-pervading. The rest he was trying to sort out as he went along.

'Boat OK, engine OK, navigation equipment OK, but all this' – Attila swept his arm to encompass the crew accommodation – 'bullshit. Owner must change the floor. You know how old this boat? Over a hundred years. Too many dead dogs.' He must have seen my expression, because he added quickly, 'Don't worry, a hundred years old but still good at floating. If not, we can always sell it to the Romanians.'

I found the captain eminently likeable, but he was also a perfectionist, and the inadequacies of the *Argo* were physically painful for him. His patience had snapped with the previous crew ('talk too much, work too little') and his first action on reaching Serbian soil had been to send them packing. It had been their departing footsteps I'd heard on the lighter's deck the previous night. But a particular aggravation that would always follow him round was his personal need for cleanliness and clean air: he'd insist on a clean tea-towel every time anyone did any washing-up, but more awkwardly he was an ardent non-smoker, which was highly unusual in the world of Danube shipping. It was a passionate stand that was to cause problems later on.

He was, though, more than happy to see his replacement crew, Vladimir and Ivica, who stepped on to the *Argo* just after breakfast, and even happier once we were under way an hour later. He was back up in the bridge, overseeing a satisfactory downstream progression of 15 knots. 'Here we are,' he smiled to me, 'you write this in your book, Mr Andrew. Me, Captain Attila, a Hungarian Serb, first mate Vlado, a Serb Serb, and engineer Ivica, a Croatian. Hungarian, Serb, Croatian work together no problem. One happy family, see?'

Certainly he looked far happier than he had been on land. He was wedged into his swivel chair on the far corner of the bridge, with Radio Croatia playing something jaunty above his head and the crew he wanted around him. On the desk in front of him were the screens for radar and satellite navigation, and the small tiller lever was nestled neatly under his hand. The echo sounder was, unfortunately, defunct, but that didn't seem to worry him unduly, even though I'd heard the river's course became increasingly treacherous as it broadened out. Shifting currents created sandbars that altered their position from one year to the next, and it was very easy to go aground.

'I've hit the sandbars before, but now I'm driving where I haven't hit them,' laughed the captain. 'And besides, how would you ever learn the course if you didn't hit a few?'

This was a far less organized Danube than it had been back in Captain Fenzl's territory, where the approved navigation channel was clearly marked specifically so you couldn't hit anything. Here the buoys were few and far between. The Serb authorities preferred to let captains make their own mistakes.

Even though I shared the forward accommodation with him, I saw little of the engineer on that first day of the journey. Ivica was tousle-haired and had the expressive face of a boy who'd never quite grown up – a face which let him down repeatedly by clouding with anxiety at the slightest provocation. If he wasn't down below in the engine room, squatting immobile with the torrent of noise raining on his back, he'd pop up occasionally like a rabbit out of a hole anywhere on the *Argo* where there was a machine room or a pumping station. Attila had also given him the responsibility for the one main meal a day, a task he carried out well, albeit reluctantly, so he'd also pop up in the galley, his oily overalls hidden under an apron bearing the legend 'Has anyone kissed the cook today?' Happily, nobody explained to him what that meant, as it would only have caused a tsunami of blushing, and I certainly wasn't going to do so. He was awkward and shy, and were he ever to find himself in female company I'd be prepared to bet he would sit silently and take the first opportunity to slink away. He and I barely communicated, partly because of his shyness and partly because I spoke no Croat and he spoke no English or German. Later on in the journey I did occasionally discover him in the cabin staring morosely at a German–Croat dictionary, because in order to progress up the Danube hierarchy he needed to be able to cope outside the Serbo-Croat world. However, I never heard a German word pass his lips.

Vladimir, the first mate, was a completely different personality. Shaven-headed, hard-chinned, earringed and vigorous, he was forthright, nationalistic, piratical and a good person to have on your side. Where Attila's moods were expressed in his choice of words and the hunching of his shoulders, Vlado put his whole body into his conversations, and initially he was confrontational towards me. He spoke good English, having once served in the Dutch merchant navy, and accordingly he took it as his task to lead a short interrogation about what exactly I was up to.

Remembering a British politician's recent description of 'The wounded carcass of Serbian pride sprawled across the Danube', I trod carefully with my answers, running through my habitual explanation about the river journey and the book. Vlado, however, assumed I was spinning him some kind of cover story.

'You are a spy,' he declared.

'Honestly, I'm not.'

I tried again, but there were several things in my explanation he found hard to understand, not least of which was the whole concept of a travel book. Then he couldn't understand why anyone would find a boat journey through Serbia, Croatia, Bulgaria and Romania remotely interesting when they had London and Paris on their doorsteps, and that they would choose a hundred-year-old barge with blocked toilets and a lingering aroma of dying dogs when they could afford to travel by five-star river cruiser with twenty-four-hour room service and the chance to create your own doilies. And finally he couldn't understand that I was there under my own steam, that I wasn't being paid and that no one had sent me.

'So if we throw you overboard, who will know?'

'Only my wife,' I said slowly. It was a sobering thought. There wasn't a lot she would be able to do on receiving a text that read 'HELP, BEING MADE TO WALK THE PLANK'.

'Are you going to do that? Throw me in the Danube?'

'We'll have to see.'

That power to throw me overboard (and I had no doubt that he both could and would, if he had thought it necessary) must have in some way reassured him that I was no threat, because after that conversation Vlado relaxed, eventually becoming my chief ally on board. A couple of days into the journey he returned to the subject of the book once more to request that Serbia and the Serbs be portrayed fairly, 'not like terrorists', and to ask if the crew were going to be in it under their real names.

'Do you want to be?'

They consulted each other and agreed they did, so they are.

Not long after leaving Bezdan the town of Apatin slipped by on the Serbian shore, its domed Orthodox church looking like an old-fashioned musical box, and then we passed the mouth of the river Drava, on whose banks I had so recently stood with Laguna. Appropriately, the previous night's rain returned as we approached

Vukovar, looming out of the Croatian bank. The town had been the focal point of one of the worst examples of ethnic cleansing in the whole Balkan crisis, when the murder of 200 civilian prisoners had been followed by a brutal eighty-seven-day siege which had killed upwards of 3,000 people and destroyed virtually every standing building. From the river the town was only partly visible and it looked only part-rehabilitated, the church still a ruin and the gaunt watertower standing like a shell-ravaged chalice. All three crew of the *Argo* – the Serb, the Croat and the Hungarian – were in the bridge as we came abreast of the ruin, and they deliberately avoided looking at it or commenting on it, gazing downriver instead. The tension could have just been my imagination, but Attila had an uncharacteristically testy radio exchange with the captain of a Croatian sand-dredger shortly afterwards.

I went to sit in the bows on my own, far away from the noise of the engine. Even here you could still tell that the *Argo* was working hard, because the bows vibrated with the pistons' beat like the tail wagging the dog. Wash from passing craft, however, made not the slightest impression on the boat's motion; the *Argo*'s 1,400 tons smashed through it without so much as sniffing, and not for the last time I found my mind straying on to those century-old steel plates and the century-old rivets that held them in place.

Towards evening the sun escaped from behind the lid of cloud that had sat on top of us all day and glared malevolently at the watchers on the bridge. The low light silhouetted the fish eagles, nonchalantly plucking from the water fish that no one else could see. It picked out passing herons heaving their bodies up and down as they flew, in a flight pattern that looked like laborious aerial press-ups. And it spotlit a wagtail that had settled on the cargo shutters, taking a breather between one shore and the other, not realizing that its supposed resting place was actually carrying it steadily further and further away from its wife and family, possibly never to return.

As we passed a mid-river island a fisherman in a little wooden boat gunned his outboard alongside and started shouting something up at me. Vlado came forward, shouted something back, and the fisherman turned his bows away.

'Catfish,' said Vlado. 'He wanted ten litres of diesel in exchange, but we don't need.'

He seemed inclined to stay, and explained how fishermen would use a short hollow stick to beat the water to attract the catfish and drive other unwanted fish species away.

When we'd exhausted that topic I felt confident enough to ask him a difficult question.

'So what did you do in the war?'

'I was at sea. I wanted to come back and fight alongside my friends but my skipper wouldn't release me. And when I did finally get off, I couldn't get another job because of my Serb passport. Which is why I am here now, on a Serb ship.'

'Did any of them die, your friends?'

'No, they had fun! It was a real party time, particularly when the whole world turned against us. Nobody cared about anything, everybody was drinking.'

'But many people died!'

'Sure. When the NATO planes hit an oil refinery in Novi Sad, my mother felt the wave of heat from the explosion at home, forty kilometres away. The night became as bright as day.'

'Were many killed?'

Vlado shrugged, as if he was the tourist, not I, and the war wasn't something he particularly cared about.

I pursued the subject. 'How about your father, did he get involved in the fighting?'

Vlado laughed. 'Not him. No, he left my mother when I was still small. Lives in Belgium now, where he's got other kids.' He seemed as dispassionate about his family break-up as he was about his country's.

'Oh. Sorry. I guess you don't see him that often, then.'

'I don't see him at all. His children in Belgium don't even know that I exist. They don't know they've got a half-brother, and I don't want to tell them until they are at least twenty years old. At that age they can make up their own minds what they want to do about it, but I'm not going to do any more damage than has already been done.'

I was about to commend him for his incredibly mature approach, but Vlado stood up.

'Come. I remember now, I came forward to tell you that Ivica has made us a fish stew.'

16

The Argo in Troubled Waters

It took a couple of days to get to Belgrade. For the most part, the journey unrolled through featureless avenues of alder, willow and white and black poplar, unbroken by any kind of habitation, although there'd be the occasional speck of colour where a fisherman had percolated through the tree trunks and now sat at the water's edge like a stray scrap of food caught in the Danube's teeth.

We'd passed through Novi Sad, the capital of Vojvodina, after dark, the street lights glistening on a newly created leisure park on the shore. Back in 1999 the city had been the scene of the worst act of government-sponsored vandalism in the modern era, when NATO warplanes had destroyed its three Danube bridges in an attempt to bring Serbia to heel. The debris had blocked the river for four years afterwards, bringing Danube shipping to a halt. A temporary bailey bridge, which opened to river traffic only a couple of hours a day, had recently been removed. And yet Novi Sad had already bounced back to become one of Central Europe's most happening places with the

EXIT music festival. Amongst young people, at least, it was burying its past faster than Linz had managed to do with the likes of the Pflasterspektakel.

Up in the bridge Attila was alone, so I stood with him for a while in case he needed company. He was clearly very tired and at one point I thought he was in danger of nodding off, so I said something to that effect. The captain just laughed.

'One eye may be sleeping, but the other is always awake. I sleep like a Dobermann. Always on guard.'

We did, however, anchor for the night shortly afterwards.

Daylight brought more variety as the southern shore rose up and revealed itself after a day of hiding away behind trees. Both banks were now Serbia, with Croatia consigned to the upriver Danube. Also finished was the Danube of castles and manor houses, which were now replaced by mean, low-slung lean-tos whose owners scratched a living from the land around them, little better off now than they had been at any time in the last five hundred years. The northern shore was flat and inhabited only by occasional herds of cows, their ankles wrinkling the water as they gathered in the shallows like groups of old ladies complaining about tired feet.

Attila, on the other hand, was full of vigour after his night's sleep. Too bad for Vlado and Ivica, who were despatched to various jobs around the *Argo*, including unblocking the forward toilet ('My boss did a very strong shit,' said Vlado). I settled on the cargo shutters in front of the bridge, to try to read and to keep out of the way, although in reality the excitement of actually being on the *Argo* still hadn't finally abated and the novelty of my situation wouldn't let me concentrate on my book.

Towards late morning Attila throttled back the insistent

272

put-putting of the jog-trotting engine and turned 180 degrees into the stream, dropping anchor just downriver from a cleft in the southern escarpment where wooden boats were drawn up on the shore.

'Fishermen?' I asked Vlado.

'More like farmers with boats,' he replied. 'They have cattle on the other side.'

It turned out we were expected, and it wasn't long before some of these farmers-with-boats were swarming all over the *Argo*. They were muscular, deeply tanned, barefooted, gap-toothed and looked like sea gypsies as they leapt aboard, shouting greetings and exchanging spirited high fives. Alarmed, I thought we were being invaded, but Vlado plainly knew a couple of them, who disappeared up to the bridge with Attila. The others roamed the length of the boat, admiring everything, before eventually homing in on the forward cabin, my cabin. Anxious to protect my worldly goods, I hastened forward, only to be greeted by a garden swing-seat emerging from the forward hatch. It was one of the three boxes that had been in my cabin, and the other two quickly followed. They were transferred one by one to lie across the thwarts of two of the rough-hewn wooden boats, now drawn together to work as a catamaran. They were then shipped carefully across to the shore.

'Boss. House.' One of the men grunted at me, pointing inland.

'Ah, the boss,' I nodded, wisely, pretending I knew him. 'The strong shit.'

Once the boxes were off, Ivica disappeared into the engine room, and a cloud of soot emerged from the chimney as the *Argo*'s put-puttering started up again. The two remaining fishermen-farmers were padding across the cargo hatches making for their own boats when an elegant state-of-the-art river cruiser came abreast of us, heading for Belgrade, its elderly passengers lining the rails of the top deck taking photos. The men stopped, unbuckled their trousers, and the passengers had the full benefit of a two-bum salute.

Captain Attila was in a good mood as we approached Belgrade, a mood that wasn't to last. A second captain was going to come aboard, he said, to be the helmsman for the lower river into Bulgaria and Romania. He himself didn't have the correct skipper's papers for this Lower Danube, where the shifting sandbars could be notoriously difficult, so a specialist was needed. The new helmsman would be on test for the company as a potential new skipper, and for this trial journey he would help to reduce Attila's own workload. 'Two captains. Better than one,' grinned Attila.

As we neared Belgrade the high sandstone escarpment hid the gradual urbanization of the southern shore, but just occasionally a defile filled with cascades of rubbish indicated the growing pressure of people, in considerable numbers, living just out of sight. There would usually be seagulls around these impromptu tips, and I remarked on them to Vlado, because they were the first I'd seen on the Danube.

'At sea we call them white brothers,' he said. 'We're always pleased to see them because they're never more than three days from land.'

Skyscrapers began to materialize out of the mist while we were still 10 kilometres away, and then I could make out the crosses on Belgrade's massive Orthodox cathedral, hauling their domes up out of the city dust.

Attila's mood had much changed when he returned from the harbourmaster's office.

'Bandit,' he muttered through clenched teeth, tossing

his briefcase into the galley. 'All he wants is money. I fuck his mother.' We stayed clear of him as he stomped up to the bridge and called his wife on his mobile phone.

A couple of minutes later the second skipper slipped apologetically aboard, a wiry, self-effacing figure clutching a suitcase. He had a hunched, hawkish and wily look about him, and eyebrows that nearly met in the middle. And although he shook us all by the hand and told us his name was Miliša, he didn't make much attempt at starting any further conversation. He spoke a little German, he agreed, but Russian was the language of the lower river; did I speak Russian? I had to confess I did not. Vlado gave him a tour of the boat, and afterwards he disappeared into the bridge with Attila.

For the next few hours I kept out of the way. We exited Belgrade through air laced with the smells of industrial chemistry. Creeks led off the main river towards various unidentifiable installations, most of them with a chimney emitting wisps of lurid-coloured smoke. Fleets of barges were anchored in the shallows, the empty ones high in the water, looking paradoxically far more substantial than the laden (and therefore low-slung). They behaved differently, too; the empty ones were far more susceptible to wind, and would swing back and forth alluringly in front of the motionless full ones, as if to say, 'I'm free, I'm empty, come and make me full.' But the full ones ignored them, not moving, not even winking, giving nothing away.

I'd sensed a change in atmosphere on the *Argo* the moment Miliša had stepped aboard, but the first sign that all was not well on board was over dinner. It was catfish again, and just Vlado, Ivica and me. I was curious as to whether we'd be pushing on through the night, now that we had two skippers, but Vlado shrugged.

'We haven't been told.'

I'd seen him and Ivica talking in low voices, steering clear of the bridge, so I enquired whether there was some problem.

Again, Vlado shrugged. 'It's the cigarettes. Miliša smokes, but Attila doesn't.'

'So can't he just step outside when he wants a cigarette?'

I'd assumed that Vlado and Ivica would automatically be on Attila's side, but it wasn't the case. 'We need to take care of Miliša. He knows the way.'

With watches still unallocated, we pushed on well beyond nightfall, through inky darkness where you had to strain your eyes for the silhouettes of marker buoys and the shapes of fishing boats. And then suddenly the engine was idling, and bright lights were close by on the starboard side. It was the Serbian town of Veliko Gradište, with a floodlit football ground and a promenade with flowerbeds right alongside the quay. The *Argo* slunk into the pools of soft light like an apologetic dog, aware that it was trespassing but desperate for warmth and company. Suddenly there were new smells in the air, smells that I realized I'd missed, of trees and flowers, and even of perfume. For although it was past midnight, there were women amongst the strollers on the quay, fascinatingly feminine, and I found myself latching on to them with the unhealthy interest of someone already too long in a world of men, diesel and cigarettes. I began to understand why seamen could be so desperate for female company on the rare occasions they came ashore.

The *Argo* quivered fearfully as we touched the stonework, and the incessant beat of the engine was cut. In the ensuing silence the noise of arguing boys on the football ground sounded delightful, mixed with the bewitching click of high heels on the prom.

It was into this silence that Attila dropped his bomb-shell. He was leaving the ship. He was tired; he'd been on the *Argo* for five weeks; he'd had enough; everything was basically shipshape, and now we had a captain who knew the way. This was his last opportunity to get off on Serbian soil and return to his wife and children. He'd be off early in the morning.

It all sounded very plausible, but that didn't make it feel right. Vlado and Ivica looked astonished.

'He knows this ship, we are his crew,' muttered Vlado. 'He called us up especially to join him.' But Attila had become emphatic in a way that brooked no contradiction, and he plainly wasn't willing to enter into a discussion. He certainly didn't want any talk about the real reasons for abandoning his ship, which I suspected were more to do with a personality clash between him and the new arrival – particularly over the question of cigarettes on the bridge; to smoke or not to smoke.

'Vlado, you will look after the paperwork,' announced the new, I-brook-no-questions Attila. 'So come, we will study it together.'

Ivica and I were left looking at each other, while Ivica's face flushed and flushed again. But there was nothing we could do, or even say. And as for Miliša, he was nowhere to be seen. So I went to bed.

By the time I woke next day, at around 6 a.m., we were already under way. Attila had gone, and I hadn't had the chance to say a proper goodbye.

I had very mixed feelings about the change of regime. Attila had been the skipper, but also the boat's moral compass. The *Argo* had been his project, and he had set the standards and the routines by which it was run. And although he was the boss, he didn't set himself apart from the rest of us; he wore his heart on his sleeve.

Most importantly for me, he had been the person who had agreed that I could come aboard his boat in the first place. For that I was very, very grateful, and I had missed my chance to express that gratitude fully.

Miliša, on the other hand, was unfathomable, the sort of character who could be harbouring a deep and nasty secret. I couldn't imagine asking him what he'd done in the war. He didn't attempt to get involved with the rest of the crew, and as soon as he came on board he'd wedged himself into the far corner of the bridge behind the tiller, the furthest away he could get from other people, from where he never came down, not even for meals. Whereas Attila had been happy to hand over to Vlado so he could take a break occasionally, Miliša was not. Steering was what he did, and he could go on doing it for hour after hour, day after day, hiding away behind a curtain of cigarette smoke. And even though Vlado and Ivica would sit up on the bridge with him, he rarely spoke. When he did, it was usually over the radio, and as we progressed downriver, it was usually in Russian. It was hard to connect with him, and crucially I had no idea what he had been told about my presence on board what was now his ship, or what he thought about it. But I was still there, and the *Argo* had officially left Serbian waters with my name on the crew list, which to some extent guaranteed my passage. If for some reason I wasn't on board at the next customs check, men in uniform would want to know what had happened to me. In the end I thought it best to continue as if nothing had changed. It was easily enough done, because Captain Miliša seemed equally keen to avoid me, but then he also avoided contact with everyone else.

There was a big attraction that day to keep us all entertained. The Iron Gate. Until relatively recently its name alone had been enough to silence even the most talkative of Danube skippers, because this was where their skills were tested to the utmost, where the land rose up in standing waves of stone and refused to let any but the most resolute pass. The name referred to the meeting point of the southern Balkan mountains with the Carpathians, a giant scimitar of a range that carved through Central and Eastern Europe. Between them, these two groups of mountains represent an almost impassable barrier, but the Danube, having traipsed 1,800 kilometres across Europe, wasn't going to turn round and sneak shamefacedly back to join its fellow north–southers. Finding a cleft between the two ranges – the Iron Gate – it slims itself down into a vigorous tree-climbing-boy of a river and squirms through a set of gorges and canyons to get out on to the flatlands beyond. There it returns to its lazy, fatso self, and ultimately merges with the Black Sea.

The Romans were the first to follow the river through the Iron Gate, carving a roadway into the steep edges of the gorges and canyons and building a bridge across the angry flood. They used this route to invade, and subdue, what was called Dacia, now Romania, but they were on foot. Waterborne traffic took one look at the rock-strewn cataracts and opted for mule trains instead.

The Iron Gate became properly navigable only after 1890, when an 80-metre-wide channel was cut through the most difficult stretch, but even in this channel the currents were so strong that, for the next eighty years, ships had to be dragged upstream by locomotive. Leigh Fermor travelled down through the 'hardly believable chasm' in 1933, and talked of rolling gravel singing audibly through the muffled flood, of boulders bounding along troughs, of the weight and force of the river 'tearing off huge fragments of rock and trundling them along in the dark and slowly grinding them down to pebbles, then gravel, then grit and finally sand'.

But in the years that had passed since then, man had finally outwitted and outmuscled nature, even in a defiantly hostile arena like this. The Iron Gate dam had been completed in 1972, and slowly the water level rose, neutering the floods, drowning the rocks, emasculating the cataracts. In places it rose as much as 35 metres, covering everything the Romans had created, and submerging whole villages, too. Around 17,000 people had to be relocated as their houses disappeared under water. The freeport island of Ada Kaleh, famous for its thousand twisting alleys and distinctive Turkish community, abandoned by the Ottomans and much relished by Leigh Fermor, was lost for ever under rising waters.

At the beginning of the chasm the *Argo* slid past the remains of the fourteenth-century fortress of Golubac, which had been built as a defence against Ottoman forces. Its towers still sat atop a formidable rock, but the new raised height of the water meant that you could row across its massive curtain walls in a puny dinghy and paddle around the lower fortifications, singing nursery rhymes. To add insult to injury, the modern road breached another part of the wall, but Golubac's towers kept on staring resolutely into the distance, declaring themselves on guard against the old enemy, too proud to acknowledge that they had been mortally breached.

Before the chasm, the Danube had been at least a kilometre wide, but now it closed in on the *Argo* to a couple of hundred metres across, and the water's surface was marked with fault lines where it had been folded together, like curds making cheese. Given the drama of the explosions of rock taking place all around us, there was something disappointing about the placidity of the river, which obeyed the bullying shore with barely a murmur of complaint. The *Argo* slid along between buttresses of rock, veering sideways into corridors whose walls rose over 1,000 feet, but there was no sense of fighting to stay on course against a maniacal current. The gorge was also strangely silent, as if we were moving along a corridor of slumbering elephants' rear ends and it was our task to do so as quietly as possible, or else the elephants would hear us and turn, and then we'd have their tusks to contend with.

Of other life on the land there was practically no sign, apart from a defunct power station with a Romanian navy gunboat tied up alongside. Man may have turned the water into a navigable highway, but he hadn't succeeded in harnessing the chasm for human use in any other way, or he hadn't until we reached the first Kazan, or cauldron, where the river relaxed into a giant scoop in the mountains and we had a brief sight of houses, fields and cars attempting to pursue a normal life. Then it was back into the chasm again, amongst shoulders of land that folded away repeatedly into the mist. As they drew nearer, someone coloured those shoulders in, first roughly, and then with a finer hand, until eventually they were alongside, and you could examine every nuance of rock and scrub. High up on the blank face of the southern mountains a modern road had been cut, but at key places the engineers had been forced to retreat inside the cliff face. The cost of the road must have been huge, and judging by the very intermittent traffic, it hadn't really been worthwhile.

Below the first Kazan we entered a long, narrow stretch where a signal station was perched on an outcrop of rock, its 'signal' a large metal puffball that could be either raised or lowered.

'Not used now,' said Vlado, dismissively. 'We have radio.'

'So what's the rule here?'

'One way at a time. The upcoming boat must wait. Because the downriver boat cannot stop.'

Cannot stop? There was no sign of any rip-roaring current on the surface, but parts of the river here were 90 metres deep, so the disturbance created by the underwater strata of schist and quartz sent towers of super-cold water soaring upwards, where they hit the surface in flawless grafts of new skin, yet to be wrinkled by the wind. In such circumstances, steering could be unpredictable.

Eventually the cliffs released their grip on the river and started to recede. We passed Trajan's monument, a stone plaque from AD 101 which had been moved to safety up the cliff. It celebrated the emperor's achievement in building a road, which was now several fathoms deep, where it was used unwittingly by Danubian suicides and admired only by the occasional passing fish.

Then came the first substantial town on the Romanian shore, Orşova, where Romanian barges used to dispose of all the goods they'd picked up from the scrap heap of Western Europe to be sold on to traders on the shore. This used to be the crews' little foray into private enterprise, and they'd pile the decks with old refrigerators, cocktail cabinets, bathtubs, bicycles, pieces of carpet, and sometimes even cars. Much of it was rowed ashore in battered dinghies for recycling into the East, but the coming of the European Union had knocked a hole in the bottom of that informal, watery bazaar, and the *Argo* passed Orşova without checking her stride.

Down below Orşova was the first of the two Iron Gate dams, so low in the water that it looked like the world's biggest infinity pool. It was a double lock system which we squeezed through in tandem with a Ukrainian push-tug, the *Kapitan Ilyushkin*, home port Izmail, covered in crew laundry and looking as if someone had tried to hide it under gaudy Post-it notes. Once in the lock, Vlado handed out family-sized bottles of Coca-Cola to the lock-keepers 'so they let us down slowly'. The drop in each lock must have been 30 metres, and as we descended between immense, weed-covered walls, water spurting alarmingly between the bricks, the climate seemed to change. It was like going down a mineshaft. By the time the mooring hooks had accompanied the *Argo* to the bottom of the pit, grumbling and moaning as they went, the air temperature had dropped a dozen degrees and a chill wind rifled across us from stem to stern.

The second lock walls were covered in Cyrillic graffiti, the work of previous crew members who'd also been descending slowly, having handed over the requisite quantity of Coca-Cola. Vlado, who was looking after the bow moorings, admired it. There was a purity to Cyrillic, he said.

'We always have one sound for one letter. It's simple. Your language may be more useful in the world, but your letters are shit.'

It took the *Argo* forty-eight hours to cover the last 360 kilometres of the journey. Forty-eight hours of nothing much at all, with Bulgaria unrolling on one side, Romania on the other. Forty-eight hours of flat, low-slung, tree-lined riverscape whose banks were so wide apart that most of the time it was impossible to pick out any detail barring the occasional wild horse. For all I knew the landscape could have been on a repeating loop, so similar did it all look. The unrelenting alley of poplar and willow was unbroken by any sign of human presence, and now that the Danube had been liberated from its last restraining barrage the towns and villages did the only sensible thing when living by an unpredictable watery giant. They kept well away.

'I call it a desert,' said Vlado, with a sweep of his arm. 'What is there here? Only trees. Only river.'

It was a strange idea, a river being a desert, but I could see what he meant. It was a vast, saturnine expanse of water moving sluggishly towards its fate, and it gave nothing back to the watchers on the bows. No feedback. No input. No detail. Supremely indifferent to our passing. This was where the sludge of Europe mooched towards the sea under a lid of khaki anaglypta.

But it wasn't sterile. There were skeins of geese, and sometimes there were solitary fishermen who supposedly even caught the occasional sturgeon. And there were boats, although fewer than before. A tug-driven pontoon ferry crabbed across from one side to the other, now that the river was far too wide for bridges. Then there'd be a fleet of ancient engineless barges hanging on to each other at anchor, high out of the water and with a small shanty house on the stern, net curtains across the windows. Sometimes there'd be a crewman squatting on a hatch cover, briefed to keep watch until the next time the barges were needed. Weeks and weeks of waiting, of fishing and, of course, of endless cigarettes.

At one point a water police launch came out from the Bulgarian side and sat alongside us, careful not to cross the river's centre line, while one of the crew raked the *Argo* with his binoculars. I resolved not to crack under interrogation; I wouldn't be the one to reveal the presence of those precious Ikea sofas.

Upstream of Lom, Miliša started to slalom the *Argo*

from bank to bank, no doubt in accordance with some mental map of underwater sandbars and in demonstration of his expertise. Certainly there were shoals of sand visible, and some of them were turning rapidly into islands. For a while we sat line astern of a Ukrainian freighter, a tactic of which Vlado approved, because the Ukrainians were the main users of this part of the river and therefore knew it best. But just as Vlado was voicing that approval, Miliša poked the *Argo*'s bows out and accelerated past, lest we should all start thinking he was happy just to tag along.

Some of these sweeping turns took us close in to the shore, so close that we were almost tangling with the overhang, and I recalled those scenes in Conrad's *Heart of Darkness* when the steamboat going to find Mr Kurtz is showered in arrows and spears from the encroaching jungle. But the only eyes I met on the riverbank belonged to three gypsies and their old nag, doing nothing in particular on the beach.

By Kozloduj we crossed paths with a proper paddle-steamer, the *Radetsky*, thumping along on a day trip, filled with shrieking and waving Bulgarian teenagers. I made a mental note to tell the owners of the *Schönbrunn*, back at Linz, that theirs wasn't the only paddler still in action on the Danube.

After a day or so the Bulgarian bank began to gather its skirts and twirl like a dervish into gentle hills tonsured with wheatfields, so golden that they were crying out for harvesting. Occasionally there'd be a small terrace of vineyards, or a small ruined fortification of some sort, and it all looked fairly well organized. Meanwhile the Romanian side remained a tree-lined blank, except now the first rank of poplars had started to pitch drunkenly forward, face first into the river, executed by a firing squad of spring floods and wind. Presumably as the front row faltered and failed in this way, so another new row was being planted somewhere at the back, in an attempt to prevent the Danube from leaving its proscribed bed. If I had been trying to assess the character of Romania from this riverbank I would have come away deeply unimpressed, but I knew better thanks to Leigh Fermor's account of walking across Transylvania, which I now wanted to emulate more than ever, if just to contradict all this emptiness.

For its part the river seemed to sense it was on its final run, and it set a fairly straight course for the Black Sea. It even accelerated, and we were regularly doing 17 or 18 kilometres an hour. When I enquired, Vlado found the extra speed hard to explain. It was possible, he said, that we were on a hydrowave, the release of a large amount of water by one of the big Iron Gate dams. It was a novel idea, surfing down the Danube on a 1,400-ton barge.

The river deviated only once from its task, turning back on itself into the wind, whipping up waves that crashed across the walkway to the stern and isolating me up on the foredeck. I was not unhappy to be alone up there, because after the drama of the Iron Gate a great lassitude had descended on the boat, the mood flattening out under the oppressively empty sky, and no one had much desire for anyone else's company.

To occupy myself I started to time our progress from one kilometre post to the next in order to calculate the boat speed and work out how much further to go, but the results were ludicrously variable, and I had to conclude that the river authorities hadn't been particularly diligent when they positioned the markers.

Miliša wasn't much more help. On a rare visit to the

bridge, and during a rare attempt at conversation, I asked him where we were.

'Europe,' he said, with a grimace.

I saw little of Ivica during these last two days, and I was beginning to understand why. The bottle of brandy I'd donated to crew supplies had suddenly started emptying itself. The level had started to drop with the arrival of Miliša on board, so initially I'd assumed it was the newcomer, but a captain risked everything if he was caught drunk in charge, and besides, Miliša barely moved from the bridge. Ivica, on the other hand, had had dismay written across his face from the moment Miliša arrived. My suspicions were confirmed when he missed a meal altogether, leaving it to Vlado to turn out a creditable spaghetti bolognaise, the signature dish of every male between Cape Wrath and Constantinople.

Vlado was the only person who didn't seem adversely affected by the change in crew dynamics. He grew into all those spaces vacated by Attila and not occupied by Miliša, and looking after me seemed to have become part of his brief. We would talk of this and that, of languages, relationships, book-writing and marriage. And although he looked like a cross between a pirate and a Bond-movie hitman, he was surprisingly romantic.

'My wife is the most beautiful woman in Europe,' he said, showing me a photograph (she wasn't). 'I always tell her exactly what I feel. That I love her. I'm like that. Not like you English, I know for you that money is number one important, the chasing of money. For me, it is family.'

I protested, but he was not convinced.

'You have so much divorce in the West. I stood before God and vowed to stay with my wife, so I will stay with her, whatever happens.'

In return I showed him the pictures on my digital camera of my journey thus far, starting right back at the source in Donaueschingen. He was amused that the Danube could look so small, and even could actually disappear. He was particularly entertained by the images I'd taken of Passau from the castle high above, showing the confluence of the Danube and the Inn. Also by the elegant church tower at Dürnstein, which he said he'd noticed many times. He knew most of the riverside locations by sight, but he'd never stepped ashore.

He wasn't, however, complimentary about Bulgaria, now on our southern shore. The Bulgarians had been too happy with the Turks as their masters, he said.

'We had them in Serbia, the Turks. I hate them, they were bastards. Don't let them join Europe. They killed thousands of my ancestors.'

Outside these conversations it was a dull, indolent passage along a section of big, wet highway that hadn't been part of my original plan, and which I'd had no real desire to see. I wished that I'd had a proper function on board that I could have got on with, but Vlado insisted that there was nothing I could do, in a way that a host insists his weekend guests relax, not realizing that 'relaxing' is the very thing that makes some people feel most uncomfortable.

In the absence of outside stimuli, one's thoughts turn inwards. Reduced to insignificance by the indifference of an unblinking sky, I began to get cranky with my own company. I began to feel lonely, tired of the smell of hot oil, cigarettes and diesel fumes, of the mesmerizing uniformity of the riverbanks and of the endlessly thrumming clippety-clop of the engine. For the first time since Esztergom I started to become homesick, after nearly two months away, and the increased frequency of

Countess Jeanne-Marie (*above*) by the Wenckheim family mansion at Szabadkigyós, eastern Hungary, where Patrick Leigh Fermor once played bicycle polo.

The plaque on the wall (*above*) indicates that the property has been bought, and left to rot, by the Roşia Montană gold mine, like most of the buildings around the main village square (*below*).

Resting by hay-makers' summer cabins in Transylvania's Apuseni mountains.

Count Tibor Kalnoky samples the plum brandy at his guest house in Miklósvár, Romania.

Rural Transylvania: no Draculas here, but there are bears in the hills – and a bull.

(*Right*) Setting out to walk between Transylvania's Saxon villages.

(*Above*) The roads may be surfaced, but who can afford a car?

(*Below*) A farmer prepares for work in the Saxon village of Copsa Mare.

(*Above*) Barbaneagra Neculai of Mila 23, in the Delta. Despite the name – Barbaneagra means 'black beard' – he was clean-shaven, unlike the more traditional Delta-dwelling Lipovani (*below*).

(*Left*) It may look pretty enough, but the boat I bought was a pig to row. Its oars were lumps of wood, secured by red threads that weren't up to long journeys (*below*).

(*Above*) Souvenirs of a more glorious era for Sulina, at the river's end.

(*Below*) The transport that meets Sulina's daily ferries is still just horse and cart.

(*Above*) Looking rough, and celebrating hard, at the end of a long journey.

(*Below*) Black Sea shipping stops briefly in Sulina to clear customs.

Dawn on the Delta; after Mila 23
it's increasingly unclear what is sea,
what river, and what land.

text messages exchanged with a certain London address only served to make it worse.

And then it occurred to me, as Ruse finally hove into sight, that I could go home if I wanted to. There was nothing to stop me. There were no rules in this travel-writing lark that stipulated the journey had to be all of one piece. I'd never intended going all the way to Ruse by boat in the first place, and I still wanted to walk through Transylvania, as Leigh Fermor had done, and that would mean doubling back on myself anyway. So why not double back a great deal further, via a set of European flight paths and that certain London address?

And so it happened that, three hours after the *Argo* finally came alongside at the Bulgarian port, I said a quick round of farewells, listened intently to Vlado's earnest warnings about how tricky the Bulgarians could be, and stalked up the metal pontoon on to dry land with a mixture of elation and relief. And somewhere between the river and the railway station I received the message on my phone I'd been waiting for: a flight was booked. All I needed to do was find a train to Bucharest.

17

Restart: the Countess and the Communists

Mark was being very cogent. 'The problem is a value vacuum. They've gone from communism to materialism, with nothing in between. It's too big a swing, from one extreme to another. Somewhere in the process there's a morality that's gone missing. Like I say, it's a value vacuum.'

He looked at both of us in turn to check we were following his logic.

'You can't blame them,' he continued. 'For decades they've had their thoughts and values dictated by the state. Now they have to subscribe to a voluntary moral code. They have to come up with their own goods and bads, rights and wrongs. That's something the government used to do for them.'

'It is very confusing,' agreed the countess, 'especially when being good gets you nowhere, but being bad can be very rewarding. Personally, I think for many of the adults it's too late, but children can regain some sense of moral responsibility.' Which was what she was trying to do with her prayer meetings.

Disappointingly, Mark and Countess Jeanne-Marie Wenckheim Teleki were getting on like a house on fire. I had been hoping for some sparks to fly at this meeting of the communist and the aristocrat, but both were finding a great deal of common ground. And now here we were having breakfast in the countess's kitchen in the former village rectory, discussing the plight of the modern Hungarian.

Jeanne-Marie was a handsome hurricane of a woman in her early seventies. She lived alone, but that didn't prevent her from agreeing to have two strangers as house guests. She'd met us off the train at Békéscsaba, the last substantial Hungarian town on the main line from Budapest to Bucharest, given us a whirlwind tour of aristocratic properties and dynasties in the vicinity ('Round here you couldn't count the counts'), and now we were in the rectory in the village of Doboz which she rented from the church. Her family manor house, just along the road, had been subdivided to become (amongst other things) the school, the village bar and the supermarket. She expressed pleasure that it was so, and although she always looked across at her former bedroom window when she passed, she had no regrets that she no longer lived there.

'I have a cousin who comes here occasionally, and it makes her ill to see all the land and the castles in someone else's hands. So I tell her – don't come. If it makes you ill, don't come, it's as simple as that.'

The countess even professed herself to be 'grateful to the Russians'. 'I really am. Running from them gave me my freedom, and freedom is more important than material possessions.' She didn't want the headache of repairing the roof on a property that size. 'Besides, what would I have become if they hadn't marched in? I would have married a cousin, as we all did in those days, just so that the property stayed in the family. I would have been stuck out here in the sticks, and he would have gone off with his mistress. And then I would have been stripped of everything by the communists. Not much of a life.'

Instead she'd followed a very different trajectory, from countess to English country wife and back again, a trajectory which had involved half a century as plain old Mrs Dickens, of The Vicarage, Spofforth, Yorkshire. Actually it was not quite so plain, because Mr Dickens had been Charles Dickens's great-great-great-grandson. It's fair to say that Jeanne-Marie had landed on her feet.

It had been three weeks since I'd left the *Argo*, and I'd picked up my journey again, feeling refreshed. I was back on my Leigh Fermor trail, and this time I was heading east from Budapest overland, not south along the river. Mark was escorting me to the border, curious to meet a countess.

The Wenckheims had started out as humble Danube Swabians from Ulm, just as Frank Flock's ancestors had done. They'd been given their title, plus swathes of cussed, mosquito-rich land, by the Austro-Hungarian court as a reward for helping to provision the imperial army. Hard work and crop innovation worked its magic and by the time Leigh Fermor met Countess Jeanne-Marie's father at Doboz and admired the great bustards he kept in the back garden, the family was very prosperous. So much so that work was no longer a priority, being mostly entrusted to the hard-working Slovaks and Serbs that the Wenckheims had encouraged to settle in the area.

Leigh Fermor's description of her father the count – slow-talking, with an anguished expression – was accurate enough, agreed the countess. She added that he had been 'a bit of a naughty boy', rather too keen on gambling for his own good. Her mother had been one of two sisters from the Teleki dynasty famous for its two prime-ministerial suicides, and her father had tossed a coin to see which one of them he would marry, not necessarily a formula for a long and loving relationship. But the children had been much cherished.

By her own admission her father hadn't been a particularly popular figure in Doboz. He'd had a bad temper, and one of his kitchen staff had even had the effrontery to slap him for being rude to her. So when the family had fled in front of the Russian advance in 1944, it'd been as much out of fear of locals taking advantage of anarchy as of what the Russians might do to them. They'd left hastily with three wagonloads of possessions and crossed into Austria, where the government had billeted them in Vienna's Hotel Bristol along with lots of other fugitive Hungarian aristocrats. Then her father contracted Parkinson's disease and her mother was killed in a railway accident, so a guardian took over the children's parenting, hiring a very strict Austrian governess who became the rock in their lives during the difficult years that followed.

She told us the next chapter as we walked around the grounds of the Wenckheim Kastely at Szabadkigyós. This was where her uncle and aunt had lived, and this was where Leigh Fermor had played his 'disreputable' but exhilarating bicycle polo, along with various Wenckheims and their footmen. The author describes the house, set in a forest of huge exotic trees, as a 'vast ochre-coloured pile . . . there were pinnacles, pediments, baroque gables, ogees, lancets, mullions, steep slate roofs, towers with flags flying and flights of covered stairs ending in colonnades of flattened arches.' All were still in situ, in a fantasia of a chateau, as were the magnolia trees and the biblical cedars in the grounds, but the family had long gone and no one played bicycle polo on the lawns any more. Szabadkigyós was an agricultural college.

Jeanne-Marie could remember her cousin, one of the bicycle-polo-players, flying off to private school – Ampleforth – in England in his own plane, which took off from the front of the house. That cousin had been killed piloting fighters in the war, and her other cousin, his brother, ended up as a lorry driver in Algeria. The remnants of the family had joined him there, and eventually Jeanne-Marie had, too, when she'd finished at school in Austria. She'd got a job in a restaurant in Algiers to learn French, moved to Paris to work as an au pair, and then to Scotland to work as an assistant for friends of friends who took in international lodgers.

Then came the meeting with Christopher Dickens.

'I was living in a flat in London with a couple of other Hungarian girls, when one of their brothers who worked in the Foreign Office brought a work colleague to visit. He was meant for Doreen, but he fell in love with me.'

So there she was, about to become a part of the British establishment as the wife of the great-great-great-grandson of one of the country's greatest writers.

'Of course Christopher couldn't stay in the Foreign Office if he married a Hungarian. I was seen as far too much of a security risk; I could have been a communist. So he had to give up his career.'

He got a job instead as the area manager for a brewery and they moved north to the 700-year-old rectory in Spofforth, brought up two children, and then hosted paying guests – Americans who liked the idea of staying with the Dickenses – to help pay the bills. For years she also ran a business making Dickens furniture, but once her husband died she started revisiting Hungary, eventually deciding the time had come to move back.

'There was no need to stay in the UK. I didn't want to live alone in a place full of memories.'

Certainly there was no sign of anything remotely English in the interiors of her second rectory, at Doboz. No antimacassars, fabrics by Laura Ashley or pictures of tea parties on summer lawns. Like many of her fellow returnees, the countess had simply closed one chapter of her life and opened the next, an ability that her life story had forced upon her, as it had upon many others of her generation.

Not that coming back had been easy. Initially she'd stayed in Doboz for a few days at a time, working on the restoration of the rectory, and she'd not found herself particularly welcome. Unfortunately she'd returned to a corner of the country that still clung to its communist ideals, a village that still had the Red Star on a monument to Soviet Liberation right at the heart of the community. A village where one man told her it was lucky her father had left when he had, or else the villagers themselves would have killed him, and where the communist mayor had told her that 'people don't want you back, they don't want to serve you again'.

That only made her more determined, and the sleepy village became something of a personal battleground. 'They'd slash the tyres of my car and break the windows. And then when the snow came they'd come over the fence and leave footprints up and down the garden to show they'd been.'

But the countess was not to be deterred. She had a big crucifix installed on the rectory door.

'Communism is the Antichrist. Communists tried to

stop people going to church. So I feel like a missionary in my own village.'

Fired with missionary zeal, she made friends in the gypsy community, invited the poor in for coffee and cakes, started a weekly catechism class particularly for children, and funded a couple of economic initiatives to try to mop up some of the local unemployment. Politically, she'd bankrolled an opposition candidate in the mayoral elections and succeeded in unseating the communist mayor. And although her own man had not got in, getting the mayor out was satisfaction enough. 'He was part of a paprika mafia that kept the price of paprika fixed, making sure the poor people stayed poor. Because if you're poor, you're timid, and you don't dare question anything.'

She'd also succeeded in having the inscription on the Red Star monument changed. The text talked of the people's gratitude to Russia for 'liberation' from the Germans in 1944, which she could just about accept, but then an additional line had been added after the 1956 Revolution, thanking the Russians again. For slaughtering tens of thousands of Hungarians. Everywhere else in Hungary the Revolution was regarded as a national tragedy, but not, it seemed, in Doboz. So she'd spoken to the village priest, who'd spoken to the newspapers, and ultimately the line about 1956 had been grudgingly erased, but the monument itself had stayed. And when she'd proposed wrapping it in the European flag on Hungary's accession to the EU, the local policeman had advised her not to push her luck.

Before we left Doboz the countess took us across the small river that ran through the village to where her family mausoleum stood alongside her family church. Both had been built by her grandfather, and both were securely under lock and key for fear of vandalism. She opened the church and showed us the frescos, the inscriptions and the first iron arch in Hungarian church architecture. Spiritually and emotionally it was clearly very important to her.

And then, climbing the winding stair on the way up to the musician's gallery, she shrieked and stumbled quickly backwards.

'My God. The Devil. Up there.'

The Devil, it turned out, was a snake. On the stone stair, where presumably it was enjoying the relative coolness after the ferocious heat outside. It was a substantial creature, a good 4 feet long, browny-yellow in colour, and probably a European cat snake. Not particularly dangerous to human beings, it nevertheless hissed angrily at being encouraged down the stairs and out of the door with the help of a brushwood broom.

The countess watched it go with trepidation. She was very shaken. It was a bad omen, she said, having a snake in her church. It had never happened before, and she hoped it would never happen again.

Afterwards, in a train rattling across the plains towards Romania, Mark and I reflected on the apparent contradiction of a woman who could face, alone, intimidation by a powerful and hostile section of her local community, but who could be so fundamentally unsettled by the symbolism of a snake on a stair.

Some hours later we were in the Romanian city of Arad, which originally had been a trading centre created by Danube Swabians and Slavs like the Wenckheims and their workers. There'd also been an extensive Jewish population here who'd ended up being accused of keeping the country back in order to serve their own financial interests. These merchants had filled the town centre with extravagant art nouveau façades, which had once been glorious but now vied with each other in decrepitude. In amongst them stood a typical communist-era monument, depicting a cowering Romanian being protected by a strong Russian soldier – a relic that no battling countess had yet found the courage to remove.

We were house guests again, and once more our hostess met us at the station, but there the similarity with the countess ended. Julia was decidedly new European, a fearsomely intelligent, composed, level-headed twenty-something. Although Romanian, she was studying Finnish at Mark's university in Budapest, and, with Romania just having joined the EU, it was clear she wasn't going to be closeted in a mud-walled house in Arad's back streets for much longer.

She certainly didn't conform to most outsiders' image of a Romanian. The commonly held view in the wider world is unflattering, and dates back to Leigh Fermor's day. When the author had crossed that very same border as we did, also by train and along the same line, he'd been carrying in his luggage a small pistol given to him by one of the Wenckheims, who had feared for his safety in the barbarous land to the east. No one had given me any weaponry for my journey, but it was plain that a similar nervousness of the neighbours still persisted amongst the Hungarians, and it was hard to cross the border without feeling some of their trepidation. In *The Glance of Countess Hahn-Hahn (down the Danube)*, Hungarian author Peter Esterhazy talks of a feeling of helplessness and defencelessness on arriving in Romania, of how 'everything is frightening here'. It was being frightening, too, in the media back in the UK, which was busy with scare stories about Romanian ruffians pouring into our cities, starting scams and looking for easy mugging victims.

So why was Romania singled out, amongst all the EU's new accession countries, for such negative coverage? Fear of the unknown must have played a big part, simply because Romania was that much further away than any other EU member heretofore. It was more primitive, so its people had more to gain from their new freedom to travel, but more significantly it had also had a very difficult extraction from a very repressive regime under the totalitarian Nicolae Ceauşescu and his wife Elena, and the West believed that it must still be psychologically scarred. We'd all seen the dreadful scenes of Romanian orphanages on our TV screens, which we took as clear evidence of a primitive society and of the continuity of man's inhumanity to man, and we'd all read the newspaper stories of political corruption and organized crime. Clearly, Romania was in a bad way.

As far as its direct neighbour Hungary was concerned, Romania's negative image had more to do with its controversial history. Border changes at Trianon had deprived Hungary of the huge principality of Transylvania, thereby incarcerating some two million Hungarians in Romanian territory. Those Trianon changes were made on the basis of a majority head-count which had taken Hungary by surprise. For hundreds of years the Hungarian Transylvanians had fought the principality's wars, erected its churches, built its castles, planned its towns, founded its schools and its universities. Meanwhile the Romanians had clung to its hilltops raising sheep and goats – and more Romanians. And although they were way further down the social ladder than the Hungarians, they had the last laugh because, when it came to the post-war head-count, they outnumbered their supposed rulers by

54 per cent to 32 per cent and therefore got the nod from the decision-makers at Trianon after putting forward a strong case that Transylvania had always been at the core of Romanian nationhood, but had merely been occupied by a foreign power for eight hundred years. From the Hungarian perspective, this was like letting the lunatics take over the asylum, but it was nevertheless democracy in action. In fact, for Transylvania it was democracy way ahead of its time, because up to that moment the region had been one of the most feudal societies in Europe. Mind you, the democratic experiment didn't last long, so there's a case for saying that Romania wasn't ready for Trianon's forward thinking.

Hungaro-Romanian relations still haven't recovered from the loss of Transylvania. Back in Budapest I'd had a conversation with a tourist guide who'd stated, quite matter of factly, that Romanians and Hungarians hated each other. Transylvanians were the guest workers of Budapest, she'd added, and they were lazy and dishonest.

Now that I was in Arad, I voiced some of these concerns to a woman who spoke practically unaccented English, as well as Serbian, French, Italian, Finnish and of course Romanian, so not much evidence of laziness there. Julia wore her formidable intelligence lightly. She plainly possessed a forensic mind that in a more arrogant society would probably have produced a withering personality, but not in Romania, where mental capacity per se wasn't yet highly prized.

'I don't consider myself dangerous,' she said, on my mention of Leigh Fermor's gun. 'And neither is Romania. I've hitch-hiked all over. As for dishonesty, we have plenty of that, but it is out there in the open for all to see. Hungary has dishonesty just as bad as us, but theirs is hidden away.'

As in Hungary, the swift succession of systems of governance – monarchy, dictatorship, revolution, communism, revolution, democracy – had each brought a new set of rules in their handbags. Romania became like a child being passed through several sets of parents, each of different degrees of strictness with different views of elbows on the table, smacking, frequency of bath, etc. So now, having had the last set of parents forcibly removed by social services, it was out on the street with the other teenagers, and it didn't quite know how to behave.

But Julia was patriotic, and she didn't appreciate the way the British newspapers had labelled Romania as 'primitive'. She believed that the education she'd had in Romanian schools was better than the equivalent in Hungary. 'Over there they have to concentrate on Hungarian identity, language and history. We get a much bigger picture.'

Sitting in the front room of the small family house in a pot-holed back street of Arad, I could see both the primitive and the bigger picture. The original house was single-storey and mud-walled and had just two rooms, although Julia's parents had added to it. In the back lived Julia's grandmother, who kept pigs and chickens and worked a vegetable garden and orchard which were so productive that she got upset if the family actually bought any food in the shops. And yet in one of the two original rooms in the front, Julia had her computer with broadband Internet, from where she communicated with the world, notably her boyfriend, who was a Serbian doctor presently working in Africa.

She was an only child, born during Romania's darkest times, when contraception and abortion had been banned by Ceauşescu. He'd wanted the population of twenty-three million to increase to thirty million by the year

2000, to boost the strength of the nation. So at around the time of her birth he had declared the foetus to be 'the socialist property of the whole society. Giving birth is a patriotic duty . . . those who refuse to have children are deserters'. And yet, on the surface of it, there couldn't have been a worse time in which to bring a child into the world. There was so little food in the shops it had become hard to feed oneself, let alone one's offspring, and Julia's parents had had to go out after dark to try to buy formula milk on the black market. As for the local jobs, they were often a sham. Her uncle had gone to work every day in a giant power station built on the edge of the town, but merely to turn the electricity on in the morning and turn it off in the evening, because the power station had never been properly operational.

Julia pooh-poohed the idea, commonly held in Hungary, that Hungarians and Romanians were at each others' throats in modern Romania. Her father was a Hungarian Romanian and her mother a Romanian Romanian, a mix which was nothing unusual in her home town. But over the border in Hungary her part-Hungarian parentage cut no ice with immigration, where she would be 'treated like scum, alongside Indians and Chinese' whenever she went to renew her student visa.

Both her parents were teachers and avid readers. Over lunch her mother, fluttery, pretty and birdlike, wanted to know what we thought of Philip Roth and Iris Murdoch, while hovering anxiously with a bottle of granny's home-made *tuica* (plum brandy). The whole street knew that the household had international visitors, and they would want to know how it had gone, and to hear that every mouthful had been eaten up.

We went out that night with her Ivy League friends, half a dozen other twenty-somethings who'd been, like

Julia, high achievers in Arad's schools. They spoke fluent English, making fun of one another if ever anyone messed up an 'if' clause, and were warily eyeing future careers. Amongst them was the dreadlocked football fan who'd been raised by his grandparents after his mother walked out; the quiet one whose sister did nude modelling on the Internet, while he took the photographs; the mayor's son who wanted to be a theatre director; and the engineering student who'd just landed his first job making railway carriages. As a group they were surprisingly lacking in cynicism, given that they'd been born into an era where anyone who didn't steal from the state was effectively stealing from his family. And in a country that was being pilloried in the European press.

They were also surprisingly unmaterialistic given that they had entered their teenage years in a post-communist free-for-all, when men with money could get away with murder, and regularly did. Somewhere along the line they'd clung on to some kind of integrity and had avoided falling into Mark's value vacuum. Most were holding to the hope that they might, eventually, find good jobs in Romania, and not have to travel the world to find the life they wanted. They believed that their generation could make something of their home country, and that intelligence like theirs would be put to good use. In the meantime, they said, there needed to be a banner on the Romanian border which read 'Eventually, Everything Will Work'.

18

Romania: Regime Change and the Politics of Gold

Despite not having a pistol, I hadn't arrived in Romania completely defenceless. In my rucksack was a device called a Dazzer, a lump of high-technology plastic which would emit a high-frequency sound that humans couldn't hear. I'd had word that a walker in Romania had nothing to fear from people, but the same didn't necessarily apply to their dogs, and an Englishwoman had recently been badly mauled after setting off alone into the hills. My walking began, however, where it was the people who were at each other's throats.

Parting from Mark and Julia in Arad, I'd caught a rattling train eastwards along the Mures valley. Leigh Fermor had dawdled through this same valley seventy-five years before, a welcome house guest wherever he went. He'd gone shooting with a blue-blooded Tibor, had attended the funeral of a countess's mother, drunk whisky with a Teleki count, swum in the river with an eccentric István and had a romp in the hay with a local girl. It was in the Mureş valley that he'd eventually fallen in love with Angela/Xenia, and borrowed a car for a romantic, whirlwind tour of Transylvania. In the book, he'd written István into the car, too, but from my Budapest contacts I'd learned that that was not strictly true; he and Angela had been alone, but he was protecting a lady's reputation.

I didn't find an Angela of my own in the Mureş valley, but I did meet a raven-haired Adriana in the gold mining village of Roşia Montană, some distance north of the river.

Roşia Montană is in the foothills of the Apuseni mountains, a straggle of a community strung like barbed wire up a high valley surrounded by the scars of centuries of prospecting, and Adriana was one of its most noticeable human features. A thirty-something geologist, her brown eyes burned with passion and her cheeks were rouged by an outdoor existence. Her mane of flowing hair needed more care than it got, and she had the unselfconsciously athletic stride of someone who did a man's job in a man's world. God knows the impact she would have had on the community if she'd ever appeared in a mini-skirt, low-cut top and high heels. The gold would have erupted out of the mountain on its own accord.

I first met this goddess of geology in the office of the Soros Foundation's information centre in the main square of the mining village. The Foundation was a newcomer to Roşia Montană, come ostensibly to keep an eye on a controversy over the settlement's future which was being debated at a national level – a controversy which was driving wedges through local families. They were there to ensure citizens' rights were being respected, the Soros people said, although I wasn't entirely convinced that their motivation was completely altruistic; George Soros has a history of snapping up ailing mineworkings for bargain prices, so he could just have been biding his time.

The problem at Roşia Montană was the gold, a metal that has always tended to bring out the worst in people. There's a lot of it in Transylvania, and it was Transylvanian gold that first encouraged the Romans to pioneer their difficult route through the Iron Gate and to incorporate the territory into their empire. The Romans had mined 165 tons at Roşia Montană before the imperial withdrawal, and some of the Roman workings were still there, still in use until very recently. In fact the gold mine could have become a key piece of archaeological evidence in the debate over who had the historical high ground in claiming Transylvania as their own, Hungary or Romania.

The back-story to that ownership debate (and a lot of regional conflict) runs thus. The Romanians maintain that Transylvania was inhabited from prehistoric times by a tribe called the Dacians, who'd started (amongst other things) the mines at Roşia Montană. This tribe had then combined with the Roman occupiers to create Daco Romans, 'more Roman than the Romans themselves'. They were billed as direct ancestors of modern Romanians and standard-bearers of Latin civilization in the East. This 'continuity theory' thus directly links today's Romanians with prehistoric inhabitants of the region.

Meanwhile the Hungarians maintain that when Attila the Hun came sweeping through, eight hundred years ago (Hussar!), Transylvania was effectively empty of everything except a few disorganized nomads, having been abandoned by the Romans, ravaged by the Tartars and pillaged by the Byzantines. Nobody wanted it so the Huns took it over, and eventually it became part of the Austro-Hungarian Empire. During this period, the more menial tasks in the principality were done by wandering Ruthenians, Vlachs and Pechenegs whose descendants eventually outnumbered their masters and called themselves Romanians. Thus the Hungarians are sceptical about the continuity theory and believe the very identity 'Romanian' to be a fabrication. They point to the fact that up until 1848 the Habsburgs acknowledged only three nationalities in Transylvania: the nobility, German-origin Saxons and Hungarian-speaking Székely, all of whom had arrived in the previous thousand years, and all of whom had comparative autonomy. There was no mention of any Romanians, or even of any Dacians.

A gold mine like that at Roşia Montană, worked from the earliest times, could have produced conclusive evidence for or against the continuity theory, particularly because a hundred archaeologists had just been crawling all over the site as a condition of the new mining concession. All civilizations have been greedy for gold, and theoretically any dominant cultures in Transylvania would have left traces here for them to decipher, but the archaeologists could find only sketchy prehistoric diggings. The Roman mineworkings were extensive, as were signs of immigrant German mining thereafter and of course of renewed activity in Austro-Hungarian times. But they couldn't identify anything specifically Dacian in between.

However, there couldn't have been a more convincing piece of evidence for the continuity theory than Adriana. Born and bred in Roşia Montană, she was completely Latin, straight off the back of a Vespa in Sorrento. Hair-tossingly impetuous, moody, good-looking and presumptuous, she met my eyes across the room of the Soros Foundation and decided there and then that she would take me in hand, show me what I needed to see and find me somewhere to sleep.

I got my briefing on the argument raging around Roşia Montană as we strode around the hamlet. Until the previous year, the mine, with its staggering 600 kilometres of tunnels and galleries, had been run by the state. During the communist era it had employed 1,000 people, or around 60 per cent of the working population of a community of 3,800, but gradually it had become less and less economic, until eventually there were just 380 mineworkers left in a community that had dwindled to 1,000. On Romania's accession to the EU, it closed with a bump. Meanwhile several outside enterprises had become interested in buying it up, because there was still plenty of gold left under the ground. Getting it out efficiently was just a matter of outside investment and deploying new technology, both elements that had just been made a whole lot easier by EU membership. That technology, however, would involve giant opencast mining which would remove the mountain tops, sweep away a lot of the existing village houses, and produce 13 million tons of ore a year, which would make it the biggest gold mine in Europe. However, the process of separation of gold from ore would require huge quantities of cyanide (the accepted method in gold mining) and the tailings pond would fill a whole valley next door.

Naturally, there was opposition. The villagers, some of whom were farmers as well as miners, had originally banded together to negotiate good prices for their doomed property, but it wasn't long before their association became opposed per se to Roşia Montană's would-be buyers, a Toronto-based company called Gabriel Resources. Much of the marshalling of that opposition was done by a whippet-thin ecologist from Switzerland who'd come to live in the village in 2002, and who plainly despised Gabriel Resources and their ilk with every fibre of her intense being. Stephanie had proved particularly good at attracting the attention of the media, and the supposed infamies and calumnies of Gabriel Resources were regularly hung out to dry in the newspapers, sometimes deservedly so. The company may have originally thought they would stroll into Romania with pockets bulging, hand over the cash and take over the concession, but they'd soon found themselves on the back foot. Meanwhile the Romanian government, which a few years earlier would quite happily have taken the money from the angel Gabriel and consigned the village to the mining underworld, was now part of the EU and subject to a whole bundle of new regulations and extra scrutiny, so it was on its best behaviour. The net result was that, many years after drawing up its first plans, Gabriel Resources was still not doing any mining, but instead still being forced to jump through hostile hoops in an increasingly bitter public-relations war.

This war was mainly being conducted in the nation's law courts, newspapers and government offices, but its casualties were piling up in the village. Around the main square were baroque and neoclassical façades that dated back to Habsburg days, but some were just façades, the rest of the buildings having crumbled away. And further down the main road every other house was a ruin, many showing the Gabriel Resources plaque that indicated they had been bought by the concession and left to rot. The company wanted to buy every property that lay within the planned development area, but not everyone wanted to sell and that had produced a split in the community between those who thought Gabriel Resources, which was offering 650 jobs, was the future of Roşia Montană, and those who thought the company was the enemy. Each side refused to talk to the other and sometimes the fissures even ran within families. Everyone was watching everyone else, and Gabriel's employees came and went in cars, reluctant to expose themselves to debate on the street. Even the Gabriel Resources visitor centre on the main square, which had various environmental reports, models and details of the resettlement zones being offered to the villagers, was empty of actual human beings when I walked in.

Adriana refused to go with me into the visitor centre. No doubt it would have classified her as fraternizing with the enemy, and all eyes were undoubtedly watching from the adjacent Soros office. She'd worked for the mine when it had been a state enterprise, so I asked her whether she too had been offered a job by Gabriel Resources.

'They offer, but I no want,' and she tossed her head, magnificently. 'I no want to work with, howyousay, hee-po-crits.'

'What about your house?'

She smouldered. She'd been offered lots of money for that, too, but she would never accept. Never.

'But eet ees very difficul living here. People fight. With words.'

We ranged around the village, past the churches and down to the Roman mineworkings, and as we walked she told me how she'd been given two years' redundancy money by the state, money which had nearly all gone. I couldn't see that Roşia Montană had any prospect other than as a mining town, so I started to say something about how she should move her life on instead of getting bitter about her past, but she stopped me, put her hand on my arm, and stared into my eyes.

'You are hungreee,' she declared, triumphantly, as if hunger explained my appalling lack of backbone.

I admitted I was.

'Come.'

She led me up a side track to a small cottage which didn't have a Gabriel Resources plaque and told me to wait outside. Moments later she reappeared with a key.

'Come.'

I trailed her down the hill until we reached a small shop, and there I stocked up on bread, cheese and tomatoes. Then Adriana was off again, with me bobbling along in her wake like a water-skier who'd fallen off his skis, but who was reluctant to let go of the rope. This time she led me to an ugly block of flats, incongruous in the mountain valley, set back from the road.

'Miner's house,' she said, 'empty now. For you.'

And there she installed me, in a three-roomed flat with an untreated parquet floor, a ceramic stove, a bathroom (but no running water) and a chicken run outside the window. We negotiated a fee, settling on an amount that made her eyes grow wide when she realized I was serious, and as soon as she had the money in her hand she vanished.

It wasn't the last I saw of Adriana. She reappeared twice more that evening, once to flop into the old miner's armchair, crying 'Tired, I am soooo tired.' And then later to tell me that the water was about to come on for an hour or two. Restricting the water supply was one of the weapons, she said, that the mining company was employing to drive people out of their homes. She, however, was not going anywhere. 'Not for money, not for no-bod-eee.'

Rows over forcible resettlement of rural communities are nothing new in Transylvania. In the first years of Romania's communist era many struggling peasant families were happy to be plucked out of their feudal existences and relocated to blocks of flats on the edges of towns, where they had heat, light, transport, shops and jobs. It looked like progress. But the jobs proved pointless, the shops steadily emptied, there was no sense of community and many learned to regret having left their traditional lives.

President Ceauşescu didn't trust self-sufficient rural households because they were more resistant to central control, so towards the end of his rule he declared his intention of flattening seven thousand Transylvanian villages to create giant state farms. When news of the plan leaked out in Budapest, forty thousand people marched on the Romanian embassy, because most of the villages concerned were ethnically Hungarian. Whether it was deliberate policy on his part or not, this targeting of the Hungarians was ultimately to prove fatal for Ceauşescu.

In its early years, the Romanian regime had looked to all the world like a new breed of a more free-thinking communism. Ceauşescu, a shoemaker's apprentice who'd risen through the ranks of the Party, had become its First Secretary in 1965. Initially he'd been popular, distancing himself from the Soviet Union, extracting Romania from the Warsaw Pact, refusing to accept Soviet troops on Romanian soil, and even welcoming American presidents. The world saw him as a bit of a maverick, a man you could do business with, a buffer between the West and the Russian bear. The national economy, too, looked as if it was working, with giant factories erected up and down the country, but productivity figures were increasingly falsified and the annual grain harvest was actually three times smaller than was claimed in official statistics. And while carefully planned socialism may have eliminated destitution, it was unable to produce prosperity, at least not for the general population. Gradually the concentration of power in the hands of the few began to corrupt, conferring great privileges on the higher echelons. To maintain absolute control, these echelons relied increasingly on the secret police, the Securitate, and one in four of the population turned informer.

It wasn't safe to think, let alone talk, outside the box. There was no opposition, no raised voices were heard, and all typewriters had to be registered with the authorities, along with a copy of their typefaces. Any conversation with a foreigner had to be reported to the police within twenty-four hours. Anything that differed from the norm was regarded as subversive. Homosexuals were sent to jail, along with a medical student who was discovered studying yoga and the workers in the Brasov tractor factory who'd complained that it was too cold in the factory to work. Pretty girls were not allowed on TV because Elena Ceauşescu feared the inflammatory effect they'd have on men, and television broadcasting was reduced to two hours per night, most of it focused on the thoughts, words and deeds of the Ceauşescus. Foreign travel was banned and birth squads spied on pregnant women to prevent abortion.

Under all these restrictions, Romania became the land of the living dead. The population was just going through the motions within a system that was mean-minded, ugly and self-serving, whose morality was absent and whose only absolute value was its own power. Individuals surrendered their autonomy completely in every part of their existence, even in the privacy of their own bedroom, where they were not meant to practise contraception. Good and bad, right and wrong, were dictated by the state. Even the church, attended by 70 per cent of a population hungry for guidance, effectively followed the state line.

So bricked-in was this Romanian jail that the news of the loosening of the Soviet grip on the rest of the Eastern Bloc in the 1980s completely passed the nation by. There was no circulation of *Pravda* or *Izvestia* in Bucharest, so Mikhail Gorbachev's speeches about *glasnost* and *perestroika* were never aired within the country. Complete central control of the media meant that there was not a whiff of liberalization in the press. In the absence of any gradual relaxation of control, as was taking place elsewhere in Eastern Europe, the only possible way out was abrupt revolution. And the spark for that came from the Hungarian connection.

Although the newly enlarged, post-Trianon Romania had granted its Hungarians, Romanians and Germans the rights to education, justice and public administration in their own language, those rights had been steadily eroded. Even in the 1930s shops that showed non-Romanian signs were taxed, and non-Romanians didn't get good jobs. For his part, Ceauşescu refused to acknowledge the distinctiveness of Romania's minorities, particularly the 1.4 million Hungarians. His line was that they were part of one nation, created by centuries of living together, and he'd ruled out running a separate Hungarian educational system, replacing it with Hungarian sections within Romanian schools and then eventually phasing them out altogether. Young professional Hungarians were dispersed to jobs in faraway places, so they would not be tempted to conspire, and in 1987 Ceauşescu banned outright the import of any publications from Hungary (which was becoming dangerously liberal in his eyes). He followed that with a decree in 1989 that henceforth all place names would be printed only in Romanian.

In December 1989, an ethnic Hungarian priest called László Tökés in the Transylvanian city of Timişoara was summarily ordered to leave his flat to take up a remote rural post where he could do no harm. Tökés had been a persistent and outspoken critic of the regime in his sermons in the city, and he'd found plenty of support in his (mainly Hungarian) congregation, so he'd stood his ground and refused to obey his bishop's instructions. On 15 December his supporters confronted the militia sent to evict him and a stand-off began. Gradually news of the confrontation spread, and the crowds increased, widening to include Romanians as well as ethnic Hungarians. Illegal songs started to be sung, and the mayor was forced to issue an ultimatum for dispersal. When the deadline passed and the crowds were still growing, the Securitate moved in, firing at will. In the ensuing melee around a hundred protestors were killed, with rumours of many more. But instead of quashing resistance, that brutality only served to fan the flames and soon the entire city was in a state of rebellion. Rumour quickly spread through the rest of the country and, in a nation without an independent press, it was passed by word of mouth, so the death toll was exaggerated at every step.

The government declared a state of emergency in Transylvania. Ceauşescu decided to assert his authority and condemn the uprising via a televised rally to be held outside the Central Committee building in Bucharest, and he ordered tens of thousands of supposedly loyal factory workers to be bussed in to make up the crowd. Standing on the building's balcony, he then embarked on a long speech about the achievements of his regime. The rally was broadcast live, so the whole nation became aware of the small disturbance in the crowd at the same time as Ceauşescu did; everyone heard the shouted insults and saw the president's sudden bewilderment at being interrupted. He tried to regain control in the manner of an angry schoolteacher – 'Sit quiet in your places' – but the anger of the crowd was increasing, as was the president's loss of face. Eventually, in full view of the cameras, he and his wife were ushered back inside the building, pursued by jeers and whistles.

A riot ensued, during which the Securitate hosed the crowd with bullets, but nobody ran away. Helicopters and tanks were deployed, but still the crowds stood their ground, despite indiscriminate killing. And when the army refused to fire on the general public any more, sickened by what they'd seen, the Securitate turned their guns on the soldiers. For the next couple of days guerrilla war raged through the city, army against Securitate, with the latter occupying any available building and shooting randomly at passersby.

Fearing for their own safety, Ceauşescu and his wife escaped from Bucharest in a helicopter, but the military closed the national airspace and forced the pilot to land. The couple were seized by the army, put on trial in front of a hastily convened tribunal and condemned to death, with the sentence carried out there and then, on national TV. The final lingering image of the dead face of the formerly omnipotent leader is something that all Romanians over a certain age will never forget. Freedom had come to them quite unexpectedly, popping out of the barrel of a gun.

The aftermath of revolution was strangely silent. A lifetime of lack of initiative meant that nobody quite knew what to do next. There had been no organized (or even disorganized) opposition when Ceauşescu had been in power, so no natural leader emerged from the rubble. How to create a workable democracy after nearly fifty years during which a totalitarian party had monopolized all public space, even the church, was bound to be a huge problem. People had reacted instinctively against Ceauşescu, and now they were dazed at what they'd just done. They'd got completely out of the habit of making their own decisions, so eventually, once they'd toured Ceauşescu's obscenely opulent palaces and cut the communist coat of arms out of the national flags, they went home to await further instructions. From someone, anyone, because that was what they had always done.

Some weeks later they raised no objection when most of the old Party sheepishly reassembled itself in the shape of the emotively titled National Salvation Front.

Given the nation's history, it was too much to expect instant democracy. Ruled variously by Romans, Byzantines, Habsburgs, Russians and totalitarians, Romania had no pattern of self-government to fall back on, no ancient formula for peace and prosperity. Its pre-war monarchy had been conjured up out of German-speaking Hohenzollerns from way upriver, and although King Michael had expressed his willingness, and had returned briefly in 1990, he was expelled after just twelve hours. Despite the downfall of Ceauşescu, many Romanians still clung to communist concepts like subsidized prices and jobs for all in nationalized industries. Opinion polls carried out in the 1990s found that 70 per cent still believed that income levels should be equal across all layers of society and that industry should remain nationalized. The heartland of that change-nothing opinion was the neo-urbanites, the worker-peasants, the people who had been uprooted from their traditional communities and moved to cities to work for large industries. That move had effectively confiscated their self-determination, removed them from their social networks and forced them to look to the state to guide and provide, so it was no use telling them to stand on their own two feet in a new, capitalist world.

Across the nation there was a reluctance to accept change, as there always is in any nation on the globe. But there was one region whose culture hadn't changed for effectively hundreds of years: the self-sufficient Transylvanian countryside, where I was headed next. It was to have been Ceaușescu's next project, but fortunately he'd been blown away before he could do too much damage.

19

Walking in Transylvania:
the Apuseni Mountains

Albac was deliciously chilly in the early morning. It was the first time I'd felt cold in many weeks, and I'd forgotten how energizing the cold could be. A tentative sun was beginning to squeeze its way down the tight valley between the steep flanks of the Apuseni mountains, producing steam from whatever it touched. It plucked the newly galvanized needle of Albac's church out of its conifer-shrouded obscurity, twiddled the biblical spike between thumb and forefinger and buffed it up so that it looked like newly minted tinfoil. Then, feeling its way towards me like a blind man reading braille, the first rays flickered lovingly over village eaves carved with stars, flowers and birds, and rippled on downwards, caressing immaculately stacked walls of firewood whose presence was as comforting to their owners as money in the bank. But then, having shown such admirable restraint, it went and spoiled everything by splashing its rays wantonly and indiscriminately across crudely painted breeze-block walls up and down the main street.

Old men in black felt hats were standing at Albac's main intersection, chain-smoking, waiting for nothing, and eyeing the slow assembly of an impromptu market of essential supplies for anyone heading for the uplands – a market that mainly consisted of peppers, tomatoes and gas cylinders. Most of the traffic that passed the intersection either jingled or barked, but the occasional angular Dacia (actually a Renault but in a style long since forgotten anywhere further west) lurched indecisively through, trailing a bronchial splutter. It was followed at a distance by the morning bread van, making slow progress because of its need to stop outside each and every one of those open doorways marked by piles of beer crates: the shops.

I'd started early because I knew I had a long climb ahead of me, and because I didn't want to mess up as I had the previous day. From Roşia Montană I'd originally intended to hike along a cross-country path to Campeni – it had looked possible on the map – but everyone, including the luscious Adriana, had advised me to stick to the road. But by midday I was so thoroughly fed up with the extra distance and the traffic that I'd cadged a lift by flagging down a minibus. It turned out to be full of women workers from a knitwear factory, going home, and I'd had to stand up at the front, holding on tight, while the more gap-toothed of the women made salacious comments and asked me personal questions I couldn't understand. Judging from the raucous way the rest of them laughed, it was probably better that way.

And so at Albac it was a release to be leaving the metalled roads and heading up through steep fields where stooks of hay, like midsummer snowmen who'd got fat and tanned in middle age, were trying to slide surreptitiously sideways into the cool shade of the field-fringing trees, to wait there for winter to return. Some were grouped in silent conference, frozen in the act of whispering. Others were just companionable couples, sagging slightly at the knees, having been too long in each other's company to care about how they looked any more. All of them shimmied with steam when the sun laid its soft hand upon them.

It was a valley of natural abundance and of timber yards, mostly fed by illegal logging. Tomatoes and runner beans flourished outside the farmsteads, the breadmaking smoke from summer kitchens hung low, mingling with the dew. A clear river ran jauntily down past me, but I had to be selective in where I looked if I wanted to miss its eddies of plastic bottles, crisp packets, cement sacks and beer cans. From the far bank an old lady talking to her two cows turned her attention, and her tongue, on me, but all I could do was smile, tell her where I was going, and point. She seemed satisfied with that.

The breeze-block architecture of the valley bottom evaporated as I climbed higher, and the farmsteads became all spruce-built, clad in shingle tiles, steadily diminishing in size in accordance with the increasing height and the diminishing means of their proprietors. Some had outhouses with floral balconies where granny had moved out to, now that the next generation had taken over the main building. Here her task was to look after the livestock and the vegetables, and I could see her resting on her pitchfork in the piggery, taking a break from mucking out, or appearing at the door of the cowshed with a pail of warm milk, while some large beast inside bumped complainingly against the wooden walls, impatient to be out.

For a while I walked in step with three itinerant gypsy

grasscutters whose portable scythes I couldn't fathom until one of them saw I was interested, slid it off his shoulder and showed how the blade swung out and locked. After a half mile or so they sprawled over a grassy bank and produced bottles of beer from nowhere, suggesting by sign language that I should join them. I demurred; I was still nervous of gypsies, and besides I wouldn't be able to walk 25 kilometres after a drink so early in the day. In order not to offend, I demonstrated the likely impact of a 9 a.m. beer on my walking stride, and they laughed and waved me on.

At Horea the last bits of patchy tarmac vanished altogether. One of the hills beside the village – the Hill of Panting – had a reputation as a place for couples who were trying to conceive, or at least it did according to the local mayor, who described it as 'natural Viagra' and had had the local timber-workers carve a heart-shaped fountain decorated with a massive wooden penis to crown the hilltop. Not all the villagers approved – the 'panting' actually referred to nothing more than getting out of breath when climbing up it, they said – but the mayor had generated new business for the two village guesthouses and the café. None showed any sign of life when I walked through, but it was still early and their guests could have been up panting late into the night.

I took the track out towards Matisesti, looping and climbing through a tartan of sloping meadows interrupted by gullies of firs and cross-stitched by home-made fences, until eventually I was up into scrubby forest, where pines were interspersed with hornbeam and oak. The main track had divided and subdivided, but I stuck with it until I reached the straggling settlement itself, trying not to pant unnecessarily. And then, using my compass and map, I struck off on a track that seemed to head due north up through a saddle in the mountain range, and which I hoped would eventually bring me down to Poiana Horea.

It was easy enough walking, with glimpses of a giant view to the east and regular stands of wild raspberries close at hand. Bilberries, too, carpeted the clearings in the woodland. The weather was warm, but not hot, the birds were flying high, and there was a pleasant breeze. Ideal for making progress, provided I was going in the right direction.

After an hour or two without meeting anyone, I began to feel nervous, not so much about my route (my compass bearing was still good, despite several diverging choices of path), but about the presence of bears, which I knew liked berries just as much as I did. I also knew they were here in quantities, with half the brown bear population of Europe (estimated at 12,000) resident in Romania, a statistic which surfaced out of my subconscious as I walked. The more I thought about it, the more anxious I became. For a hungry bear, this path was stacked with temptation.

And then, around virtually the very next corner, I nearly collided with an old lady in a headscarf, a pail of bilberries at the end of either arm. Her lips were blue, indicating either a weak heart (a close encounter with a bear?) or that she'd been snacking while she picked. When I asked whether I was headed in the right direction, she simply nodded and walked on. I felt reassured. If there was any real danger, she would have said something, I felt sure.

Half an hour later and the track threaded between a handful of glorified mountain huts that were plainly occupied, judging by the laundry and the well-tended flowerpots. I didn't see their occupants until a few minutes later, when my eye was caught by movement through the trees when I'd nearly crested the ridge. I could make out a family in a rough clearing engaged in making hay, the father scything a poor crop, the children tumbling over one another in his wake, and the mother raking and stacking. On the surface it made an idyllic picture, but on spotting me they stopped and stared, and the family dog, until then unaware of my presence, came hollering down towards me through the brush. The family stood and watched without attempting to call it back, so as it came lurching downhill I felt for where I'd hung the Dazzer on my belt, and when I judged it close enough I gave it an electronic squirt. Instantly the dog skidded to a halt on its haunches, turned and hared back uphill to its owners. For my part, I hastily turned and walked away up the track, acutely aware of their eyes on my retreating back. Whether they'd seen or understood what I'd done I couldn't be sure, but I very much doubted it. They certainly wouldn't have heard anything from the Dazzer and nor had the dog yelped as if it had been hurt. From their perspective the little scene had probably been a touch mystifying, but from mine it had been an unqualified success. I was impressed.

The path eventually emerged into grassy flatlands at the saddle of the ridge at 1,400 metres. Here a handful of sleek, fat, hobbled horses galumphed slowly about, grazing steadily, plainly too good to be hauling timber. Their owner, sitting with his shoulders against a stockaded shrine to the Virgin Mary, seemed completely unsurprised to find a foreigner materializing at his shoulder. He confirmed that, yes, this was the way to Poiana Horea. I just needed to follow the valley down, and he waved his finger in the general direction that my compass also suggested I go.

By now I was getting used to the idea that, unlike in Western Europe, these mountain tops were settled and busy. They had yet to become a leisure facility, as in the Alps or the Pyrenees, and instead presented the opportunity of yet more, albeit seasonal, back-breaking work. Accordingly there were more wooden houses scattered over the edge on the other side, and a couple more dogs which came at me baring their teeth through gaps in wooden fences. Whether they intended to do more than just encourage me on my way I don't know, but I wasn't prepared to wait and see. When they were close enough a judicious squirt stopped them in their tracks. I was starting to get an idea of the Dazzer's range: if they were more than 5 metres away, they would just look mildly surprised.

Descending steeply now, with a whole new range of aches in muscles that had just spent the last five hours climbing, I passed whole families out haymaking, constructing stooks around the spine of what had once been a small fir, with several branch stubs left intact. This skeleton would be supported by staves and as it was piled higher with hay, a couple of the children scrambled up and walked around the top to tread it down, dodging the pitchforks raining new hay in their direction. The adults may have been doing all the hard physical work, but the children were an integral part of the whole operation.

The track became more substantial. Now that I was descending I could see it looping through the trees below me and could therefore judge where to cut the corners by plunging down through the scrub, as many a walker had plainly done before me. Eventually it stopped its hyperactive pirouetting and settled into the groove of a valley bottom that ran it down directly into Poiana

Horea, a scattered village of summer hill-farmers. In the village shop I bought a large and ludicrously expensive bottle of lemonade, and feeling that its price earned me the right to ask for information, I quizzed the proprietor about somewhere to stay. Despite having listened to, and repeated from, a teach-yourself-Romanian tape for much of the last couple of days, my Romanian was still extremely basic, and in the end we resorted to sketch maps, from which I understood there was indeed such a place. I needed to ask for 'the engineer'.

The engineer's tin-roofed house was about 2 kilometres east of the village, and it reassuringly carried a *Pensiunea* sign. Its dog was there, but its owner was not. Fortunately, unlike the other dogs I'd encountered, this one was calm and welcoming, so I settled down outside the porch and the dog settled with me.

We didn't have long to wait. A few minutes later a moon-faced middle-aged man, a touch too overweight for a farmer, came ambling through the garden gate dressed in what looked like his pyjamas, his trousers pulled right up over his belly. He looked extremely surprised to see a stranger on his doorstep.

This was Charley ('Don't call me Carol, it's a girl's name') Nemes, who turned out to be not from the mountains at all, but an Anglophile university professor from Cluj, the city that was my end destination for this part of my walk. In very good English, he explained that he was known locally as 'the engineer' because he worked in the university's faculty of electronic engineering. During the long summer holidays he and his wife Monicka retreated to his cabin in the woods and made a little money out of renting the rooms to whoever could afford them. And although tourism in the Apuseni mountains was increasing, I was the first foreign walker who had arrived independently at his doorstep. 'So you can see, when I see you at my gate I was surprise.'

The interior of Charley's house was a bit like a chalet in the Alps. Everything was wood-lined, organized and insulated. Every little bit of wood had been fiddled, turned and twiddled in a lathe by a carpenter with too much spare time, and looked like a house built out of ornamental chair legs. Sitting down over a cup of tea and a biscuit in true British style, he explained that it had been built with the help of an English friend who came out every summer. And while most of the houses around were effectively illegal – built without planning permission – his at least was completely above board. Of that he was very proud.

'The main business of these mountains is forestry. It's not legal. But what if you took it away? The community would be dead, completely dead. The foresters need houses, so they built houses.'

I said I'd been surprised to see so many, so high up, and Charley explained that it was traditional for families who were short of land in the valleys to move up into the hills in summer to make hay and to graze their animals. 'So you get more houses, it's not legal, but it is traditional.'

It was an annual upwards migration that used to happen in the Alps and the Pyrenees too, a migration that no longer takes place.

'So are there holiday houses as well? Other than yours, I mean?' I told him how, elsewhere, tourism had taken the place of tradition.

'Certainly there are,' said Charley. He said something to Monicka, who disappeared off up the track, returning fifteen minutes later with half a dozen middle-aged Romanians, all also from Cluj, all of whom spoke some English and who were curious to see the foreigner who'd appeared out of the hills. And so we had a little English-speaking tea party in the Apuseni mountains, complete with McVitie's finest biscuits, which Charley had been keeping for special occasions.

That evening I retired to bed with a slim volume by Mihai Eminescu, Romania's national poet of the 1880s. It turned out he'd been pretty outspoken when it came to the treatment of passing foreigners:

> If any shall cherish the stranger
> May the dogs eat his heart
> May the weeds destroy his house
> And may his kin perish in shame.

A hostile sentiment that only the dogs seemed to have remembered, thank God.

The next day's route was largely cross-country, along forest paths that I'd discussed at length with Charley, who was touchingly concerned I would get lost and end up wandering around the Apuseni for days on end. When I'd told him about my encounters with dogs, he'd not been surprised. Everyone kept dogs in the hills, he said, principally as protection against bears, which was why they let them be aggressive. But there weren't many bears in the Apuseni, so I didn't need to worry on that account. Which was why, when I heard something ahead of me on the track that morning, my first thought wasn't to run and hide.

It was a belly-aching, rumbling sound, clearly an animal, and probably one with a stomachache or a sore head. I didn't pay it too much attention as I rounded the corner, but as I did so I found myself making direct and sudden eye-contact with a bull. A large, free-range, leery-eyed, dribbling one, complete with horns. The real McCoy, right down to the hanging testicles. I stopped. The bull did the same, as we debated who was the more surprised. And then it started pawing the ground, as all good bulls are meant to do.

We were probably a good 50 yards apart when it first lunged forward, and happily I had the uphill advantage. Casting around me, I thanked my lucky stars that this stretch of path led through young, thick woodland. Thinking it was always a good idea to keep the height advantage I darted upwards into the pines, scrambling steeply into dim, mossy undergrowth, blood pounding in my ears.

The bull quickly reached the point where I'd disappeared. Pressing myself flat into the moss, I watched it as it stopped, turned and took a couple of paces upwards to stick its head into the gloom of the forest. I knew that British bulls had poor eyesight, so I relied on staying still as much as on being hidden. Any child playing hide-and-seek would have spotted me easily, but the bull was flummoxed, or perhaps it was so crosseyed with testosterone that it could no longer think straight. It stood there, swaying its head and belly-aching to itself, contemplating whether it was worth the effort of trying to force its way upwards, while I lay there motionless, listening to my heartbeat, and praying that it didn't. Out of the corner of my eye I was sizing up the climbability of the nearest trees.

In the end it didn't come to that. The longer the bull hesitated on the threshold of the forest, the better my chances were of its losing interest, so as the seconds ticked away I felt increasingly calm. Down below me, the animal took a step backwards on to the path to check whether or not I had sneaked back down again, and once he'd reversed back out into the daylight he seemed to forget where I'd gone. He paced up and down, bellowing a challenge, and for a split second I was tempted to bellow back, to see if he really meant it. But when I didn't emerge to fight he eventually gave me up as a complete waste of effort and continued his rumbling progress up the path.

As soon as he was out of sight I dropped down and took off in the opposite direction as quickly as I could. In the distance I would still hear him, grumbling, and I came to the conclusion that it wasn't a stomachache or sore head making him complain like that. He was a red-blooded male with a full set of balls and he was looking for a girlfriend to do a whole hill of panting.

Some hours out of Charley and Monicka's, after some difficult choices between diverging paths, I finally descended into a hamlet called Dobrus, at the meeting point of two valleys. That day Dobrus's population had been swollen dramatically by an encampment of gypsies, who'd constructed box-like shelters along the banks of the river junction and made them watertight with big sheets of plastic. There were perhaps a hundred of them, mainly women and children, all sleeping, playing, cooking, feeding and excreting in the same area. It was a harvester's camp for the forest fruit and mushrooms, and a couple of clapped-out vans down by a ford in the river were being washed down by the gangmaster, who nodded gruffly when I asked whether I was on the route for Măguri. Apart from him, however, the whole community of gypsies didn't take the slightest bit of notice of me walking through, even though I knew a foreigner with a rucksack was a very rare sight in these mountains. And even though I'd been told repeatedly that gypsies would prey on easy targets like me.

But that wasn't the last I saw of gypsies that day. In Măguri I was joined by an olive-skinned young man with a wisp of a beard and wearing a Chicago Bulls tracksuit, who caught me up, fell into step and seemed inclined to communicate in any way we could. By that time it was mid-afternoon, baking hot, and I was feeling pretty tired, having already covered something approaching 20 miles that day, so I wasn't feeling tremendously talkative, and besides, the limited Romanian I had learned was only about eating, sleeping and travelling, and it was soon exhausted.

Măguri turned out to be a long, high settlement strung along a series of tracks at 1,200 metres, and it took over an hour and a half to walk through it, with very little shade. I'd made a couple of mistakes in route choice early on, which must have added 3 or 4 miles to the day's total and certainly added to my weariness. But it was easy to see why this place had been chosen for settlement, amidst rich grasslands on a high plateau. The large timber houses, horse-carts and stockades reminded me of images of Amish country in the United States, although the Amish probably didn't have satellite dishes, as some of these houses did.

It was at one of these larger steadings that the young gypsy said he had been working, or at least that's what I understood him to say. He'd been scything hay, apparently, but I wasn't sure whether I believed him; all the other gypsy haycutters I'd seen had carried their own scythes, but this young man seemed to have no possessions at all apart from a packet of cigarettes and a mobile phone. Now the harvest was largely over, he said, his intention was to head back to his family in a town the other side of Cluj, which made his lack of any kind of baggage more worrying.

Suspiciously, too, he didn't seem to know the path any better than I did. It was I who asked whomsoever I passed whether I was on the right track, while he ambled on ahead, dropping the pace of his loping, path-skimming, light-limbed walk so that I was bound to catch him up. And when eventually the path slid down off the side of the plateau, leaving Măguri behind, he was still by my side.

By that time I'd decided that my end-destination that day would be Racatau, involving 5 or 6 miles of steady descent through what was increasingly remote, mainly forested country. If my gypsy was looking for somewhere to knock me on the head, then I was about to provide him with a whole series of perfect opportunities.

As I walked, so my suspicion turned slowly into a real anxiety, even fear, of what he might be planning – a paranoia that was made worse by my tiredness. I was aware, as I walked, that this feeling was comparatively irrational, being based entirely on what others had said and not on my own experience. After all, I told myself, fear of gypsies is a sentiment that Eastern European governments encourage, because it frees their hand in gypsy management. For their part the gypsies' main crime is the disinclination to obey their governments, fearing being enumerated, labelled, ordered and put into a system that they are unfamiliar with. A system where they work when someone else wants them to, for someone else's profit, and where they can be rendered redundant at someone else's whim. To them such a system is unacceptably proscriptive, but for us in the West, being shackled to others like this has become the basis of our working lives. It is called being a team player, and if you're not a team player then there must be something wrong with you.

As we walked, my gypsy – I'm ashamed to say I didn't

learn his name – talked pleasantly of this and that, ignoring the fact that I rarely understood anything he said and gave him little encouragement. He was very interested in whether I had a car and a house, and where that house was. When I told him it was in a place called Anglia, he said he knew where that was – it was in Hungary. He knew, he said, because he'd picked asparagus there. Then he embarked on a passionate exposition of how poor he was, and how badly paid everyone was in Romania. In between whiles he chain-smoked, checked the strength of the signal on his mobile phone, and plucked occasional fruit off what looked like young beech trees, which he tried to encourage me to eat. I refused. For my part, I tried to always keep him in sight, to make sure he wasn't using the fruit-picking as a cover to pick up a branch from the trackside with which to bash me over the head.

And so we progressed down through the trees, he composed, and me agitated, wondering when and where an attack would come. Eventually, after an hour's fast and hard walking, the Racatau valley bottom came up to meet us, complete with proper tile-roof houses, the noise of dogs barking and children crying. The sanctuary of civilization. When it reached the valley bottom the path from Măguri turned a sharp corner and spilled us out on to a roadway with a hardware shop on the corner. With a great sense of relief, I headed straight for the doorway and asked the shopkeeper if he could direct me to a place called Ionel's Cabana, which I knew to be somewhere in the valley. Once we'd established it was a couple of miles up the road, I turned, expecting to see my shadow waiting for me as usual. But the gypsy grasscutter was a good 500 metres away and disappearing fast, loping away downhill in the direction of Cluj in that same loose-limbed, skimming stride, without once looking back. He hadn't hit me over the head. He hadn't asked for money. He hadn't even said goodbye.

Instantly I felt bad. All that paranoia had proved completely unfounded. I had made mistaken assumptions based solely on his ethnicity in a way that I never thought I would. I felt as if I'd libelled him in public, and that I should publicly apologize. I wanted to summon him back and thrust some *lei* into his hand and tell him to take the bus home to speed him to the bosom of his family, but it was too late, he was already out of sight. So I turned and trudged up the track in the direction the storekeeper had pointed.

I didn't realize it at the time, but the moment I turned to head for Ionel's Cabana, I was walking into new-enterprise Romania, which had started to infiltrate the valley I'd arrived in and which was unexpectedly to dominate my next twenty-four hours. For my part, I was still blithely assuming my path would be strewn with colourful rustics and close encounters with over-romantic bulls, but I hadn't bargained for the way that Romania had already changed in cities like Cluj, and how the fallout of that change was already pushing its way up nearby mountain valleys like this.

I had a foretaste of that new-enterprise Romania at Ionel's Cabana, which turned out to be composed of two large, purpose-built buildings separated by a courtyard and a kitchen. It was in full occupation by a group of well-heeled twenty-somethings who'd come out from the city in company cars and on quad bikes, and were now having the sort of frat party I'd never have associated with Romania. The girls were in bikini tops, the guys in Hawaiian shorts with beers in their hand, and the imported music system thumped out a kind of Romanian rap, which bounded off the walls of the valley. I arrived just as they were firing up the barbecue for the evening, and I was all but ready to turn away and collapse under the nearest hedgerow when one of the group's alpha males hauled me back. There was, he said, a loft with mattresses in it, and I was welcome to sleep up there. And so I spent the night high up in the roof space above the party crowd, feeling the floor bounce beneath me, peering down through a loft window and watching the couples pairing off. The faces of local farmers appeared on the fringe of the firelight, looking on with a mixture of fascination and alienation as their new-look countrymen partied into the night in a way they must have seen done on cheap American TV, but could never have imagined in their wildest dreams fifteen years before. Mercifully, I was too tired to let the music's heavy and insistent beat keep me awake, although I do remember some kind of middle-of-the-night procession where the group were bashing saucepans with spoons, and then later I became aware of sharing the loft with a couple having sex. Exactly how that woke me up I'm not quite sure, because they were being very discreet, but a man's antenna are finely tuned when it comes to certain sounds. Needless to say, when I slipped away early the following morning there was no sign of them, or even of anyone else.

That day's walking was a culture shock, too. Accumulated fatigue meant that I'd changed my plans from valley-hopping to Cluj across the mountains to bearing straight down the Someşul Rece valley from Racatau to the main road, a distance of around 20 kilometres, and then looking for a bus. What I'd not bargained for were the weekend picnickers out of Cluj, and as I progressed I met a steady stream of cars coming up the valley on a summer Saturday, looking for grassy banks to spread out on and to spoil. The more populated the river became, the thicker the tide of litter that spread across its banks and accumulated in its pools, where it threatened to throttle the rapids. The Someşul Rece had become a conveyor-belt of used packaging.

It was hard to understand the rationale behind singling out a beauty spot for weekend picnics and then abusing it in such a way. It had to be the hangover from communism, which had never had any respect for conservation. That, plus the unaccustomed trappings of consumerism – specifically, in this case, non-biodegradable plastic bottles, beer cans and crisp packets. The net result was a local ecological disaster. In the bad old days the picnic wrappings would have been either glass, which had to be returned, or cardboard, which either decayed or was otherwise useful. By contrast the wrappings of new consumerism were throwaway, but not going to go away, so the litter-lined river became an emblem of Romania's new freedom and its new purchasing power: 'I am free, therefore I choose to throw my empty can of Carlsberg into the Someşul Rece.' And who was I to criticize? The likes of my country, after all, were the ones who persuaded them to buy the cans of Carlsberg in the first place.

Reaching the main road at Gilau I encountered another after-effect of capitalism. It was a Sunday, so there were no buses. There used to be, said a shop assistant, but now people had cars. So I hitched a ride with a middle-aged boy racer in his souped-up Renault who was working the short stretch of road between Cluj and Gilau for the afternoon. In new-enterprise Romania, hitch-hikers pay a fee.

In Cluj I fell into the care of a welcoming hospitable couple who were new-enterprise Romanians through and through. Carmen and Adi had new-look jobs, a swish company car, and lived in a new-look apartment in a condominium with shiny floors, broadband Internet, a designer open-plan kitchen and a great view. In another age and another country you'd have called them yuppies, and they'd have been proud of it, too.

Mark, whom I'd left behind in Arad, had put me in touch with Carmen, a teacher of English whom he'd got to know on one of his courses. But now she worked in an environment which he would have struggled to approve of: a private school, one of the first in Transylvania. This new school was a symptom of the democratizing onrush of contemporary Romania, but not everything about it was completely democratic. Carmen told the story of how, when he'd learned that the school was full and therefore couldn't take his daughter, a local businessman had leaned on a high-ranking policeman who'd in turn leaned on the headmistress, and a space had duly been created. Carmen was frustrated. 'Why do we need to fear the police any more?'

Over dinner we talked about their memories of the last years of communism, when they'd still been very young. Adi, who worked for a Hungarian-owned company selling computer software to supermarket chains, said he'd relished the friendships made.

'We spent a lot of time in the streets. There was no TV. My grandparents thought communism was a good thing, but my parents didn't commit themselves. Afterwards, they told me they never criticized the regime in my hearing for fear that I would repeat that criticism outside. In those days, suspicion was everywhere. You couldn't say what you thought even in your own family.'

For her part, Carmen remembered the shortages that forced her to do her schoolwork by the light of a candle, wrapped in a blanket to keep warm. She recalled her father's clever ruse of forming an association in their housing block in order to buy a video cassette player – an association was necessary because an individual buying a VC player would attract official attention – and wiring it up to all TVs. The whole block could then watch movies smuggled in from Germany, lapping up anything they could get, no matter how poor the quality. Anything was better than the two hours of state broadcasting dished out every evening, two hours entirely devoted to the lives of the Ceauşescus.

'The movies were mainly Kung Fu and soft porn,' she said. 'And because I was always good at English, I was given a microphone and I had to translate. But then word leaked out and the Securitate came calling, so it had to stop.'

She too remembered playing outside while watching for the next lorry to arrive at the shops. Her job had been to ascertain whether the lorry contained sugar or meat or bread, and then to alert her parents to see whether they wanted her to join the queue.

'Even now I can't understand,' interrupted Adi, 'how it was that with everybody working we had nothing in the shops. And how, now, with some unemployment, we have shops that are overflowing.'

Overflowing shops made good business for him, of course, particularly as new international retailers were starting to open flagship stores up and down the country. But the liberalizing regime also meant that he worked long hours, often at weekends, and didn't participate as fully as he would have liked in the life of their son.

'We're going to have a social problem with this,' he predicted. 'With the children of parents who go off to work, leaving their children without love and guidance.'

I nodded. It was one of many social problems facing a rapidly advancing new-enterprise nation.

'I think you probably are.'

Walking in Transylvania: the Saxon Villages

A day later and I was back immersed in Transylvania's timeless rural life. I'd dropped south from Cluj on a local train and emerged at a tiny rural halt, along with a handful of other passengers who all dispersed in different directions across the fields. I turned south across the fields towards the village of Atel, aka Hetzeldorf, an easy 5-kilometre walk through very different land forms to the Apuseni.

Where the Apuseni had been a high, raging sea, spumed with forest, this was a gentle, rolling swell whose downy flanks had clearly been lovingly groomed by industrious farmers for several centuries. In places the steeper sides had also been layered into terraces which had once hosted vineyards, but these terraces were now just empty shelves, adorned with the occasional vine-emulating thistle that grew to head height. Above them, the ridges were crowned by ordered copses of trees, and everything else was cloaked in a light covering of meadow grasses and wild flowers, which, if you examined it closely, proved to be a tessellation of colour, of gentian, clover and nodding sage. Here there were no plastic bottles in the streams, and the profusion of wild flowers suggested that no artificial fertilizer had ever been used. It was a hillscape which had clearly been thoroughly cared for, in a thoroughly organic way, and all that was missing were the people.

This was the heart of the Saxon Lands of southern Transylvania, a region of around 230 villages which were once home to tens of thousands of German-speaking farmers and their families. As an ethnic enclave it pre-dated the Danube Swabians by hundreds of years, because the Saxons first settled here in the twelfth and thirteenth centuries at the invitation of King Géza of Hungary. Transylvania had just become a Hungarian principality, and the king had wanted to bolster its security against possible invasion from the east, so he invited farmers and traders from what is now Flanders, Luxembourg and the Moselle Valley. He granted them effective self-rule and tax advantages as well as land, just as Empress Maria Theresa was to do many years later with the Danube Swabians in the Banat. Soon afterwards the king also settled a Hungarian warrior tribe called Székelys in the wilder country to the east, where they too still remain.

The Saxons, who were hardworking and innovative, turned a thinly populated straggle of hills into a fertile homeland. The farmers concentrated on the vineyards, maize fields and meadows, and the traders on the new fortified cities like Sighişoara, Braşov and Sibiu so that the farmers had somewhere to take their goods to market. For a while, it was a medieval garden of Eden, enlightened and egalitarian. Accordingly the population grew steadily over the centuries, reaching a peak of around 800,000 in the 1920s and becoming a major force in Transylvanian society. As part of the German-dominated Austro-

Hungarian Empire – which recognized the Saxons, the Székely and the nobility (but not the Romanians) as the three 'nations' of Transylvania – they felt secure. Like the Danube Swabians, they were scrupulous about maintaining their German culture and traditions until twentieth-century politics happened along and upset the applecart.

As he had with the Danube Swabians, Adolf Hitler saw the Transylvanian Saxons as his advance guard in the east, and he recruited many of them into his army, with promises of returning the much-valued Saxon independence that had been lost at Trianon. So when the war ended badly for Germanity as a whole, the Saxons suffered too. Soviet forces marched through the villages, rounding up most of the adult population on the basis of collective guilt and transporting them off to Siberia for six years' hard labour. Many didn't survive, and those that eventually returned home found that some of their land and houses had been handed over to Romanians, Hungarians and gypsies. During the rest of the Ceauşescu period they mostly kept their heads down, leading their traditional lives and trying not to attract attention – a strategy that nearly worked. But then in 1988 the president, who was becoming increasingly intolerant of Transylvania's ethnic minorities, went public with plans to demolish all Saxon villages, as well as thousands of Hungarian ones. As a strategy it spectacularly backfired on him, because this was the trigger that started the riots in Timişoara, and thereby the chain of events which ended in the president's death.

But the Saxons hadn't stuck around to do much celebrating. A 1978 agreement between West Germany and Romania had allowed for them to return to Germany as citizens, and many had grabbed the opportunity, even though it was many centuries since their families had originally left. This voluntary cleansing wasn't a fast process because the German government had to pay Romania 10,000 Deutschmarks for each and every one of them, ostensibly to repay all the money Romania had invested in their education. By the time the Wall came tumbling down, 250,000 had left, and most of the rest swiftly followed. But I wasn't surprised to see Atel's only street dotted with cars with German numberplates, because in the summertime they came back to check on the family property, to do a bit of painting and decorating, and to change the locks to make sure the gypsies didn't get in. My German was going to be useful again.

Atel turned out to be pretty quiet, and it was constructed in a way quite unlike the villages I'd seen before. Each house was end-on to the street, either sharply peaked or blunt-roofed, often with some kind of motif under the eaves: a date, a cross, painted flowers, ears of wheat. Between it and the next house ran a wall, sometimes with a flourish of tiles, into which was set a normal-sized door and a large double gate big enough to drive a horse and cart through. Only when that gate was open could you see the extent of the property inside.

The house sat to one side of a cobbled courtyard, where it dwindled away into low barns and storage. Opposite it stood the haybarn, of crucial importance in the difficult Transylvanian winters. Beyond it were animal pens, a well, wood piles, a large vegetable garden with geese, and an orchard, sometimes with a horse or two in a paddock.

The only variation to this pattern were the houses of the merchants or the community leaders, which would present their full frontages broadside on to the street in an uninhibited declaration of wealth. But these apart, there was a feeling of conformity in the ground plan of the village; each householder had been allocated the same sized plot, hundreds of years ago, and it was still sufficient, today, to lead effectively the same life as their medieval ancestors had done. A life based on a couple of cows, a couple of pigs, some geese and chickens, a horse or two, shared maize-cropping and lots of vegetables. Effectively it was a 500-year-old housing estate of smallholdings, so self-sufficient that communism had made little impact. They didn't need central government in any form, so when the new system had come knocking the villagers could afford just to shrug their shoulders and turn the other way, which is what had so irritated Ceaușescu.

The day was drawing on as I wandered up Atel's main street, so I was thinking in terms of finding somewhere to stay. I made enquiries at the ubiquitous Magazin Mixt (as the name suggests, rural shops stock everything) but the proprietress shook her head. Outside, I followed a horse and cart and queried the owner when he stopped. A *pension*? Yes, I said, a pension. He looked uncertain, but yes, he said, there was a pension here, and there, and over there. And he knocked on a gate, hard and loud, until eventually a little old lady, half blind, stumbled out into the daylight, like a dormouse that had been rudely woken. I apologized as best I could in my broken Romanian; plainly, the man had thought I wanted to meet *pensioners*. I mimed what I really wanted, and happily the old lady, once she'd understood, seemed relatively amused at the misunderstanding. Being hauled out on to the street by a foreigner was plenty of entertainment for one day.

And then I met the village policeman. Not only was it a surprise to find a policeman in such a small, sleepy place, but this one hailed me in English, from a street corner. When I explained what I wanted, he walked me across to knock on the door of the old people's home, where the traditional courtyard layout had been in-filled with new construction. Here a ruffianly looking man with a bunch of keys, who spoke fluent German, took me under his wing. The church had a parochial house where guests sometimes stayed, he said. I could sleep there. It would cost me 5 euros, was that OK?

And so I found myself in occupation of my own house, with my own cart-gate (locked), my own vegetable patch (neglected), my own fruit trees (ripening nicely) and my own well (full), and I could sit in my own window, as the old ladies did, and watch the occasional horse-cart tripping by. The only thing I lacked was my own cow. I felt I'd been pretty lucky again.

The house was sparsely decorated, but I didn't need much. There was an old German hymnal on the fridge, and a motto on the kitchen wall which read:

Wir kochen und braten mit Fleiss und Geschick
Wenn's köstlich Euch mundet, das ist unser Glück.

Which roughly speaking meant 'We cook and we fry with skill and talent and if you like it we feel happy.'

There were, it seemed, just thirty Saxons left in the village, and twenty-seven of those were in the old people's home. They hadn't wanted to leave with all the others, so money had been invested in the home by the younger generation, the generation who returned every year in their smart German cars to check on their houses and their relatives.

This snippet of information came courtesy of Hans, a seventy-something dipsomaniac wearing a leather blacksmith's apron who had plainly been lying in wait for me when I stepped back out of my gate on to the street. Did I want to visit the church? he asked.

Transylvania's Saxon villages are famous for their fortified churches. King Géza had been realistic with his settlers: he needed them to be medieval speed bumps, to slow down any hostile Tartars and Turks heading west, and they accordingly had prepared their settlements with fortifications into which they could retreat when anything fierce and hairy turned up at the gate. Being pragmatic, God-fearing people, they combined their fortress sanctuary with their most valuable building, their church, which would supply them with spiritual strength while the enemy gnashed its teeth without. It would give them physical refreshment, too, because within its massive walls they constructed storerooms in which to hang their air-cured hams. Placing them there must have been the medieval equivalent of putting money in the bank.

Hans, who had only one tooth and cackled unnecessarily to give it maximum exposure, threw open the gates and led me through the massive entrance bastion under the inscription *'Ein' feste Burg ist unser Gott'* (literally 'A strong fortress is our God'), the first line of one of Martin Luther's favourite hymns. The church stood in the courtyard inside. It dated from 1380, although its gates were a comparatively young 1798. Massive, whitewashed walls rose to an ochre-tiled roof plated like a dragon's back that undulated as if it was breathing, but inside all was quiet apart from a wincing floor. The interior was bewitchingly simple and dusty, but it did have a neo-baroque altar plonked down at the far end, a beacon of colour amongst pale unvarnished wood. Plainly, everything needed work, but equally plainly everything could probably last several more centuries, as long as the roof remained intact. There was a service every second Sunday, said Hans, but the musicians' gallery, he agreed, was no longer used. He didn't want to disappoint me with lack of tradition, however, so he added that he rang the church bell at 7 a.m. to encourage the men into the fields, again at midday to tell them to lay down their tools for lunch, and again at night for lights out. And occasionally to ward off thunderstorms. Did I want to climb up? I certainly did.

A set of glorified ladders zigzagged up through the well of the tower, which smelled of woodworm and bat shit. Each new floor was littered with the remains of owls' nests, and although the ladders felt sturdy enough under foot, they would never have passed any health-and-safety examination, which was possibly why Hans declared that he would stay at the bottom and wait for me. Eventually I arrived under the pagoda-like tower, in a belfry exposed on all sides and with daylight glinting through between the tiles above my head. On the eastern side the castellated roof-ridge rippled away like a fairground ride, long since having lost all its youthful straight lines. To the north I could look out over the medieval grid plan of the village. To the west rose the next hills, and to the south I could look down on an ox-cart creaking back from the fields. The whole thing looked like an illustration from a children's book, or a model village from a history museum. I blessed my luck that I had it all to myself.

Back at ground level, Hans was quick to ask for money for the church and money for him, both of which I gave, hoping that it didn't all end up in the same pot, being transformed into alcohol. He beamed, an expression which wasn't lost on another elderly man in a leather apron, this time with two teeth rather than just one. Leaving his bench outside the old people's home, this second man too asked, in German, for 'a donation', in a way that suggested that merely speaking German was a party trick which he would do only for a cash incentive.

I gave him a token amount, and later came across him in the Magazin Mixt waving his coin at the shop owner, trying to persuade her to give him a couple of swigs of *palinka*.

By the time I set out next morning I was truly in love with the place. I'd slept on a mattress on the floor, waking to the lowing of cattle heading out for the fields, the murmur of voices under the window and the insistent rhythm of the occasional horse and cart. It was a dull, drizzly day, but I still found my surroundings compellingly beautiful. Life had slowed down around me to match my pedestrian pace, and I felt in harmony with it, savouring everything, even the crunch of my boots on the gravel road. I belonged. As I walked, I exchanged mumbled greetings with every villager I passed, most of whom regarded me with a mix of curiosity and benevolence.

I headed out of Atel in a southerly direction through orchards heavy with plum trees, chickens in chicken runs and peonies in peony-filled stockades around religious shrines. Whole bushes were vibrating with stonechats and whinchats, the hedgerow was deep in downy round-wort, thickened with tall feathery grasses, and topped with explosions of yellow buds. There was slender yellow rattle hidden in the verges, along with blue creeping bell-flower and purplish pink knapweed, trying to compete with the more brutal ruderals like greater burdock and marsh mallow. *Rudus* is Latin for rubbish, so these were plants that grew in rubbish land, but they had their uses despite the derogatory name; the mallow's soft flowers were used against sore throats and the dried seed-heads or burs from the burdock used to be placed on the strings of suspended hams in the church stores to deter mice.

The track quickly decayed, fraying at every twist in the

valley and sending off confusing side-branches to probe every fold in the hills. The tread on my boots clogged up with mud, and I slipped regularly, to the amusement of a mewing bird of prey. My map insisted there was a proper road to the next village, 7 kilometres away, but it was clearly wrong. So I hauled out my compass again, and discovered that its polarities had been completely reversed by sitting in the rucksack pocket alongside my rechargeable torch. It was still effective in its upside-down way, and with its help I stuck to the trail whose heading conformed closest with the direction I wanted to go. It was worryingly under-used for an arterial route between villages; I could see only one set of cart tracks since the overnight rain, but once I'd crested a set of hills and descended the other side, union with another track produced a horse and cart loaded with hay and children, who found the sight of a foreigner with a rucksack very amusing. Tagging along behind them, I entered Richis with the tolling of the noonday bell, the sign to down tools and eat lunch, so I sat outside the Magazin Mixt and hacked into bread and salami.

From Richis it was an easy afternoon's walk down a river valley, along a proper metalled road, to the village of Biertan, aka Birthelm, one of the best known of the Saxon villages.

Biertan, which has a UNESCO-listed church, is in all the guidebooks, whereas Atel is not, so I arrived full of expectation. And certainly it had a feeling of importance, with a handful of grander buildings around the main square, where the largest market in the region used to be held. The square was dominated by the multi-turreted church (effectively a cathedral in its day), castle-like on its own little hill, surrounded by sentinel towers.

But there were tourists here, and money, a craft shop,

an information centre and a restaurant, plus a regular flow of cars, which completely changed the feel of the place. There was even a white line in the middle of the road. After the innocence and the virginity of unknown Atel, Biertan felt commercial and worldly wise. People arrived here at 30 m.p.h., spent a couple of hours and a couple of dozen *lei*, summed the place up, and left. The village was indifferent to their passing, which was fair enough, but by this stage I'd been getting used to the idea of being a walking curiosity in an unsullied land, where life was led at medieval pace. However, Biertan's lack of interest in me worked both ways; two could play at the indifference game.

Its image in my eyes wasn't helped by the first two accommodation options I tried being (a) unfriendly and (b) full. But then, in the village's themed 'medieval' restaurant, I found myself talking to someone who was plainly a manager, well versed in customer care, who persuaded me that I should stay in the newest opening, which turned out to have a TV, minibar and hydromassage shower. Lovely, but inconsistent with my experience thus far. And so I ended up wandering around inside Biertan's celebrated church feeling out of sorts, out of kilter and unappreciative. As for the latter, it was too big for a church, too small for a cathedral, and its tracery-veined ceiling, oriental carpets and tattered guild flags didn't do much to rectify a fundamental lack of elegance. Even the news of a 'divorce room', where couples intending to separate were locked up and forced to share a single room, single bed and single plate to make them see sense, failed to impress. It also didn't help that in this, the most famous Saxon church, visitors weren't allowed to climb up a single one of its multitude of towers, no doubt for very good reasons of health and safety.

Happily, normal service was resumed next day, as I found myself climbing another rickety set of ladders in the tower of the fourteenth-century church at Copsa Mare, aka Grosskopisch. Here there were gaping holes in the plankwork floor that would have been lethal on a dark night, but there was no suggestion of stopping anyone going up, and the view was if anything better than at Atel. From the tower, Copsa Mare looked like the skeleton of a leaf that had been dropped into the valley many aeons ago. It had decayed a great deal over successive centuries, but you could still see the basic outline. Smoke rose gently from summer kitchens with the sound of chickens and barking dogs, and there was a horse-cart of newly scythed grass standing outside the Magazin Mixt. The farmer emerged, slapped his mare on the rump, and they clopped off home, the mare's foal skittering alongside. There was nothing in the picture that didn't belong to any of the last five hundred years, although sharp eyes might have spotted a familiar label on the beer bottle in the farmer's hand, and even sharper might have spotted the condensation, too. It had just come out of the Magazin's fridge.

'Your Prince Charles was here.' The church-keeper had accompanied me up the tower.

'Oh?' I knew this, but perhaps he knew more. 'When?'

'Last year, maybe.'

'He has a house over in Malancrav, doesn't he? I'm heading there, via Nou Sasesc.'

'Ah, Malmkrog and Neudorf,' said the church-keeper, gently correcting my Romanian names with the original German.

'And I heard he walked this way, like me?' I'd got it from a reliable source, but the church-keeper wasn't to be drawn.

'*Das weiss ich nicht.* But here, I'll show you the route you need to take.' And he pointed out a trail that rose through maize fields towards a hill topped with ash, elm, false acacia and willow.

A couple of hours later I was relying on my skew-whiff compass again. The weather had deteriorated, producing a strangely muted day where birds on the wire were not bothering to sing and flowers on the mallow couldn't decide whether to be out or in. The hilltop woods were drenched in low-slung cloud, and as I neared them I could hear them slow-handclapping as it started to rain. The track top deteriorated into sticky clay and I was grateful when it merged into a grassland track, although I felt guilty, too, about stepping on wild flowers, some of which might well have been rare, with my muddy feet. Despite the weather, it was impossible not to feel uplifted by just being there.

I spent ages trying to cross a stream without getting wet, only to emerge into neck-high reeds which drenched me from head to foot as I pushed through them. The compass took me straight up a hillside, along a ridge and down through a crowd of umbellifers, which soaked me once more, and delivered me into Nou Sasesc. Here there were several German numberplates in the village, as expected, and a group of men talking about what exactly needed to be done. The first one I queried for directions spoke only Romanian and suggested the only way into the next valley was by going all the way down to the main road and back up again, a distance of at least 25 kilometres. Another butted in, this time in German. No, he said, there was a *Feldweg* – field path – over the top and down the other side. It was not far.

The track led me up through a belt of oakwoods into a beechwood forest of some substance. It was tall, sombre and silent inside. Dark, slender trunks reached up and up, finally flinging out suppliant fingers at the sky somewhere way above my head, trying to grasp enough daylight to survive. Down below, the effect was of walking through a giant cavernous room where daylight struggled to make its presence felt, of threading through an echoing forest of Moorish arches, like in the great mosque at Cordoba. Unfortunately, unrestricted by any ground-level growth, the path completely unravelled, frittering itself away amongst the proliferation of trees. Once again I was left with only the compass as my guide, but fortunately it wasn't long before the ground started to fall away again and I was back out on to the springy turf of rolling meadows, feeling that I should have a set of panpipes or a flute to hand and do a little jig as I emerged from the trees.

Malancrav was ringed with apple orchards. By Saxon standards it was a large village, pleasingly arranged around two intersecting valleys with a stream at its centre, and served by a poorly surfaced road that brought very little in the way of motorized traffic. It had an old-fashioned sweep-well, and some of its houses were still the original mud-walled and lime-washed variety, where succeeding coats of paint struggled to cling to the uneven surface, giving the overall effect of trendy rag-rolling. And yet there was plenty of activity here, with talkative children on bicycles and happy geese in the stream, and I knew that it still had an eighty-strong Saxon population, a German-language school and its own Lutheran pastor who'd originally come here on holiday from Germany, never to leave again. And besides the house belonging to Prince Charles, it was also the focus of efforts of an organization called the Mihai Eminescu Trust. Despite being named after the nationalist poet who wrote that stuff about being hostile to strangers, the Trust was actually the brainchild of very posh Brits, with Charles as their patron. Its aim was to preserve built and natural heritage, so it had snapped up a handful of the vacated houses in Malancrav, restored them, and now rented them out on a low-key basis to anyone they considered suitably respectful. I managed to creep in under the bar.

It seemed Malancrav was used to wandering foreigners. I found the house with the help of a sassy girl in her twenties who'd just come back from a waitressing job in Germany, and who happened to be in the village shop when I asked about the Trust. As we walked through the village together, she greeted everyone who passed with 'This is my new man.' When I, too, grunted in amusement, she looked alarmed. 'You can speak Romanian?'

'I can't really speak, but I can understand.'

I wished I hadn't said anything as we walked on in silence.

She handed me over to a pretty teenager who had the house key. After Atel, I knew what to expect in terms of interior layout: the cart-gate and the main door, the end-on gable, the yard rising to orchards, the outhouses and barns. Inside, the house was stripped back and austere, with all the comfort of a museum, but there was a spirituality in its simplicity; a coat of varnish would have been frivolous. Simple wood floors and furniture, an oak table and dresser, and on the wall the same Lutheran line as above the church in Atel, *Ein' feste Burg ist unser Gott*, in stern Gothic lettering. The only concession to modernity was the bathroom.

The teenager returned an hour later, once I'd made the place more homely by draping my damp clothes all over the furniture. This time she was with a friend and bearing a dinner of salad and chicken soup cooked by her mother over the road, which I ate while the two of them stayed in the kitchen giggling furiously. If I hadn't had a teen-age daughter of my own I might have thought they were laughing at me, all by myself at the oak table with my beatific grin and surrounded by my smelly socks. Perhaps they thought I was Prince Charles.

When they'd gone I sat in the window and watched the evening cow parade, which I'd come to recognize as a key feature of daily life in Transylvanian villages. Cows in these parts were credited with intelligence and responsibility, and once given the command to go, they took themselves up to the pastures in the morning and brought themselves down again in the evening, like members of the family going to work. For me, their return helped to pick out the houses which were still occupied, because gates would open and owners would step out over the threshold into the street and wait, chatting to their neighbours. Some of the returning cows would put on little cameos, like the one that found its gate shut and had to bellow to be let in, or the buffalo that browsed a neighbour's flowerbed and found itself under attack from the neighbour's dog. Many would be welcomed home by a slap on the rump and a clip around the ankles with a birch switch, as the householders bid good evening over their shoulders to the rest of the street. I could almost envisage some kind of verbal exchange once the gate was shut behind them.

'Did you have a nice day in the fields, dear?'

'Forget the small talk and for God's sake get your hands on my udders.'

Next morning I left before sunrise, but one of Malancrav's pigs had departed this world before me and the gutters were running red with its blood. A funereal mist shrouded the valley, but as the sun climbed so it initiated a slow striptease, revealing some parts, and leaving others veiled in wisps and wreaths. Those parts it illuminated looked pretty delectable, the low sun picking out overnight dew on the cobwebs, turning them into lacy hedgerow lingerie, much to the irritation of the scowling spiders sitting spotlit at their centre.

A man on an old bicycle came bouncing down the hill, his scythe strapped to his back, greeting me as I stood aside to let him pass. I daresay he'd have been pleased to see the change in the weather, because there'd have been no haymaking work during the previous days of rain. I followed his tracks upwards into woodland, but concluded eventually that he'd been cycling along the ridge, looking for a way down, whereas I just needed to keep heading east, up hill and down dale. So I retraced my steps for a while and resorted to the compass again.

It was rougher walking that day, and I spent a lot of the morning getting wet and dry again as I passed from meadows that were still in the shade to meadows that had spent some time in the sun. Perhaps because of the rougher terrain, I came across a couple of horsemen, too. The first was a large, swarthy man seated bareback on an equally broad-shouldered beast, on the outskirts of the village of Cris. The rider was having a shouted exchange with a cowherd up in the hills a good three-quarter mile away. He released a couple of words at a time, elongating the vowels, letting them roll up in the hill in the still air. Then he'd wait for the reply to come barrelling down again. With the distortions of this long-distance talking I couldn't pinpoint the language, and the two men may well have been gypsies, but I could tell that all was not well. The horseman looked grumpy at the outcome. I'd guess it was a kind of 'Where did you put my wallet?'-type conversation, where the answer is invariably 'I haven't touched your blessed wallet.' The sort of conversation I usually have when I too am riding out of town.

The other horseback communication was directed at me. I was halfway down the road from Cris to Sighişoara, leaving the Saxon villages behind me, when two horsemen appeared on a ridge to my right, and started to hulloo downwards. I felt pretty sure that they were asking for information about their route, and I felt bad that I couldn't understand them. I'd asked for, and received, so much help myself in the last few days that I would have liked to have returned the favour, particularly now that I really did know where I was. But my ear couldn't make sense of those elongated vowels, so in the end all I could do was wave and shout cheerful greetings in English in the hope they'd realize I was a foreigner.

Not long afterwards a farmer came down the road in his beaten-up old Dacia and offered me a lift to Sighişoara, so in the end I made my exit from the Saxon villages at 30 miles per hour.

21

Transylvanian High Society

A couple of days later I was back in the tender care of the aristocracy, in the shape of the familiar welcoming figure of Tibor Kalnoky, the Transylvanian count who had so impressed me on my first-ever visit to Romania. Tibor was an urbane, sophisticated European aristocrat in his early forties who had flawless manners and spoke flawless English as well as German, French, Hungarian and Romanian. His family pedigree dated back to the twelfth century, and his great-uncle Gustav had been prime minister of the Austro-Hungarian Empire. His charm, integrity and family history had been one of the catalysts for my journey.

After the Saxon villages, I'd only lingered long enough in Sighişoara to let my boots dry. It was a handsome place, for sure, particularly the medieval section atop Castle Hill, where it was ringed with towers erected by various guilds, amongst them the tinsmiths' tower, the butchers' tower, the farriers' tower, the tailors' tower and the shoemakers' tower – this last a peaked fairytale effort which was now the home of the local radio station. Cobbled and ribboned with flags, with music echoing down the streets, Castle Hill was officially a UNESCO World Heritage site, a sort of Mont-St-Michel of Transylvania, with a daily migration of tourists that started as soon as the sun warmed the cobbles.

It was also the birthplace of Vlad Ţepeş, aka Vlad the Impaler, definitely not a cobble-warming sort of a chap, although the building that claimed to be his birthplace was actually built a year too late. Vlad had been the model for Dracula, but the town seemed equivocal about cashing in on the whole Vlad thing. Dracula souvenirs didn't leap out from every street corner, there were no themed tours, and it wasn't easy to get marinaded on Dracula cocktails. This may have been because in Romanian eyes the fifteenth-century prince was, contrary to his literary reputation elsewhere, a bit of a national hero, thanks to his military successes against the Turks.

The Impaler part of his name derives from his trademark method of torture and execution of his enemies. He'd have his men insert the sharp end of the stake into the victim's anus and, sometimes with the assistance of a couple of horses, haul it all the way up the body to emerge at the mouth. Death was always slow. Even visiting ambassadors were risking their lives, because a perceived insult could result in their hats being nailed to their heads in such a way that they'd never be doffing them again.

By all accounts Vlad divided his panache for spectacular execution even-handedly between would-be invaders and fellow-countrymen, male and female, boy and girl. One legend has him leaving a gold cup in the street and returning to pick it up the next day; so fearful were the locals of his wrath that no one had dared to touch it. In many ways he was the Saddam Hussein of his day.

Certainly the Ottomans got to know him pretty well, and there were stories of whole armies turning back when they came upon rank upon rank of stakes on which were impaled thousands of rotting carcasses of fellow-soldiers who had previously attempted to unseat him. When he was finally defeated, he was decapitated and his head was sent to Constantinople, where the Turks had it preserved in honey and put on display to demonstrate that he was properly dead.

The 'Dracula' name actually belonged more properly to his father, Vlad Dracul, where *dracul* meant 'of the order of the dragon', although it has since come to mean 'devil'. The exact back-story didn't really matter to the author of *Dracula*, Irish writer Bram Stoker, who probably mixed a lot of Vlad the Impaler with a bit of the legend of Elizabeth Báthony, a sixteenth-century countess who abducted and tortured hundreds of young girls and was supposed to have bathed in their blood in an attempt to preserve her youth. Either way, the resulting book is a piece of great storytelling set in a land which no one knew anything about, where there were certainly no vampire bats and whose natives were very unlikely to object.

Bram Stoker wasn't the only one to take advantage of Transylvania's perceived exoticism. Jules Verne, whose Danube book appears earlier in these pages, took a similar approach with his *The Castle in the Carpathians*, using Transylvania as the setting for an unashamedly Gothic tale where an evil baron incarcerates a beautiful opera-singing countess in his remote castle, keeping the villagers and shepherds away with ghostly special effects. The Transylvania of his book is a place of gloomy forests, ruined castles, mountains with tumbled rocks, and shepherds who can forecast the weather from feeling the wool of their sheep. It's a place which, according to a line in the book, 'lends itself so naturally to all sorts of supernatural imaginings', largely because nobody amongst the readership knew any better.

Modern Transylvania still has something of the Transylvania in these storybooks – the forests, the castles, the mountains and the shepherds – but its aristocracy doesn't sleep in coffins. Count Kalnoky carried none of the threat of his fictional predecessors, although there was a certain air of mystery about him, driving as he did through semi-medieval landscapes in an immaculate Range Rover with diplomatic numberplates, on account of being a Knight of the Order of Malta. He was more Da Vinci Code than Dracula, and it wasn't so long ago that he'd first come to work in Romania as a mere marketing executive in a pharmaceutical company, albeit an executive with a title.

The count's return was almost happenstance. The family had first fled westwards into Hungary in 1939, escaping fascism, and from there they had been driven further west still by communism, eventually ending up in the United States. Some time later they'd returned to Europe, and Tibor was born in Germany, where his father had risen through the ranks of IBM to head the computer giant for the whole of Eastern Europe. In 1987, with the tide turning against communist ideology, the twenty-year-old veterinary student persuaded his father that the time had come to revisit secretly the family heritage in the Hungarian-speaking region of Transylvania. They'd travelled discreetly and with little or no expectations, but were exhilarated to find 'very, very nice villages', with equally nice villagers attached.

'My father was recognized as soon as we set foot in Miklósvár. By the time we came out of the church, half the village was assembled outside. We couldn't communicate with them – in those days we no longer spoke Hungarian – but it was a very, very emotional moment. And then someone said that a convoy of cars was coming. There were no cars in rural areas in those days, so it had to be the Securitate.' They escaped by driving through the forest, and to their credit the villagers never gave them away, despite days of questioning. Even decades of anti-gentry propaganda hadn't erased ancient respect.

After that the young count resolved to return and to fight to get back the family's two manor houses and half a dozen village houses. He went to Budapest to learn Hungarian, and then a large pharmaceutical company keen to expand into emerging Eastern Europe offered him a post in Bucharest. From there he began the legal process of seeking restitution, suing the state for eight long years, a process he finally won in 1999: 'Just a year before Romania passed a law which would have given everything back anyway.'

The properties he recovered were in a bad state, particularly the two manor houses, which had been used as Party headquarters and then community halls. It would take many years, great determination and considerable funds to bring these buildings back to what they once were. Without revenue from land – 'to keep one square metre of manor house, you need one hectare of forest' – Kalnoky decided to seek income from tourism. He restored some village houses in Miklósvár and opened them as oak-beamed guesthouses, with oil lamps and wood-fired heating, antique furniture and hand-embroidered textiles, as well as the latest in low-voltage lighting and some of the only bidets in Transylvania.

The project had worked well. Miklósvár was in the heart of Székely country, that warlike Hungarian tribe whom King Géza had settled in the eastern Carpathians. Their villages were more low-slung and had less architectural flourish than in the Saxon lands, but their lifestyle had the same compelling simplicity, and here at least whole communities were largely intact. A population of 700,000 was still in place, in defiance of Ceauşescu, and, in defiance of anything digital or even mechanical, still operating a horse-and-cart economy in a landscape with bears in the forests and wolves in the hills.

Miklósvár was a particularly good example. Here there had never been any recorded crime, and tradition still had the upper hand. This was a place where the old wives' tales came true, where you literally didn't count your chickens until they were hatched, and you made sure you made hay while the sun shone. In fact you made a cartload of hay for every leg of a cow, and two extra cartloads for every leg of a horse. And given that those two beasts were the prize possessions of most families in Miklósvár, everyone and his auntie seemed to be out scything hay in the days that I was there.

On my previous visit I'd drunk *palinka* with wood-cutters up in the forests, sitting on their horsedrawn sleds. I'd been wolf-tracking in the snow, knowing that the wolf population worried the farmers. And I'd discussed the bear problem with the local women who worked in Count Kalnoky's kitchen, where they prepared the pork stews, dumplings and smoked cheeses.

This time their opinion was that the problem was getting worse, and an American girl had already been killed by a bear earlier in the year. There'd also been a 'wolf child' found, a feral boy who'd spent years living with wild animals, Mowgli-style, and had forgotten how to speak. Stories like these could have belonged to Bram Stoker, and I found myself listening to them with sympathy, but without fear, now that my wilderness walking was done.

The count's social connections and the uniqueness of his home-stays had the reputation for attracting an interesting mix to his dinner table, because although the accommodation was spread out through the village, all guests converged on the main house to eat together at the end of the day. Diplomats were fairly frequent visitors, and there was even the occasional heir to the throne in the shape of Prince Charles, who had become something of a friend, and who was relying on the count to assist in the restoration of his Saxon houses. The count called these his 'Agatha Christie' dinners, partly because of the gathering of different social stereotypes in an isolated closed community, and partly because usually most of the guests were British. They certainly were on this occasion, and I found it disconcerting to step straight into British society after having forged my own solitary path across fairly wild country. But, sadly, there were no royals or diplomats amongst them, nor even any feckless curates, chancers, penniless aristocrats, or doctors with histories of alcoholism, as Agatha Christie would have had it.

This new social environment threw up a new difficulty for me: I had to make sure I still had a supply of sufficiently clean clothes to look presentable as I went from one titled household to the next. For his journey, Patrick Leigh Fermor had carried two pairs of dark flannel trousers, a 'decent-looking' tweed jacket, several shirts, two ties, a pair of pyjamas and a soldier's greatcoat. I was travelling a lot lighter, but I still had a clean shirt and clean trousers for special occasions somewhere at the bottom of my rucksack. Fortunately, at my next stop, the Mikes estate at Zabola, everyone was wearing jeans.

This was still Székely land, and the Mikes and the

Kalnoky estates were relatively near neighbours. The difference was that while Kalnoky's guests were effectively accommodated within the village, those at Zabola were hosted behind private gates within the massive estate grounds, so it was a taste of life as it must once have been.

The estate's parkland and mature woodland had been planned by a celebrated French garden designer to cradle the main manor house, which dated from the seventeenth century. In the nineteenth century a huge lantern had been added to the roof and a tower-like portico bolted to the front, commensurate with the family's growing wealth and importance. Eventually a whole new villa, just as big but not quite as decorative, had to be built a short distance from the manor to accommodate all the guests. The two buildings were then connected by an underground tunnel so that guests could make their way across to the main house without exposing their formal dining dress to inclement weather.

Back in those days the reception of visitors was a full-time activity for established Transylvanian families like the Mikes. As with their close cousins in Hungary, they had little need actually to do any work, relying instead on their large landholdings and teams of managers to relieve them of day-to-day issues, so that they themselves could concentrate on the likes of hunting, or horse-breeding, or library-building, or throwing great parties. These life-styles (the rump end of which was experienced by Leigh Fermor) were chronicled by a Transylvanian aristocrat called Miklos Bánffy, writing at much the same time as Leigh Fermor came wandering through and staying for lunch, tea, dinner and several days thereafter.

Bánffy is the George Eliot of Transylvania, and he chronicles archaic society life in a trilogy of books that doesn't spare on the sumptuous detail and which could belong to any of the last three or four centuries. The image he creates is of an endless round of grand balls, of family visits to big houses, of gargantuan meals and of romantic intrigue. Households of that era were surprisingly Anglophile, often sending sons and heirs to British public schools – as the Wenckheims had done with Ampleforth – using spoken English in clever asides in conversation, and adopting English fashion trends. They even had an institutionalized teatime, when ladies sat waiting for visitors around plates of hot muffins and thin sandwiches, dressed in loose flowing tea-gowns 'in the English fashion', with necklines and sleeves sewn with festoons of old lace. These women were far from emancipated; many wives were unhappy in their marriages, cooped up in remote manor houses while their husbands had affairs with women in town and in the villages. Meanwhile their daughters vied spitefully with each other for the hand of the most eligible of the bachelors who came calling, so desperate were they to leave home.

The men, meanwhile, would do a bit of studying in their youth, although it was unthinkable that they would ever prioritize exams over the likes of the first pheasant shoot of the season. So there was a succession of tutors and governesses (usually from France or England) who despaired of ever teaching them anything. Mind you, every house was invariably proud of its library, which would contain essentials such as the works of Voltaire and dissertations on Palladian architecture, printed on vellum and encased in the family's own leather bindings.

The position of these families in Transylvanian society was nothing to do with personal achievements or wealth, but all about the quality of their bloodline. Thus the descendants of conquering Magyar warlords had higher social standing than the children of a Greek banker who had spent all his life polishing the seat of his office desk and had become very rich as a result. The true old crusties considered politics to be shoddy muck-raking, and they adhered rigidly to family tradition in their voting habits. Bánffy describes how one old fossil 'managed to overlook the fact that Balint [his main character] was an MP only because . . . he knew that the Abady's first ancestor had been a Bessenyo chief from the Tomai clan, who had settled in Hungary as long ago as the reign of Prince Géza.'

These honourable gentlemen would move from banquet to banquet, race meeting to race meeting, being waited on by liveried footmen in tailcoats. Bánffy describes these manorial social occasions with great relish. How, on sitting down at table, an awed silence would descend on the gathering to give the food, the wine and the well-trained staff due respect. 'Not a plate clattered, not a glass tinkled; the solemn hush was broken only as the butler or head footman poured wines with a soft murmur of mysterious words. "Chateau Margaux 82?"' Then would begin the avalanche of dishes. Capercaillie, venison, turkey stuffed with herbs, hare pâtés, home-cured hams and whole pike without bones (regarded as a great culinary *tour de force*). Battleships of fish platters, sauceboats of gravy and relish, and snippets of gossip. This would be followed by towering cakes, compotes and tarts, piled with whipped cream, after which the elder gentlemen would adjourn to cigars on the terrace and then gambling in the basement, while the younger men would drink until they vomited.

At the larger occasions there'd be dancing: waltzes, square dances, stately French *cotillons*, and traditional Hungarian *czardas*, starting slow and getting quicker and quicker, to music provided by a gypsy band. Then there'd be a light supper at 1.30 a.m. to maintain the momentum and help the party through till dawn.

Male conversation on these occasions invariably rotated around each others' hunting stories, and a good estate always made sure that the guest of honour had the best shots standing on either side of him, to ensure that a good bag would be placed at his feet. That tradition continued into the communist years, where the likes of Ceauşescu and Honecker were regularly pictured standing triumphantly over the carcass of a giant bear or a twenty-pointer stag. There'd be no mention of the fact that some of Honecker's stags had only just been defrosted before being propped against a tree, and Ceauşescu's bears had been slowed down by secret agents who'd pre-doped them with pots of honey laced with Valium. On one day in the autumn of 1983 he shot twenty-four.

On his journey, Leigh Fermor got a whiff of the tail-end of this lifestyle, which had only half a dozen years to run before it was swept away. At Zabola I did too, because such elaborate socializing must have been a priority on the estate, given the sheer size of the guest villa and the elaborate tunnel arrangements. Years of misuse (variously sanatorium, school and children's home) had effectively wrecked both buildings, and everything of value had been removed, even down to the rows of sinks wrenched off the wall in the schoolboy bathrooms. So now the family guests were reduced to staying in the Machine House, a third building down by the lake which had once contained generators and a small textile factory, but which had been converted into high-ceilinged accommodation and decorated in post-colonial shabby chic by the returning family. The result looked like a coming together of Indian hill station, Tudor-beamed British cottage and Austrian lakeside villa, which was a fairly close reflection of its creators: two brothers with an Indian father, who'd grown up in Austria but who'd attended British public schools.

On the afternoon I arrived the thirty-something Gregor Roy Chowdury of Ulpur, the elder of the two brothers, presided over afternoon tea set out on linen-covered tables on the summer lawn outside the Machine House. Despite the name, he looked more Italian than Indian, and his English was measured and stately, as befitting nobility, although technically he wasn't titled at all. I couldn't see him raising his voice at the cook, the maid, the butler or the underfootman, as his forefathers must have done, but he plainly had inherited a certain steely determination to put Zabola back together again.

His father, Shuvendu Basu Roy Chowdury, had been from a Bengali family that had lost its landholdings in the partition of India, and had met his mother, the Countess Katalin Mikes, at Graz University, where they had both been students. Two dispossessed people coming together from two very different cultures. They'd had two sons, Gregor and Alexander, who'd spoken German to each other, Hungarian to their mother and English to their father. With a young family to feed, the countess had become a university librarian, while her husband had become an oil trader, shuttling back and forth between Austria and London. It was the latter's death that had precipitated the family's return to Romania.

The Countess Katalin, whom I guessed to be in her mid-sixties, had plainly been very attractive in her prime, but she'd had a tough start to life that must have rocked her self-confidence. The communists had burst into Zabola in the middle of the night when she'd been just three years old, and loaded her and her mother, the only remaining residents, into the back of a truck. Her mother had ended up working in one of the labour camps in the Danube

Delta – camps for enemies of the state who were tasked with creating rice fields, and where the expectation was that many inmates would die. Her mother had indeed nearly perished in the harsh conditions, and eventually her health had become so chronically bad that after a couple of years she was released. Many other relatives were not so lucky.

Meanwhile the little girl Katalin had been removed from the Delta-bound truck at the last minute and taken in by villagers in Zabola, from where she'd eventually been moved to Cluj to live with another branch of the family. Even there her background had excluded her from all but the most basic education, but her family connections meant that, when Ceauşescu started doing deals with outside nations over ethnic minorities, relatives in Germany were able to produce sufficient quantities of Deutschmarks to 'buy' her and get her out.

The family were to come back regularly to Transylvania over succeeding years, but it wasn't until after the Romanian Revolution that they started to think about making a claim to all the property they'd once owned and looking for relevant land-registry papers.

'When we were children we used to spend hours sitting in mayors' offices all over the region,' remembered Gregor, 'while my mother asked the same questions over and over again. Papers would appear and disappear, and to get the originals sometimes required going to court. As kids, we didn't understand a lot of what was going on.'

Eventually the countess's persistence was rewarded, and the parkland and houses were officially returned in 1997 – in theory. In practice it was to be another eight years before the sanatorium patients and staff finally left, before the meadows could be used for horses again and before the woodland emptied of its wandering lost souls.

The burning question for the Mikes/Roy Chowdury family was what to do next. What could be done with it all, now that they'd got it back? There was no time for eccentricities: two massive buildings in a poor state of repair represented a cash-flow bottomless pit. The deceptively languid Gregor, who'd been the first to come and live here permanently, had taken the initiative and converted the Machine House into upmarket guest accommodation to stem the losses. Although the family was slowly getting land back, revenue from forestry and agriculture to support the buildings was a long-term solution, which was why I found myself at dinner that night with two international bankers – one Dutch and one Argentinian – and their assorted families and nannies, plus a Romanian public relations entrepreneur and her journalist partner. They were representatives of the new capitalists who were profiting at the heart of Romania's emerging democracy, and they were invaluable to the Mikes estate, because they had the inclination and the spending power to escape the heat and the soullessness of Bucharest and treat Zabola as a weekend retreat. No doubt eventually they'd secure themselves country cottages elsewhere, but meanwhile Gregor, Alexander and Countess Katalin could once again play at being host.

So the estate that had once welcomed floods of important personages, and which had had a long intermission in the company of the young, the destitute and the insane, had once again become a sanctuary for Romania's elite. Only this time they were paying.

22

Bucharest's Royal Pretender

In Transylvania my route diverged from Patrick Leigh Fermor's to the point of no return. After his whirlwind romantic motorized tour of the likes of Deva, Sighişoara and Cluj he'd hastily escorted the glamorous 'Angela' back to her married life, lest scandal should catch up with them, and then resumed his solo journey on foot, heading due south across the Carpathians from Deva until he eventually hit the Danube again at Orşova. This was where he was to make his final crossing of the river before heading on to Constantinople through Bulgaria.

I'd already sailed through Orşova on the *Argo*, so following the Leigh Fermor trail any further would have only had me doubling back on myself. And besides, my book was about the Danube, not about a journey to Constantinople, so I cut my metaphorical ties with him and left Transylvania in a far more mundane way: by train, following a literary path of my own. I had a river to finish and an appointment with a royal family to keep – an appointment which was to be the last of my aristocratic encounters and one which had a pleasing symmetry with my very first. That first encounter had taken place in a castle on a rock in the pretty town of Sigmaringen, some 2,000 kilometres upriver and 90,000 words ago, in the early weeks of early spring; this one was to take place in one of Europe's most charmless capital cities in the torrid humidity of late summer, with 400 kilometres to go. But both men were Hohenzollern.

Bucharest is a brutal, soulless, insipid, traffic-filled city with a pestilential summer climate whose merciless heat cracks the concrete and turns the tarmac to soup, and then proceeds to fill its buckled bowls with occasional torrential rain. It has a huge stray-dog problem that creams the ground with turds and results in several maulings a year, and biblical plagues wouldn't be out of place. Guidebook authors and brochure writers do their best, trotting out the clapped-out cliché about 'Paris of the East' and then struggling to find anything interesting to say thereafter. The city may have been stylish once, but it sure isn't now, not unless you count the swanky modern estates to the north where the new rich live, to escape city-centre strangulation-by-concrete. In most Romanian towns you can penetrate through grim suburbs and find something rewarding nestling inside, but not here; Ceauşescu saw to that, sweeping away the old city centre to make way for massively egotistical urban planning, the whole purpose of which was to emphasize the power of the state and render the individual totally insignificant. As a front door to a country it is totally unrepresentative and it saddens me to think that visitors might come here, judge the nation on the basis of Bucharest and never come back again, missing out on the whole bewitching panoply of Transylvania.

It is edgy, too. All the way through Eastern Europe

I'd been warned about the dangers I'd face in Romania, dangers which had never actually materialized, provided you don't include dogs and bulls. But I felt most at threat in Bucharest.

The unease started on the train into town, a modern double-decker of considerable sophistication whose guard examined my ticket, which I knew to be bona fide, and then tried to enter into a discussion with me about it. After he'd gone, leaving me not a little bemused, someone across the aisle took a look at it for me and explained why: the printing of the date was sufficiently indeterminate, he said, as to be easily altered. I'd thought I was being accused of doing something wrong, but the guard had been offering to buy it off me, for re-sale.

Bucharest's Gara de Nord was full of hungry eyes. It was one of those places where you need either to march straight through looking like you know exactly what you're doing, or else to make a beeline for the nearest wall and stand with your back against it whilst you ponder your next move. Hesitate and stop uncertainly in the main concourse and you risked becoming a victim, because the bouncers on the entrances were susceptible to the occasional bribe to let in the more organized pickpockets. At least the hazards were more visible on the forecourt outside, where packs of dogs and gypsy children swilled around the doorways of ropey casinos, side-stepping the spivs who worked the crowds by first asking you something obvious like the time, but whose real interest was to probe your composure and assess your vulnerability, to see what you might want, or what they might be able to get for you or from you. Not a place to come unless you've got an appointment with a man who would be king.

I'd called Prince Paul prior to arriving in Bucharest and

had ended up making all my arrangements with Princess Lia, who sounded like a character out of *Star Wars*. We'd arranged to meet in the foyer of the Athenee Palace Hotel, once notorious for the quantities of spies who'd openly stayed here, and for the extensive bugging, drugging and phone-tapping of its guests. Variously home to British spies, the Gestapo, and the Securitate luminati, it had had a corrupt staff who had been ever ready to procure prostitutes and change money at black-market rates – at least they were until the government re-staffed the whole place with informers and installed a Securitate colonel as the director. The secret police even peopled the hotel with free-speaking *bon vivants* and supposed intellectuals, to create an atmosphere that would encourage indiscretion. Ultimately the Athenee Palace witnessed some of the worst violence of the 1989 Revolution, which took place in the small square outside, but since then it has had a makeover by the Hilton group and become a gathering place of people who need to be seen at the best and most infamous address in town.

Princess Lia was unmistakable when she swept in out of a summer thunderstorm. Cloaked, gloved and in a black felt hat, rakishly angled, which never left her head whether we were inside or out. Under it was a strong face, once beautiful and now heavily made up in late middle age, from which issued an incessant, gracious and practised stream of words simultaneously expressing interest, concern and welcome. She was American to the (invisible) roots of her hair, had the aura of a movie star who was not getting quite enough work any more, and she spoke with the deliberate articulation of someone who habitually uses her own language amongst those who have difficulty understanding it.

I gathered, by the way I was swept up and escorted to

a shiny black chauffeur-driven Range Rover outside, that the hotel had served its purpose as a rendezvous only, and that I was to be taken to meet the prince in 'the Home', as Princess Lia called it. There followed a short, twisty ride down various shortcuts that, if I'd been more suspicious-minded, I would have concluded was deliberately intended to confuse. Eventually the massive electronic gates of a nineteenth-century townhouse clanged shut behind us and I found myself in a high-ceilinged room cluttered with portraiture, formal French-style antique furniture, and a grand piano whose main purpose seemed to be the bearing of serried ranks of photographs of HRH Prince Paul in the company of various important personages. They reminded me of the official plaques at the source of the Danube, and they performed the same function. Through them, he existed, he was a prince. Unfortunately, in every one of them he mugged at the camera in a way he presumably thought was princely, but which I thought made him look like a satisfied badger.

The man himself, Paul-Phillipe Hohenzollern, turned out to be small and dapper, bushy-eyebrowed with a twinkling, birdlike (rather than badgerlike) gait and a manner of speaking which involved unburdening himself of achievements and perceived injustices all at once, and in no particular order. No time for niceties or chit-chat; straight on with the matter in hand. After barely more than a minute in his company I felt that I had been dumped right into the middle of a conversation which had been running on a loop for some while, and it would have helped me a great deal to understand it if only I'd been there at the beginning. I think the princess appreci-ated my predicament, for several times she stopped her husband in his tracks, or sent him off to ferret around in a back room to find the letter from the Pope, from the

King of Morocco, or from Clarence House (all of which basically seemed to me to be just acknowledgements of his own letters to them, and all nicely presented in a folder complete with their envelopes, like trophies), while she patiently unravelled what had just been said.

The essence of the whole conversation was that Prince Paul saw himself as the legitimate heir – the 'first line of succession' as he put it – to the throne of Romania. And he saw me as somebody who needed persuading towards his view of that fact. There was no doubt that his lineage went right back to Karl Hohenzollern, the twenty-seven-year-old who'd been invited by the Romanian government to travel down the Danube from Sigmaringen in the latter part of the nineteenth century to become the first Romanian king. But Paul's problems started with his grandfather, King Carol II, who'd married aristocrat Zizi Lambrino without his father's approval while still just the heir to the throne. The marriage was later annulled by the Romanian government and declared morganatic – i.e. a marriage between two persons of unequal rank whose offspring would therefore not inherit any parental titles or privileges. His grandfather had meekly accepted the annulment and remarried someone more in keeping with his status – Princess Helen of Greece – but not before he'd fathered a son with Zizi: Carol Mircea, Paul's father.

Although he was the eldest son of the man who became king, this Carol Mircea was excluded from the line of succession by the annulment, so the spotlight shifted across to his half-brother, now King Michael. Michael is an old man living mainly in Switzerland, and it is his offspring who are back in Romania, living in the royal palaces; they are accepted as the legitimate line, even though they are all girls, a gender which would have disqualified them in the past.

Carol Mircea never seriously took issue with the annulment of his parents' marriage, and never attempted to reclaim the throne, although he did go through the European courts to assert his entitlement to use the family name Hohenzollern and to his share of his father's assets. Meanwhile King Carol II doesn't seem to have taken any further interest in his firstborn, proceeding with his life as if his first marriage had never taken place.

'It was Magda Lupescu,' chipped in Princess Lia, 'his mistress. She made sure he never saw his son.'

Carol Mircea's apparent lack of interest in the throne was frustrating for Paul, but the inheritance ruling in the European courts was pivotal to his case. Combined with the 'illegal' annulment of his grandparents' marriage, he saw it as proof that his claim to the throne was legitimate, and I could see his point. It meant that whenever the monarchy was restored in Romania, his would be the first line of succession – no matter that any such restoration was highly unlikely, and that he was sixty and that Princess Lia was not far behind (fifty-nine, I reckoned), and they didn't have any offspring to hand anything on to, rendering the whole obsession pointless. But when I dropped this observation into the mix the prince became momentarily frosty.

'The princess and I hope to have children.'

His case was not helped by a personality that I can't help but feel lacks *noblesse oblige*, despite the battalions of photographs on the piano, the folders of celebrity letters and the drifts of newspaper cuttings. Evidently he didn't cut much of a dash in Romanian society, either; in fact, I'd been warned off seeing him by some. Nor does he appear to be particularly popular at grassroots level, for when he tried to run for president, back in 2000, he'd won only 0.49 per cent of the vote.

He was justifiably proud of being the first royal to return to Romanian soil, scurrying off into a back room and coming back brandishing the front page of the *Daily Telegraph* from 11 January 1990, showing him on the tarmac at Bucharest airport, smiling manfully and tightly clutching his bag of duty free. His biggest moment.

'The first royal to return to any East European country. And ours was the first royal wedding in Eastern Europe.'

In fact he'd spent much of his life in the UK, where he'd gone through the public-school system. It wasn't clear how fluent his Romanian actually was, and he put me in mind of another returning royal I'd visited in Serbia a couple of years before – Crown Prince Alexander, who was back in his palace in Belgrade, waiting for restoration of the monarchy there. Alexander, too, had grown up in the UK and his Serbian was basic, or so said the bodyguard who'd driven me back into town after the interview. But that wasn't necessarily a bad thing, continued the bodyguard, because when the crown prince went walkabout he couldn't understand what was being shouted at him from the back of the crowd. I wondered if the same happened with Prince Paul.

He was a perfectly nice man, I reflected, as I tried to juggle the papers he fed me with the china cup and saucer on my knee, which a solicitous Princess Lia regularly replenished with cold coffee. But that line about him and Lia having children was slightly optimistic, and I had my doubts about his judgement, too. He had, for example, declared his uncle, King Michael, responsible for the deportation and killing of Jews during the Second World War, and asked that he be shot as a war criminal. Although they didn't want him back as a monarch, Michael was respected by the Romanian people, so this looked misguided at best. When I asked Prince Paul about it, he didn't deny it, but he gave his reasons.

'There was a massacre of Jews just after his visit to Iaşi [Romania's third city], and my point was he should have made a declaration denouncing it. To be honest, the press got it a bit wrong. I said "The chap should be shot", you know how they say it in England, you know "That chap should be shot". I didn't mean he deserved to be *executed*.'

Ho hum.

'How do you get on with King Michael's children, the princesses? They're here, aren't they?'

'We try to avoid each other,' said the prince, bluntly.

What a mess: two families circulating at the top end of Bucharest society trying to pretend the other didn't exist. It must have been a minefield of protocol for charities looking for patrons and for high-profile overseas visitors looking for somewhere to pay their respects. But Prince Paul did seem to have just cause for avoiding Prince Radu, the husband of King Michael's eldest daughter and designated heir, Margaret – a woman who also had the odd distinction of being an early girlfriend of the young Gordon Brown while they were both at Edinburgh University. Anyway, it seemed from certification and clippings in the prince's possession that this Radu had been using the title 'Prinz von Hohenzollern-Veringen', and had even faked a document purporting to be from the Hohenzollerns of Sigmaringen, bestowing that title on him. Paul had a copy of a (genuine) letter from Sigmaringen decrying this 'illegal behaviour' and threatening Radu with court action if he didn't desist from using the family name.

'My cousins the Hohenzollerns', Paul said, 'were very scrupulous about such things.'

After ninety minutes of these and related outpourings, punctuated by the more soothing voice of Princess Lia, during which the prince would flicker rapidly across the back of the room from one antechamber to the other like a character from a bedroom farce in search of his trousers, my audience with this particular branch of Romanian royalty was adjudged to be at an end. The princess would drop me back, she said, and once we were in the Range Rover again she asked the driver to take a detour around the city centre so she could show me the sights.

To be honest I'd already seen what I wanted to of central Bucharest, but it's not every day you get invited by a princess to tour a city centre, and I was intrigued by Lia and how she'd come into Prince Paul's life. Amongst the images on the piano I'd spotted a much more youthful (and quite stunning) image of her meeting the Dalai Lama, suggesting some kind of high-falutin previous existence. So as she showed me Ceaușescu's massive folly, the Palace of Parliament, the second-largest building in the world after the Pentagon, I established that she'd had a Romanian family background herself (Arad, where I'd stayed with Julia), although she'd been born in Michigan and had grown up in California. She said she'd been an aide in the White House during the Carter years, but most of her activities seemed to be charity-fundraising related, and she'd met Prince Paul at a UNICEF do in London.

'I find Bucharest very elegant,' she enthused, talking up the glum highlights of a rainsoaked city (the thunderstorm hadn't completely moved away). 'But of course she's in need of brushing up. Like a lady who hasn't washed her face for fifty years.'

Frankly, that was kind. A lady who'd lost her teeth and most of her hair, more like, and her bodily hygiene left something to be desired, too.

At this point Lia's mobile phone rang and the princess greeted her caller with a cheery 'Hi dearest,' but then her smile froze, and I couldn't help but hear the voice on the other end enter upon what sounded to me like a female's hysterical rant. The princess quickly switched to emergency Romanian, before signing off as early as she could with a promise to 'be there soon'; during all this the smile never left her face.

'Of course, we're not living in a fairy tale,' she commented, more soberly, as the Range Rover swept down Ceauşescu's attempt to emulate the Champs-Elysées. I wasn't sure whether this was an opening into a more confessional level of conversation, given what had just transpired, so I kept quiet. But it wasn't to be; after a quick order to the driver, Lia embarked on an explanation of how the legal process of getting property back occupied a great deal of their time, although she had the generosity to add that she felt sorry for those who had only had small property holdings and had been unable to get anything back. Either they didn't have enough money to pay a lawyer, or a lawyer wasn't interested anyway because the deal wasn't big enough, or else they still felt intimidated by the people in the system and therefore didn't even dare try.

And that's as far as the conversation went, because I was suddenly back at the hotel. The Range Rover deposited me on the pavement outside, and the princess was gone, a perfumed silhouette with a rakish hat and a final black-gloved wave.

That wasn't quite the end of my Bucharest interlude. I was intrigued by the whole Paul–Lia dynamic, particularly by that near-hysterical phone call from a female voice the princess had addressed as 'dearest', so I stopped at an Internet café round the corner from the

Athenee Palace and Googled Princess Lia of Romania, as one does.

And what a cruel and deadly thing the Internet is! There she was, in her previous life as Lia Triff Belli, where Mr Belli – Mr Melvin Belli, aka the King of Torts – had been a celebrity lawyer, famous for defending the likes of Mae West, Zsa Zsa Gabor, Errol Flynn, Tony Curtis and even Jack Ruby after he shot and killed Lee Harvey Oswald.

Belli had been married five times. He was sixty-four, orotund and wealthy, loved public attention and was at the peak of his career when he first met the very pretty twenty-three-year-old Lia Triff, then a student at the University of Maryland, and was asked, 'You're a very famous lawyer, aren't you?' Their marriage lasted fifteen years, through numerous high-society parties, and produced one daughter, but ended with a typically public display of scandal and acrimony. Lia accused her husband of violence, and he accused her of sleeping with all and sundry. The net result was an estimated $15 million settlement for Lia, and a further $1,000 fine for Belli for supposedly throwing their pet dog and subject of their custody dispute, an Italian Greyhound named Whelldone Rumproast IV, off the Golden Gate Bridge. The fine was also for Belli famously calling his wife 'El Trampo', a nickname which still reverberates around the Internet, twenty years on.

For a woman, 'El Trampo' is the kind of monicker that pursues you across the world, and across the decades, however much you change your life. For a travel writer, sitting in an Internet café in Bucharest, it made a recent encounter even more colourful, as well as a little bit more surreal.

23

The Danube Delta

Twenty-four hours later I was in the Delta, a paying guest in the house of Barbaneagra Neculai, a man who had no aristocratic pedigree whatsoever but who strutted around his property as if he was Danubian royalty, ribbiting like a bullfrog. Blackbeard (for that was the literal translation of his name) had a face like a pug and a gut like a Buddha that he was happy to show to everyone, giving it a friendly slap every now and then to keep the flies off. He wanted to know everything about me, and repeated every morsel of information he acquired in a cracked, high-pitched voice, for the benefit of the neighbourhood. Our topics of conversation were necessarily limited, but that didn't stop him giving me his opinion on everything under the sun, swelling up and up with increasing excitement as he did so. It was fortunate we didn't have much of a language in common, or else he would have gone on swelling and swelling as the discussion developed until he finally burst. I'm glad he didn't, because without Barbaneagra

Neculai I wouldn't have been able to finish my journey as I wanted to.

I'd come to the Delta hotfoot from Bucharest. In so doing I effectively missed out 400 kilometres of the 2,840-kilometre river, for which, dear reader, I apologize, but most of that 400 kilometres was hard to access from the land, and from talking to the crew of the *Argo* I knew it to be more of the same Danube that I'd seen at Ruse: the Danube of sluggish, torpid, turd-coloured Anaglypta, over a mile wide and only in motion because of its enthusiastic younger sibling pushing it from behind as you'd push a broken-down car, but from many hundreds of kilometres inland.

This indolent Danube had been travelling for so long it had forgotten it even had a destination, and it couldn't really be bothered with being a river any more. It wasn't the Danube I wanted to remember, having been adulterated by wealthy countries upstream who should have known better, leaving it a cancerous waterway, murky, bloated, soulless and unrecognizable. It had lost its motivation, had had its living force extracted and turned into hydropower, and now that it had nothing more to give, it was shunned by the land it travelled through. The sooner it drowned itself in the Black Sea the better.

The only thing I regretted not seeing in that missing 400 kilometres was the Black Sea Canal, the 'Canalul Mortii' or Canal of Death, whose first attempt at construction through a malarial swamp had resulted in the deaths of tens of thousands of 'undesirables'. The idea was to provide a shortcut for shipping in a serious hurry, but in reality it saw little traffic. Those deaths had been for nothing.

The Delta, on the other hand, was abuzz with life. Water, reed, forest, dunes, in infinite combinations, strangled in lianas, vines, bulrushes and wild apple and pear trees, broken up by stands of poplar and groves of willow. A massive resurgence, a primordial natural wonder, an Everglades without the crocodiles, a UNESCO biosphere reserve. This was where the sorry river completed its last about-turn, threw out its arms in relief and sprawled like a teenager on the sofa over 6,264 square kilometres of land, some of it in the Ukraine, some in Moldova, but the vast majority in Romania. The resulting area of swampland and reed was the size of a substantial British county, and apparently pullulating with 160 species of fish (including sturgeon) and 325 species of birds, some of them very rare. Described by Claudio Magris as 'a great dissolution' and by Patrick Leigh Fermor as 'the vast whispering labyrinth where the Danube falls to pieces', it was where the Danube went into rehab and learned how to be living water again.

It all sounded wonderful. I was expecting a place where tribal fishermen lived on islands, survived on fish and spoke in ancient languages as they lived out their ancient rituals. I saw it as a transplanted slice of Africa, or possibly Asia, or at the very least somewhere very exotic and far away, and a suitable climax for my journey.

The reality was not quite so picturesque. The 160 species of fish were, not surprisingly, all but invisible, fish being fish, and the 325 species of birds did their darndest to do the same, birds being birds. The tribal fishermen didn't look very tribal in their jeans, and as for the whispering labyrinth, it had three main channels, the Chilia, Sulina and Sfântu Gheorghe, with the Sulina – the most direct route to the sea – being a big, straight, stone-walled ditch. However, if you ventured away from any of the three, life could become devilishly tricky if you didn't happen to be a bird or a fish, or have a satnav and a super-powerful outboard motor to blast through the soup of sedge.

Faced by all this territory to conjure with, the Danube absented itself to play at being everything from lake to swamp, and mankind spent millions of man-hours cutting canals to try to track it down and bring it to heel, while extracting reeds, growing rice and catching fish at the same time. This is the sort of place you needed to float over in a hot-air balloon to get any sort of impression of its size and variety. In a boat you moved in man-made corridors from *ghiol* to *ghiol* – lake to lake – with little idea of what lay either side. Hopefully it was the Danube, learning to have fun.

I embarked into the Delta from the port of Tulcea, on the last bit of dry land. From here, onward travel had to be by boat, so the long bend in the river as it swept through town, smelling of sewage and engine oil, was the focus of a great deal of activity.

Towering over the far end in the distance were the shipyards, which still turned out boats that could cope with both river and sea. Closer at hand came ugly balconied blocks of flats which had been painted Neapolitan blues and greens to try to soften the ghastliness of their architecture. Between them and the river stretched a long, sweeping promenade in rippling concrete, sticky with melted ice-cream, which at various points in its progress also doubled as a car park. Its edge was lined with all varieties of floating creations in various states of undress, some of which looked like junkyard scrap until you saw them take on passengers and push their noses out into the stream. Entrepreneurs had converted barges into shore bases with restaurants and bars, and they all advertised tours and fishing trips. Around them clustered speedboats, ambulance boats, pontoon boats and little ramshackle flit boats, ready to take a paying customer anywhere, as long as it was within rowing distance.

Every now and then a big whale of an oceangoing hulk would steam up past all this chaos, covered in rust and peeling paint, dribbling ribbons of bilge water from spear-holes in the hull and frothing fetid cappuccino at the stern. These ships were usually headed for the steel mills at Galati, a bit further upriver, and their names and home ports suggested far-off places in the Crimea and out beyond the Bosphorus – in other words the big wide world outside.

But Tulcea was concentrating on the Delta dwellers. They were the target for its louche cocktail bars, retired seamen's clubs and dilapidated discos along the back of the promenade. Alongside them were more utilitarian outlets, too: import–export agencies, shops that sold chainsaws, outboard-motor spares and bits of modern plumbing. There were several clinics to give the sick and injured a choice as soon as they staggered off the boat: a choice between medical attention, or the reviving delights of the Ambiance cocktail club, with its rotting sunshades.

Tulcea's big moment in the day was the departure of the three main Navrom ferries, substantial ships the size of small cross-Channel ferries that headed off down the three main Delta channels at 1.30 p.m. Reconditioned Russian hydrofoils made these journeys too, tinny metal lozenges that buzzed in and out through the morning, but their fares were too high for the average Delta-dweller, so their passenger list comprised handfuls of officials and business people whose time was precious and whose ticket was being paid for by somebody else, and who didn't mind the claustrophobic, sweaty interiors. Besides, the majority of villagers had cargo to carry, so they stuck to the ferries.

As the time approached, the promenade became increasingly choked with men pushing trolleys piled high with boxes. Beer was being shifted in big quantities, gas cylinders were being delivered by lorry, crates of bottled water were moving east and mountains of sweets and crisps were going west. I tagged along in the wake of a cart piled high with luggage being hauled towards the *Dnieper Star*, a river cruiser from the Ukraine that was making ready to head out into the Black Sea for Odessa, Sevastopol and Kiev. And just astern of it I found what I'd been looking for: a small ferry destined for Mila 23, a prosaic name for a fishing village at milestone 23 of the original sinuous course of the Danube, in the days before the Sulina Channel had been cut straight to the sea.

Taking the Sulina ferry would have been the fastest way to complete my journey, but also the most tedious. The Sulina Channel was the Delta's high street, busy, developed and full of outside settlers who'd built new holiday homes along it. By contrast Mila 23, I'd been told, was an original Lipovani settlement, home to the descendants of Sea Cossacks who'd fled there after a fissure in the Russian Orthodox Church in the seventeenth century. The Tsar of the time (Peter the Great) had insisted on modernization, demanding that the Old Believers cut off their beards, and when they'd refused he'd sent the army after them. Many had fled into the forest (*lipa* is Russian for lime tree) and ultimately ended up in the Delta, which was a particularly good place to hide. There are still five Lipovani villages here, of which Mila 23 is one. I was expecting a rustic, old-Russian Venice, but that was not how it turned out.

The ferry journey took three hours, across lily-carpeted *ghiols* and down increasingly narrow canals. It seemed a hazardous selection of shortcuts; the bows burst repeatedly through clusters of overhanging willow, klaxon sounding, the skipper roundly cursing any boats coming the other way, until we finally emerged on to what was plainly the old course of the river, reminiscent of the Danube as it had looked way back in Austria or Hungary. And there was Mila 23, straggling around the inside of a big bend in the river, the roofs of its houses only just visible behind a high embankment.

Anchored to stakes along the water's edge were lines of slender fishermen's skiffs, clinker-built and tarred on the outside, and I wanted one as soon as I saw them. Bigger boats had to tie up at Mila 23's two pontoons, one for Navrom boats and one for private vessels, alongside its main shop, which also served as the village bar (it had the village's only substantial fridge) and therefore the centre of its social life. From here, hard-baked dusty tracks ran off in all directions, upriver and downriver and at diagonals inland.

An isolated shop like this played a major community role; it provided the villagers with luxuries and bare necessities, and although most of Mila's households were effectively self-sufficient, the shop's stock served every purpose from birthday presents to what would be under the tree at Christmas time. Its hard-drinking regulars dominated village gossip. Given this limited sphere, I could begin to see the appeal of the diversity (and the anonymity) of Tulcea's shanty town of bars and discos.

The village centre itself took a moment to locate, away from the river's edge across open patches of ground on a slightly higher elevation, where it had been moved after catastrophic flooding in 1960. Here a small estate of skew-whiff, reed-roofed, timber- or mud-walled houses sat in little compounds within stockades, their eaves studded with many decades of swallows' nests, whose presence, Lipovans believed, was a defence against fire. Each home had its own vegetable garden and fruit trees, a run of geese or chickens for when they needed to pay the doctor or celebrate a special occasion, and a patio area roofed with vines where the woman of the house usually sat, shelling peas and talking to the neighbour or the cat.

There was lots to talk about, for the narrow paths that constituted the village's main thoroughfares were being dug up for the installation of a proper sewage system, replacing the existing practice where everyone made their own arrangements in thunder boxes at the far end of the garden. The sewerage money came from Europe, and the demand was being driven by the two biggest buildings in the village, both nearly complete, and both of them small hotels. It seemed that I'd got to Mila 23 just before the rest of the world; somebody had woken up to the fact that this Lipovani village, on a river rather than a ditch, had major selling points for tourism, and there was about to be a helluva lot more shit flowing about. Next year, I found myself predicting, there'd also be a helluva lot more beards and fewer jeans, because it needed to look the part, too.

Of course the downside of being in the village before the hotels opened was a shortage of places to stay, which is how I ended up entering into conversation with Barbaneagra Neculai, who was resting his belly on his stockade opposite the village church, shirt off, watching the world go by. He listened to me in silence, let the silence extend well after I'd finished while he looked me up and down, and then offered me a room in his house, for a fee. Judging by the expression of glee when I accepted it, the price was outrageous, but it seemed eminently reasonable to me, especially when I insisted that it included meals.

His house was long and low and had smooth, thick walls of straw and mud. It was more modern than most and had obviously been added to, eccentrically, over the years by Mr Barbaneagra himself, with some rooms accessed through others, and even more (the bathroom, for instance) by going round the outside. Half the bathroom's floorspace was occupied by a giant mud-brick stove, fired from the outside, to heat the water. The kitchen stood separate and open-plan, connected to the main building only by a corrugated-iron roof, under which fishing rods were stashed. Given the nature of the Barbaneagran diet (fish, fish and more fish), keeping the kitchen at a distance was undoubtedly wise, although the Barbaneagras had a gas cooker and no longer used the stove fired with old maize husks, as many of the more primitive houses did. A transistor radio sat on the outside of the bathroom window, permanently on but veering delinquently between stations. The Barbaneagras never paid it much attention, and I suspected its main purpose was to drown out any unfortunate bathroom noises.

Mrs Barbaneagra was a large, calm shamble of a woman with a long tumble of greying blonde hair and a nice smile that showed a good display of gold teeth. She reminded me of an Indian squaw, particularly when her grandchildren came round in the early afternoons, clambered all over her and pulled her hair, to her evident delight.

'Lipovani,' explained her husband, nodding towards his wife, and adding that he himself was not. He'd been a ship's engineer out of Galati until he'd retired. He didn't mention it, but he'd obviously had some kind of accident in the engine room that had made a mess of his right hand. I wondered if another accident was responsible for the high-pitched voice, or maybe that had been the only way he'd been able to make himself heard over the barracking diesel. Anyway, his previous career conferred a special status on him in a village that still essentially survived on what it could catch, barter or grow, because he had cash. He had an income in the form of a company pension, and people like him were important in making the whole Mila 23 economy go round, as was I.

The Barbaneagras seemed pleased to have a guest. They gave me a room that was basically a corridor to their grown-up son's room, making me understand that he 'only slept there' and spent most of his time in some other unspecified location. I never discovered what that unspecified location might be, but the son did exactly as his parents said he would: he arrived late at night, only to depart again early in the morning, and each time I pretended to be asleep.

Now that I was in the house, Mrs B was very concerned at what I might or might not eat. She walked me through her vegetable patch, pointing out aubergines, potatoes, peppers, tomatoes and onions, checking whether I had any objection to any. And then, in the evening, I'd have fish *ciorba* (a cold thick soup, usually with potato and pepper) and fried fish (with another token vegetable) and she and I would have an exchange of smiles and pointing, indicating exactly where in the garden the potato or the pepper or whatever it was had lived out its happy life before dedicating itself to my needs. During these meals Mr B would absent himself to a seat on the other side of the stockade, out of sight but not out of earshot, and Mrs B would pass comment about my table manners for his benefit. It would then be repeated from the other side of the stockade, with greater emphasis.

'He's spitting out the bones,' she'd say.

'HE'S SPITTING OUT THE BONES,' he'd reply.

'He doesn't like the eyes,' she'd say.

'HE DOESN'T LIKE THE EYES,' he'd reply.

'He's dunking the bread,' she'd say.

'HE'S DUNKING THE BREAD,' he'd reply.

'I don't think he wants any more,' she'd say.

'THEN TRY HIM AGAIN,' he'd reply.

Mr B, to give him his due, was very keen to help in any way he could, so when on the morning of my second day I told him of my plan – that I wanted to find a suitable boat so that I could row the last 23 miles to Sulina – he didn't laugh. In fact he didn't believe me at all, so it took a mixture of mime, drawing and repetition of basic words to drive the point home. Even then, he couldn't understand why anyone would want to travel like that when there were passenger boats there for the asking.

'Mr Andrew, *multi canali*, *multi canali*,' he kept repeating. There were so many canals he was sure I would get lost.

But I persisted, and in the end he pulled on a shirt as a tribute to the seriousness of the mission and took me with him to see a man about a boat.

I hadn't appreciated that the village was effectively surrounded by water. An inlet from the river filled a lagoon around the back, a rather rank lagoon that turned out to be the village's parking place, full of more of those finny tarred skiffs that I'd seen on the riverside. Three men were sitting on an upturned wreck fixing fish-traps, and one of them looked up when Mr B called his name. We all shook hands, and they listened attentively while he explained what I wanted. But when it came to the final question – would any of them rent me a boat – they had no hesitation: it was out of the question. Mr B didn't seem in the least surprised.

'OK then,' I said, not discouraged, 'let's forget rental.' Boat hire was clearly an unfamiliar concept amongst Lipovans. 'I'll buy one. A wooden one like that. How much?'

This time there was more of a murmured consultation, and then one of them turned to me and said in English, 'No.'

'What do you mean, no? I haven't made an offer yet.'

But apparently 'no' meant 'no'; none of them would sell me a boat, however high the price, and they didn't know anyone who would. The problem was that, without their boats, explained the one who'd said 'no', they couldn't work and a Lipovani man needs to work. So no one would sell.

I had to admit that this was not what I was expecting. Plainly, there were plenty of boats in that lagoon, more than enough to go round, and not many of them looked as if they were in regular use. So I began to produce money from my wallet, money in what I considered suitably copious quantities. But the three men just stood, shrugged their shoulders and looked embarrassed. Eventually I was forced to admit defeat, and I couldn't really understand why. Mr B, who had an I-told-you-so expression on his face, didn't offer any insight or encouragement, so in the end I thanked the three men and we started back towards the house.

We'd almost reached the gate when we were hailed from behind. It was one of the three, and he said something to Mr B, who turned to me.

'He has a boat,' he made me understand. 'A boat for sale.'

Which is how I came to be the proud owner of a green plastic bathtub.

I have no idea how this boat ended up in Mila 23, but

it certainly didn't belong in a fishing community. It was large, heavy, broad in the beam, fat in the bottom and high in the water. A brute to row, a brute to steer and all in all quite out of keeping with the setting, which is presumably why I hadn't seen it in the lagoon. I reckoned, on looking it over, that it must have fallen off the deck of a passing ship, being the sort of boat that would have been quite good at bobbing about in rough water with a lot of people in it until rescue came. A happy family on one of Disney World's watery rides would have been quite content with it, too, but any self-respecting Lipovani fisherman wouldn't have been seen dead rowing around in it, which was why it had been secreted away. And why they were happy to sell it to me.

But it had oars, and it was dry inside, and I would have the current behind me pushing me on, so I wasn't fussed. In fact I was secretly elated, because I'd begun to accept that I wouldn't be able to complete the journey as I'd wanted to, which would have been a major disappointment. However, rather than seem too keen and settle the deal there and then, I said I'd give the boat a half-day spin around the neighbourhood, and provided it performed satisfactorily, we'd agree a price.

That half day was beguiling. Conditions were dead calm, and it was a pleasure to be under my own steam at last, pottering around on the river I'd been stalking for so long. It was like the consummation of a prolonged courtship. A union long awaited. I sculled up and down side canals, nosing through reeds and dawdling across secret lakes, bothering frogs and scattering flocks of waterbirds like a dog chasing sheep. I didn't go far, both for fear of getting lost in Mr B's *multi canali*, and because I'd agreed to report back at the inlet in the early afternoon.

When it came to that negotiation, I entered into it

well prepared, armed with my favourite Romanian word, *scump*, meaning expensive: s*cump*, *scump*, *scump*, delivered with the emphasis of a pile of bricks hitting a sand dune. But the Lipovans had already seen how ready I was to part with my cash, so however much I scumped, I still ended up paying 220 euros for something I was pretty damn sure had fallen off the back of a lorry. Or a *Dnieper Star*.

24

Rowing to Sulina

I used to row competitively before my lower back forced me to give up, so I know that a racing shell can cover 2 kilometres in around seven minutes, even without a stream pushing it along. At that rate, 23 miles should only take a couple of hours, but I'd allowed a whole day to do Mila 23 to Sulina in my green plastic bathtub with the current behind me. If the worst came to the worst, I could camp out; I had a mosquito net, basic food and water, and a drybag.

To give myself the best chance I set off at dawn, a dawn so misty that I could feel the moisture prickling my skin. Emerging from Mila 23's inlet, assuming the water was all mine, I found the grey veil already peopled with fishermen, bending, waiting, turning and cursing, like furtive actors getting into position in front of the safety curtain before the lights went up. Sadly, there was no chance of my slipping between them unnoticed, clumping along in my club-footed bathtub, but only a handful of them softly returned my greeting, even though I was prepared to bet that they all knew full well who I was and how much I'd paid. Even Mila's dogs seemed to be having a laugh about it, and it took ages before I was properly out of barking distance.

Even then it was never silent on the river. Every now and then there'd be a big thump and a splash as something substantial ate something not quite so substantial: a pike chasing a perch, a beluga sturgeon swallowing a Danube mackerel, or a carp thrashing its tail. Occasionally there were cattle on the bank, some of them standing contemplatively up to their ankles in the water, and my approach would trigger a mini stampede, and that in turn would give me a heart attack. And in between whiles there'd always be a frog, abandoning its lilypad with a startled plop.

It may sound obvious, but the big disadvantage in travelling backwards is in not seeing where you are going. On a familiar piece of water you know instinctively where you should be pointing, and you can usually judge your forward course by the drift of your stern, but here I didn't know what lay ahead. Initially I tried sculling along in the middle, but it felt exposed and lonely, and I noticed that all of the fishermen stuck to the sides, so in the end I did the same. Being in touch with the bank was comforting, but it was also irritating. From the middle, it had looked relatively unbroken, but from the edge it was full of little deceptions: the floating islands of reeds that demanded a diversion; the mats of lilies that snagged an oar; and the little bays that drew me in, unwittingly, until a casual glance over my shoulder revealed I'd been suckered and there was land dead ahead.

The bank also played host to fish-traps, and I quickly became adept at spotting them. Mostly they were hooped and strung between stakes in or around beds of weed so that only the top curve emerged from the water, like the half-submerged ribs of something that had long since died. A couple had their owners in attendance, and I watched them pole the boat around, drive a stake into the riverbed, up-end the trap into the boat, and then reposition it at a different angle if the catch wasn't considered sufficiently good, all of it with barely a ripple. How I envied them their boats.

Harder to spot were the nets, with upended 7Up bottles as floats, and these required a wide berth if I wasn't going to end up wrapping them around my bows. I nearly didn't see the first one, and had to dig my oars hard into the water to stop. As I backed away, I spotted a boat hauled up under a nearby willow; the fisherman's, no doubt. I couldn't see him, but he'd presumably been watching me as I so nearly made a mess of his livelihood.

So on I plugged, in my clumsy way, stamping an untidy set of puddle-shaped rivets along the old course of the Danube, and taking careful interest in what I passed. I was deliberately taking it steadily, monitoring my body for signs of wear and tear, stopping every hour or so to tie up to the low branches of a white poplar and stretch my back by lying down in the bottom of the boat in an attempt to head off those old rowing injuries. By midday, blisters had started to form on my fingers, so to delay their onset I pulled a pair of socks out of my luggage and used them as gloves. An hour later I was digging into the drybag again, this time for a pair of boxer shorts; I'd lost my hat somewhere in Transylvania, and now the sun was getting savage. Resuming with socks on my hands and pants on my head, it occurred to me that I might even start a fashion amongst the Lipovan.

It wasn't just my physical state I was concerned about; I had a weather eye on the state of the boat, too. Most worrying was the crude system for the rowlocks, where the oars were secured to metal spigots by thongs of thread. As a system it didn't fill me with confidence, but all the Danube oarsmen used it, so I made a mental note not to work it too hard. In any case, in the event of a problem there was a bow-rope which could be improvised as a replacement. I had no such doubts about the oars themselves; they were big slabs of timber, and they may have been crudely fashioned and poorly balanced, but they'd be the last things to break.

The wind started at around noon, just as I was beginning to feel tired, and just as I came in sight of the main Sulina Channel. I was already discouraged at my slow rate of progress across the map, so a head wind that stiffened steadily came at the worst possible time. The boat, with its high sides and shallow draught, proved very vulnerable. It had no grip on the water, so it crabbed and swung, and it began to be an effort just to keep it pointing in a straight line. I could feel the stiff waves slapping against the bows, and every slap reduced my forward progress and made the next stroke more of an effort.

Originally I'd been looking forward to catching the stream as I hauled out into the Sulina Channel, but it was clear that conditions were only going to get worse, because as any ship's captain will tell you, wind against tide is not a happy combination. The wind was coming straight up the channel, creating standing waves to which the Sulina's episodic boat traffic added its own wash, bounding back and forth off the stone embankments. To make things worse, I now had an audience, for where previously I'd been in my own little world on the old river course, now I was on a thoroughfare whose southern bank was surprisingly built up. Clumping doggedly along the shore to try to avoid the worst of the waves, I was aware of critical eyes on my boat, my technique, my pants, my everything.

After an hour on the Sulina, I was seething. The boat was banging and yawing in the chop, so it was all I could do to get my oars in the water, let alone get any purchase, and every time I took them out again to prepare for the next stroke, the wind blew me backwards. My surroundings were depressing, because I was now in the heart of one of the Delta's biggest villages, Crişan, a ribbon development with a couple of garish hotels, whose guests sat out on deckchairs on pontoons in the (for them) pleasantly cooling breeze and laughed at the curious foreigner, sweating and swearing as he clubbed his way past. I was trying to think positive, telling myself that the one advantage of my boat, as against one of the fishermen's wooden boats, was that at least it wasn't going to be swamped, and even if I did end up in the water I'd be able to climb back on board comparatively easily, and it was at this point that I suddenly ended up flat on my back, staring at the sky. I'd been hauling at full power to try to make some headway, and the strain simply became too much for one of the thongs that held the oars. It snapped.

I got ashore and sorted out a replacement from the bow-rope, a process than forced me to acknowledge that I was in far worse shape than I'd anticipated. I was trembling with fatigue and my hands were barely steady enough to use my knife with safety. It forced me to think rationally, because to continue at that rate – barely one mile an hour – was requiring so much effort that it was effectively pointless, and yet I still had lots of hours left in the day. So I consulted my map and identified a place not far ahead where a channel dropped south and linked with the Canalul Imputita, which ran parallel with the Sulina. I reckoned there'd be more tree-cover from the wind and the sun along this side-branch. Best of all there'd be no audience for my sorry performance, so I could retreat and lick my wounds.

Two hours later I was reconciled to not reaching Sulina that day. The Canalul Imputita was, as I'd hoped it might be, far more intimate and sheltered, carpeted with green sedge and lilypads and lined with mace reed, yellow waterflag, Brooks mint and Dutch rush. In fact it wasn't clear that there was any dry land anywhere near. But my improved forward progress was balanced by increased anxiety about getting lost in Mr B's *multi' canali*, and if it wasn't for the occasional reed-cutter and fisherman out drumming the water for catfish, I wouldn't have gone on. They confirmed I was heading in the right direction, and once I had accepted that I wasn't going to complete my journey that day, I began to feel less frustrated. The afternoon was wearing on, the wind dropping, and the dragonflies and the birds were appearing again. The waterway smelled of sulphur, suggesting the presence of a volcanic spring, and the occasional boat passed by laden with reeds for roofing and for winter fuel.

I was on the lookout for otters, but the only swimming thing apart from the flash of fish was a snake, sashaying across the surface across my bows. Along the main river I'd identified egrets and shelduck, and now I distracted myself by following the movements of a black-headed, dart-shaped seabird, silver in colour – possibly a tern – which was such an expert flyer it could practically hover as it took fish at will from just below the surface.

Then there were the herons. The tall, somnolent, hunch-shouldered military gentlemen, like something out of the colonial service dozing by the fire. Their yellow cousins didn't really look yellow at all until they took fright from their favoured positions, standing on the exposed ribs of the fish-traps and staring down. They could, and did, spear the trapped fish inside, but they couldn't pull them out once they'd killed them. I saw only one solitary pelican, even though the Delta has thousands, but towards evening the cormorants started to amass in colonies in the trees and shriek at each other. These colonies were loud and intensely smelly and the trees that hosted them were bleached and skeletal from the acidity of their guano. As for the birds themselves, they'd never really graduated from flying school with much distinction – the adults looked like avian bombers, clawing through the air in desperation to reach their target and offload – so their arrival amongst the upper branches usually ended in an explosion of feathers and much squawking as they dislodged a youngster, who'd come crashing down through the trees and into the water below.

With less imperative to make progress, I rested regularly now that I was away from the main drag, and by early evening I'd started to look out for somewhere to stop and sleep. After some miles of just reeds on either side, one shore was now solid ground supporting a healthy population of poplar and willow, and I eventually spotted a tiny bay which gave access to a small clearing under the trees. It was a recently abandoned fishermen's camp, one of those impromptu campsites where friends from the mainland had come to drink beer, chain-smoke and swat mosquitoes, while getting in touch with their inner man.

The tiny bay was sealed on one side by a wall of tree roots bearded with filigree hairs, roots which came alive with a salvo of little frogs as I approached. I tied up and climbed up the bank to find a fireplace littered with freshwater mussel shells, a carpet of fishscales and a half-eaten bag of potatoes. Beyond them lay an outer ring of wrappers, crisp packets and empty cans of beer, and beyond that a pathway that led away into the bush behind. It proved to be brutish and short, leading past the scattered remains of dead fish and into a tangle of reed that had been decorated by bits of stained tissue paper, where it abruptly stopped. The fishermen's toilet.

I returned to the fireplace with mixed feelings. The smell of dead fish was bound to attract animals – the undergrowth was already busy with frogs – but then the stink of human faeces should keep away anything substantial like wildcat, wild boar or lynx, but would it deter snakes? Given that I didn't have the means to light a fire, my question was would I be better advised to sleep in a makeshift reed shelter on the land, or stay in the boat?

In the end I plumped for the boat. I spread a mat of rushes on the bottom to take the edge off the hardness and stretched my mosquito net across from gunwale to gunwale. It was the first time I'd used the net in the whole journey, and it was worth bringing it, not because of any plague of mosquitoes – I'd barely seen one in a zone that was supposedly famous for them – but for the feeling of security it produced. Then I ate some of my biscuits while watching the sun go down, before crawling inside.

Back in Mila 23 I'd bought a litre of home-made wine from a Lipovani household, and now, in the bottom of that green bathtub with the ghostly white mosquito net making the sky over my head, I set about consuming it. It tasted more like grapefruit juice than any wine I'd ever drunk, but the alcohol certainly hit the spot. If there was any kind of wildlife abroad on the bank that night, I never heard it.

*   *   *

The next morning everything hurt, especially my head. I got going as soon as I woke, shortly after dawn, in very still air. I was grateful for the mist, grateful for any protection I could get from the sun. My back was sore, the tendons in my wrists were stiff from gripping the oar handles, and I made decrepit progress. It took me as long as an hour to feel loosened up and effective, to regain any rhythm and fluidity. But without any kind of wind to impede me, an hour was more than enough to get me out of the Canalul Imputita and back on to the Sulina at a point where I knew I had only 7 miles to go.

That last part of the journey lured me on – and then threw me a sucker punch. At first it was a completely different experience to the previous day, partly because I'd rejoined the channel where it had returned to the original river course and was now without stone embankments or houses. And partly because there was no wind, and thereby no waves, so the stream carried me along at a steady pace. I can't say it was exactly pleasurable, the river was so broad and featureless, but in the distance over my shoulder I could already see signs of Sulina: a watertower and the shapes of warehouses.

And it was at this point that the wind started again, blowing away the mist to reveal a blazing sun, and within fifteen minutes I was cussing like a navvy as the boat started to slap and bang on rising waves and the sweat-and-suncream combination started to sting my eyes. A string of freighters came past. The *Alle*, registered in Belize City, the *Yuri Primov* from Izmail, the LS *Concorde* from Gibraltar – each made me feel horribly puny as I bounced around on its wash.

It lasted only two hours, that final stretch of the journey, but it was hell. I had to dig deep, physically and psychologically. The only way I could see I was advancing was by isolating some landmark on the bank – a shrub, a willow – and watch it pass, congratulating myself on its progress. Sometimes it would go easily, and I'd look back five minutes later and it was already distant, but at other times it would exert a malevolent magnetic force and it took for ever to pull away. On these occasions I told myself to grit my teeth and hang in there. I could feel the blisters popping on my hands, the discs grinding in my spine and the tears welling up in my eyes – although I'd always claim these last were the stinging of the sweat and suntan cream. I cursed this stupid idea. I cursed the stupid river. I cursed the stupid boat. I cursed the wind and water that wouldn't stay still. I cursed this stupid way I had of making a living.

And it was in this terrible frame of mind that I crawled slowly past the watertower, past the sign that said Sulina, past a large floating crane, past concrete bunkers on the shore, past various rusting hulks and decaying cabin cruisers stacked on dry land, and into a gully of telegraph poles and houses roofed with rusty corrugated iron, where the stony shore turned eventually into a long concrete wall, and where there were boats moving from one side to the other. This was Sulina, the end of my journey, but I felt no elation, and curiously no desire to jump ashore. It was a forgotten place, dusty and run down. Many of the turn-of-the-century warehouses on the northern shore looked long since abandoned, and many of the communist-era apartment blocks on the southern shore were also clearly empty. It was as gap-toothed as a boxer's mouth at the end of his career, a career for which he had nothing to show. I knew it counted as a port, but there was no harbour per se, just a long quayside with occasional boats. I plodded on, past scruffy old pilot boats, past the silhouette of a mosque, around a gas-canister delivery boat and up abreast of two Russian hydrofoils, where I pulled in just astern and tied up to a ring on the shore.

Immediately one of the heavy men leaning against the first hydrofoil came lurching in my direction, saying something emphatic, but two could play at that game.

'Look, sunshine,' I said in English, equally emphatically, 'I know you're telling me I can't park here, but I'm telling you I bloody well can.' And I glared, not just at him, but at the whole bloody place, adding as an afterthought, 'Oh, and by the way, do you want to buy a boat?'

The crewman stood for a moment, assessing me, my boat, my rucksack and my tone of voice, and then, mumbling something, he turned away and left me alone.

I sat for a full half-hour on that quayside, my legs dangling over the edge, unmoving, unblinking, not even thinking. Shut down. And then a freighter, the *Sea Way* (home port, Malta) hooted as it went past and I had to move my legs sharpish to avoid them getting trapped as my own boat lunged malevolently towards them on the *Sea Way*'s wash. Suddenly I was standing up.

Now that I was up, I realized I needed to do two things: find somewhere to stay, and get rid of the cursed green bathtub. Frankly, I was in a state of mind where I would have happily just walked away from the latter, delighted never to see it again, but the memory of 220 euros spent still grated on me. So, gesturing to the loitering hydrofoil crewmen that I would be away for ten minutes, I shouldered my rucksack and wandered off into Sulina's dusty streets, taking care to give its big population of stray dogs a wide berth.

Two roads in from the riverside I found a guesthouse and a young man who spoke some English. I explained what I wanted, he thought for a moment and then made a phone call, and ten minutes later there were three of us standing on the water's edge, staring down at my boat: the young man, a middle-aged woman and me. The young man had ascertained from the hydrofoil crew that I had indeed arrived in the boat that I claimed was mine, and he and the woman conferred. Eventually he turned to me.

'No money,' he said, 'but she will let you stay in an apartment for three nights. In return for your boat.'

Which is how I ended my journey in a flat in one of those brutally ugly communist apartment blocks, rent free.

25

Blue River, Black Sea

The end of a journey, and the end of a book, is a discombobulating experience. If you'd have asked me beforehand, I would have said I was expecting to arrive in a blaze of glory, to experience some exhilarating emotion, and to express some major profundity. But for the rest of that day of arrival I felt nothing, said nothing, and wrote nothing. I was numb.

I guess my mental state wasn't helped by the bottle of hooch I bought to celebrate, and which sent me almost instantly to sleep. I only finally emerged from my apartment in the early evening, where I could have been seen standing on the wasteland outside the apartment block sniffing the air like one of Sulina's scores of under-fed and dazed strays, preparing to lift my leg.

My temporary home was a couple of streets back from the river. It was square and had high piggy-eyed windows covered in rugs to stop the sunlight getting in. The stairwell was streaked with rust, stank of stale cigarettes and its walls were studded with nails, bolts and other embedded bits of metal, the shrapnel of Romanian utilities. My temporary home was up on the third floor, where it had two bedrooms, a small concrete balcony for the drying of family laundry, a bathroom and a tiny kitchen whose only tap I could never quite turn off. The only other occupants of the block lived directly above me, and their wastepipe ran straight down through my main bedroom, so that whenever they took a shit during the night, it passed within a few inches of my head. It would be in the Black Sea before I was.

That apart, I liked having the anonymity of my own front door, and pretending to be a local, pretending that I could abandon all my responsibilities and stay here for ever, where no one would ever find me. I felt as the Lipovans must have done when they first went to ground in the Delta; where better to hide oneself than a little island of decayed civilization on the edge of the known world? Sulina was a backwater of backwaters, the last resort of European sediment, where the European shit came to rest. It was the bung in Europe's stern, the pimple on the arse end of the continent, wedged between one kind of watery wilderness, the Delta, and another, the Black Sea.

It was a crazy place to try to build a town. The urbanization had been assembled around two long quays, like extra-long railway platforms, facing each other across the channel. The view from one side to the other created the illusion of a metropolis, whereas the reality was little more than a façade, like one of those cowboy ghost towns put together for the cinema. And as in a cinematic cowboy town, it didn't take much to penetrate through the façade and out into the sand on the other side, except here that sand quickly became a brackish swamp which was neither river nor sea, but somewhere in between.

Nevertheless, the township put up a good show

of solidity. The far bank was populated by (empty) warehouses of some size and substance. Between them stood (empty) merchants' accounting houses in the style of late-nineteenth-century colonial bungalows, and a Chantier Naval that hadn't been doing any chantiering for some decades. The near bank had the empty streets, the desultory handful of shops, the cinema that had been closed for years, the empty market and the packs of feral dogs. The roads were dirt, and the occasional vehicle – for there were one or two – would kick up a dust cloud that settled on everything, turning it all the same drab beige. But this was no shanty town; it had once had real gravitas. Some of the larger waterside buildings carried memories of grandeur in the fanlights above their doors, the fancy scrolls and decorative columns around their windows, their French shutters, ironwork balconies and brick chimneys, suggesting ambitious and wealthy residents. These days, however, they were rarely lived in above the ground floor.

In its appearance Sulina didn't belong to anywhere else on the river, certainly not to anywhere in Romania, which anyway had only taken possession of it in the 1930s. It could have been a colonial trading settlement on a river mouth in Africa, or in Asia, and even more plausibly a river mouth in literature, straight out of Joseph Conrad. Except that in Conrad such settlements were always sophisticated and busy while the wilderness was inland, in the continent's dark and lonely heart. Here, the opposite was true: the heart of the continent, upstream, was the sophisticated and busy end, while the river mouth was the former outpost of progress that had since regressed into a monument to forlorn hope. It looked like a filmset created for some long-forgotten epic which never quite made it to the global cinema, and I was happy that it was so. It would have been a bugger to have ended my journey in a shed on the bypass.

It was nearly a century since Sulina had had its moment in the limelight. Originally a Byzantine, Genoese and then Ottoman naval toehold, its grandest flowering came in the nineteenth century, when it became the focus for an ambitious multinational scheme of the sort that has since become commonplace EU fodder but in those days was something truly revolutionary. The focus of that scheme stood at the top end of the town quay, its grandest, most pompous building, the occupants of which had been charged with turning dreams into reality. This was the echoingly empty head office of the very first Danube Commission, or the Administralia Fluviala Dunari de Jos, according to the lettering above the entrance. It was established by the Treaty of Paris of 1856, a treaty which settled the Crimean War and made the Black Sea neutral territory, and which set about opening up the river as an international waterway. Sulina was designated its gateway port.

In the years before the Commission had set to work, Sulina had been a wide, open seaboard strewn with sandbanks and wrecks, whose hulls and masts were used by mariners as a guide to where the deepest channel was to be found (provided of course they had managed to avoid the prowling navies of the Ottomans and the Russians). At times of high water, nearly all dry land completely disappeared here, leaving only a few wretched hovels built on piles on narrow patches of European sediment. This pale landfall provided only the flimsiest shelter from wind or tide, so any transhipment of cargo from seagoing to rivergoing ships could only take place in calm conditions. But it was still busy, despite these hazards: in a storm in 1855, twenty-four sailing ships and sixty lighters were blown ashore here and three hundred people died.

The Commission changed all that. It was an amalgamation of national representatives, the ancestor of other, more familiar European bodies. Its first board, some of whom had full diplomatic status, were an English noble, a Turkish Pasha, a French civil servant, an Austrian ex-army officer, a Prussian bureaucrat, a Russian baron and a Sardinian marquis, and they didn't have any one language in common. The Turk spoke German and Turkish; the Prussian, Austrian and the Russian spoke Russian, German and French; the Frenchman spoke no language but his own, but could read German; and the Englishman spoke nothing with any skill, but claimed he could understand most of the rest. It must have made for interesting meetings.

Undeterred by these Babel-like complications, the Commission leapt into action like polyglot plumbers whose instant task was to unblock Europe's main drain. With the priorities of shipping in mind, they built two long moles out into the Black Sea to mark and protect the channel, dredged out the middle and erected lighthouses to assist navigation. To the inland ends of the two moles they added the town jetties, those long railway platforms parked on the swamp, around which the new town of Sulina took shape.

The result was an overnight success. Unfettered by any one national interest, and with no vindictive warships to dodge, Sulina became a reliable transhipment port across whose wharves Black Sea freighters could offload into Danube barges at any time of the day or night. There was a sudden demand for manpower as shipping lines and freight agencies of many nationalities – including large numbers of Greeks – set up branches here. Merchants followed, along with consuls and ambassadorial representatives, and in their wake came rabbis, imams and priests to look after everyone's spiritual needs. Soon there was a mosque, a synagogue, and three churches: an Armenian, a Catholic and an Orthodox, in architectural styles that straddled East and West. The swelling community of children was educated in two Romanian schools, two Greek and one Jewish, and there was a French academy for young ladies, along with a ballroom for the elite to socialize and a casino for gentlemanly recreation. In short, a Hong Kong on the Black Sea.

And like Hong Kong, this gathering of multinational, multicultural commercial interests must have created an interestingly exotic society in that isolated community, which at that time was still two days' journey from proper dry land. I could imagine the dinner parties, hosted by the Greek consul and his lovely daughter, where the guests would pretend to be delighted at the prospect of eating yet more caviar (here virtually the staple diet). The guests of honour would have been a couple of the higher-profile representatives from the Commission – the Russian Baron d'Offenberg, perhaps, or the Sardinian Marquis d'Aste – and the remainder of the guests drawn from the collection of has-beens who'd been given a posting that no one else had wanted to the furthest end of Europe. Along with the baron or the marquis there'd be the doctor who'd fled here after making some dreadful medical mistake, the sallow Jewish merchant whose commercial power everyone feared, the tubby cleric with a weakness for young boys, and the lean and caddish Austrian soldier who'd been sent here to spy. And making up the numbers would be a couple of keen young shipping agents, split between desperation to move on and desperation to catch the consul's daughter's attention. And they all would have spoken French, albeit pretty badly.

It didn't last. Eventually even the society of misfits unravelled as the Danube Commission progressed its grand bit of plumbing, deepening the river inland and improving navigation to such an extent that the Black Sea shipping no longer needed to stop at Sulina, but could travel upriver to Tulcea and Galati and unload where there was proper industry, roads, railways and dry land. Meanwhile the Commission, having done its job at Sulina, abandoned its offices and moved inland too, taking with it most of the community's glamour, and a lot of its commerce. Sulina eventually lost its freeport status, becoming officially part of the Romanian mainland.

Since then there'd been various schemes to try to keep the settlement alive, and the communists had briefly been keen on Sulina's strategic significance, creating barracks and radar installations and sealing off the outer moles to casual visitors. But even that was being wound down, and now the only intermittent pulse that showed that sleeping Sulina was still alive came from the arrival of the ferries from Tulcea, which brought handfuls of tourists, curious to see what happened at this arse end of the European world.

I sat amongst them in a coffee shop by the water which was little more than a minute from the apartment, enjoying being smiled at by a nice waitress, who seemed to understand my semi-catatonic state. From here I looked out at the river with new respect. It may have looked like a dirty ditch straitjacketed between the Commission's two quays, but I knew from personal experience that it was far from being a spent force, and still had a savage integrity that man's attempt at replumbing it hadn't managed to extract. Here, at the very end of my journey, it had managed to produce its wildest, most extravagant display.

And now, contrary to the main-drain impression

given by quayside Sulina, only 16 per cent of the Danube made its final exit here. The rest of it was happily consummating its union with the Black Sea along a 150-kilometre front, witnessed only by the occasional passing fisherman, having evaded man's last attempt at control. After 2,840 kilometres of barriers and abuse, it was finally breaking free. If man wanted to claim that he'd sheathed and fettered it by building two platforms on a swamp, then the river wasn't going to deny it, but you needed only to climb one of those Danube Commission lighthouses to see how big the delusion, and how insignificant the town.

Once I'd recovered sufficiently from my unexpectedly gruelling bit of rowing, I ranged further away from the apartment, busying myself like an addict trying to feed his addiction. I didn't want to admit my journey was at an end.

I wandered out into the wasteground beyond the town, where rusting turn-of-the-century steamships had been marooned by epic tides alongside cabin cruisers whose cabins had tipped forward into their hulls, burying their faces in their hands.

I mooched along the prom amongst the old men in their habitual positions on the sea wall. Speaking a dialect that blended Russian with Romanian, they were telling each other things that each of them already knew, the same things they said last year, and the year before.

I peered down into the river water hunting for well-travelled litter that might connect me with the river of my 20-euro bicycle, of the Danubian aristocracy, of a horse called Laguna, of a barge called the *Argo*, and of a floating green bathtub, but I found none.

I discovered the demilitarized zone, now reduced to

416

empty foundations, where feral puppies played in the burnt-out shell of the car where they'd been born, and where they'd grow up and die. Theirs was going to be a short life in a strictly proscribed world, but they nevertheless practised being fierce at the stranger walking by.

I browsed around the graveyard, where the Greeks had the most ostentatious monuments but were massively outnumbered by the Ukrainians. There were a few Germans, a couple of Italians, an Englishman, and a separate cemetery where Muslims and Jews had been interred within the same walls, the unlikeliest of bedfellows. Their graves, and Sulina's architecture, were all that remained of the port's big moment on the European stage.

And finally I ended up at the beach, where the Black Sea speculatively put its elbows up on the bar at the back end of the town and belched a gentle froth, like an old regular with a Guinness moustache. It wasn't a particularly impressive sea, as seas go, and it wasn't black, it was brown – but I wasn't going to blame it for that. My blue river hadn't been blue.

In the distance the sea had a proper maritime horizon with occasional smudgy ships, but close at hand it didn't make a big song and dance about being any different from the land. The shore was flat and featureless, the waves short and stuttering, the sand more like silky silt than sand, and weed in the shallows laced itself round my ankles in a feeble attempt to stop me wading out. But a sea is a sea, and I'd spent a long time getting to this one, so I knew what had to be done.

When does a journey like this finally end? There is no fat lady who sings. No banner that welcomes, no official delegation that pins a rosette. Nobody waves a flag, stops a watch or fires a gun. I didn't have to ring in to report to anyone – no one knew where I was – and I didn't bump into the Greek consul's daughter or even granddaughter; they'd long since gone to heaven. I'd come to a stop at sullen Sulina simply because there was nowhere further to go.

Looking back upstream, I could visualize my own route compared to that of the Danube, and the adventure we'd enjoyed together right across Europe's midriff to where I now stood. From this perspective, looking back from the beach, it looked like a drunken, emotional, lover's journey, with both parties setting out inseparable, kissing and canoodling as we'd weaved erratically across the first 1,000 kilometres, too wrapped up in each other to be paying much attention to where we were going. Then came the first tiff and trial separation, followed by a more cautious reunion as the relationship changed gear, and as both parties came to understand the other was more complicated than each had previously thought. Each had had its own needs; the Danube had a Mother Baar to obey, a sea to get to, and gravity as its lord and master, while I had had all sorts of ideas tugging me this way and that. It was my course that had been the more fickle of the two. I hadn't stuck faithfully to the riverbed, but instead had veered away, surging, tumbling and stalling, like an unreliable tributary. Like the Danube, I too had brushed the sediment off bits of history, tugged at the roots of a handful of cultures, and toppled a few overhanging preconceptions of prejudice. And then the two of us had come together at the end, finally reunited in the Delta, like a couple of careworn old lovers who knew that the spark had long since died between us, but who'd resolved to meet again in order to part.

Overall, I reflected, I was the one who'd got the most out of our three-month relationship, but then I'd been the one who'd been the most naïve at the outset and had

had the most to learn. Thanks to the Danube, I'd been touched by moments of beauty, rewarded with flashes of insight and carried onward by a sense of adventure, while the Danube had just been going through the motions, as it had always done, and as it always will.

Thanks to the river I now understood a great deal more about the downriver half of my continent. I'd discovered that Europe is not just the bit between the North Sea and the Mediterranean, that it has a horizontal dimension as well as a vertical one, an East to go with its West, and a whole new slice of history lurking up its sleeves. I'd discovered that Europe was a joined-up place after all.

As for the river which had showed me all this, it had variously been fêted, abused, imprisoned and ignored along its length, but now it was free. It had completed its journey, done its duty, and accordingly it terminated our relationship there and then, without so much as a backward glance. At Sulina it discarded its identity and left me on the shore with my memories, like a *femme fatale* who'd allowed me to dabble with her awhile, but had dropped me as soon as she had caught sight of bigger and better things.

I regretted the river's passing, but I'd known this moment was coming ever since I started out, 2,840 kilometres ago, so it wasn't as if I'd come unprepared. I dug into my bag, burrowing past the socks I'd worn to meet Karl-Friedrich Hohenzollern, the waterproofs I'd worn on the cyclepath, the Dazzer that had discouraged the Transylvanian dogs, and the trousers I'd worn to meet the Romanian prince, finally to lay my hands on the swimming shorts that had last seen action in the spas of Budapest.

And ten minutes later, emerging exhilarated and dripping, I could finally say that the river and I were even. I'd baptized myself in the Black Sea, and now I too was free.

Index

426